# On Two Legs and Three Wheels

## The Travel Adventures of a Couple Overcoming Age and Disability

# Cary D. Lowe

Black Rose Writing | Texas

©2025 by Cary D. Lowe
All rights reserved. No part of this book may be reproduced, stored in a retrieval system or transmitted in any form or by any means without the prior written permission of the publishers, except by a reviewer who may quote brief passages in a review to be printed in a newspaper, magazine or journal.

The author grants the final approval for this literary material.

First printing

Some names and identifying details may have been changed to protect the privacy of individuals.

ISBN: 978-1-68513-558-4
LIBRARY OF CONGRESS CONTROL NUMBER: 2025930280
PUBLISHED BY BLACK ROSE WRITING
www.blackrosewriting.com

Printed in the United States of America
Suggested Retail Price (SRP) $23.95

*On Two Legs and Three Wheels* is printed in Book Antiqua

\*As a planet-friendly publisher, Black Rose Writing does its best to eliminate unnecessary waste to reduce paper usage and energy costs, while never compromising the reading experience. As a result, the final word count vs. page count may not meet common expectations.

## AUTHOR'S ACKNOWLEDGEMENTS

I dedicate this book to my wife, Patricia (Trish) Butler, whose love of travel and determination to overcome obstacles made possible our scores of adventures at home and abroad. Together, we have experienced more people, places, and cultures than most people even imagine. And we have done so despite her mobility limitations and our gradual aging. This book tells our stories, with the goal of inspiring others to replicate our experiences.

Others also have played important roles in making possible our travels and this book. My colleagues in the San Diego Professional Writers Group—Mark Jackson, Heidi Langbein-Allen, Margaret Lang, Tim Kaine, Lee Polevoi, Jim Riffel, Helen Davis, Jack Innis, and Bonnie Bracken—reviewed and commented on each successive chapter as I produced it. My two beta readers—Bob Leiter and John Kelly—provided invaluable input for my final editing of the entire work. Innumerable airline flight attendants, hotel staff, tour guides, restaurant servers, taxi drivers, and simply helpful individuals all contributed to making our travels memorable and worth recounting. And the staff at Black Rose Writing ultimately brought this book to fruition, allowing me to share our stories with you.

Cary D. Lowe

# On Two Legs and Three Wheels

# CONTENTS

THE CHALLENGE

| | |
|---|---:|
| Chapter 1 - THE FIRST FALL | 1 |
| Chapter 2 - AFTER THE GOLEM | 10 |
| Chapter 3 - NO NEED FOR A SCOOTER UNDERWATER | 31 |
| Chapter 4 - IT DOESN'T GET ANY LOWER | 48 |
| Chapter 5 - A TALE OF TWO WINTERS | 62 |
| Chapter 6 - FIRST SCOOTER TO THE ARCTIC OCEAN | 77 |
| Chapter 7 - CRUISING COLD AND HOT | 93 |
| Chapter 8 - LET'S TAKE A ROAD TRIP | 112 |
| Chapter 9 - FINDING RELIGION IN THE CARIBBEAN | 123 |
| Chapter 10 - WE'LL ALWAYS HAVE PARIS | 135 |
| Chapter 11 - A WEEK IN PROVENCE | 149 |
| Chapter 12 - WATER, WATER EVERYWHERE | 161 |
| Chapter 13 - TWENTY-SIX MILES | 184 |
| Chapter 14 - TAKING IT EASY | 195 |
| Chapter 15 - DESERT MAGIC | 205 |
| Chapter 16 - TICKETS BUT NO RESERVATIONS | 215 |
| Chapter 17 - STAIRS ARE NOT A PROBLEM! | 228 |
| Chapter 18 - NOT SO EASY IN THE BIG EASY | 240 |
| Chapter 19 - THE LOOK OF LOVE | 254 |
| Chapter 20 - A TRAIN, A PLANE, AND AN AUTOMOBILE | 265 |
| Chapter 21 - DO YOU SPEAK ENGLISH? | 278 |
| Chapter 22 - TRAVEL IN THE TIME OF COVID | 294 |
| Chapter 23 - HOMECOMING | 304 |

THE CHALLENGE MET

# THE CHALLENGE

Travel can be as exhilarating as falling in love, as exciting as winning a lottery, as satisfying as dinner at a great restaurant. Not always, but even if it fails to reach those heights, it's usually an enjoyable experience. For most people, it just requires picking a destination or an itinerary, booking transportation, making hotel reservations, and maybe arranging for a rental car. But not for everyone.

For disabled travelers, especially those with limited mobility, the joys of travel are tempered by special needs and by the knowledge that obstacles abound, often at inconvenient times and in unexpected places. A single high step blocking a wheelchair from reaching a spectacular viewpoint. A highly recommended restaurant turning out to be located on the second floor of a building without an elevator. A jetway out of service at a destination airport. A ramp that won't deploy on a city bus. A hotel room billed as accessible but lacking a roll-in shower.

The world has become far more user-friendly for disabled travelers in recent years, though that varies considerably from country to country and even within individual countries. Such obstacles can be especially frustrating for travelers who once were fully ambulatory and now must deal with limitations on their mobility. Also for their spouses and other traveling companions, who must learn to join in finding solutions to these problems.

Yet, once it becomes clear that nearly all such problems can be resolved and that most obstacles can be overcome, the world of travel reopens. Perseverance and ingenuity, combined with equal measures of patience and flexibility, are miracle cures for most of the travel ailments associated with reduced mobility. The Rolling Stones said it well: "You can't always get what you want, but if you try…you'll get what you need."

Personally, I've been lucky. My legs have carried me around much of the world. Early in life, I hiked Swiss Alpine trails, climbed to the top of the Statue of Liberty in New York, and walked narrow lanes in Venice and boulevards in London. As an adult, I hiked switchbacks to the peak of Mt. Whitney and stone steps up Mayan pyramids, wandered sunbaked trails through the Grand Canyon, ran a marathon in the crowd-lined streets of San Diego, and walked around cities from bustling Tokyo to luminescent Paris. Now in my seventies, my legs have held up well, allowing me to keep walking in fresh places.

But what if my legs had quit working at some point? How could I have kept traveling? To answer that question, I only need to look at my wife, Trish, who lost her personal mobility to multiple sclerosis but has continued to travel with me to far-flung places.

She received an MS diagnosis in her late thirties but didn't show significant symptoms for a decade. When I met her, she was still fully ambulatory. Still, it would likely be just a matter of time. We felt encouraged when her condition remained stable while we traveled both domestically and internationally during the next few years.

Then Trish's condition worsened. On our first trip together to Europe, she relied on a cane and my arm to negotiate urban streets and plazas. Soon after, she began using a wheeled walker. That worked well enough around the house or the office, and even for some travels. It even aided her in walking down the aisle at our wedding. But, as Trish's walking ability continued to deteriorate, the walker proved too slow and cumbersome for travels involving exploration.

In preparation for an early excursion, Trish acquired the first of a series of mobility scooters—a bright blue, three-wheeled, battery-powered vehicle with hand controls and an adjustable seat. I became experienced at checking in the scooter for airline flights and retrieving it at our destination, as well as assisting Trish to and from her seat aboard the plane. Similarly, I learned to anticipate questions about the scooter from airline personnel and how to deal with airports that offered only stairs for disembarking.

Through experience, we figured out what kinds of motor vehicles can accommodate the scooter, and how I can load and unload it with the least stress on my back. At home, we fitted our cars with lifts for that purpose, but those typically aren't available in rental vehicles. Depending on location, we have rented SUVs, hatchback sedans, and even pickup trucks. Although our blue handicapped parking placard technically is not valid outside the United States, we have used it successfully in a score of other countries and never had it challenged.

Through experience, we learned the capabilities and limits of the scooter. With an occasional push, it can climb surprisingly steep slopes. Hard surfaces consume less battery power than grass or dirt, but some, like cobblestone streets, make for a bone-jarring ride. Unpaved pathways are negotiable, except that scooter wheels lose traction if they sink too far into loose sand or gravel. And a scooter carrying a passenger cannot climb or descend stairs. Most of what we have learned about scooter-assisted travel applies to wheelchairs, as well.

All of that forced us to be more creative in our trip planning. We learned what questions to ask hotel staff about the features of their "accessible" rooms—whether they have a roll-in shower, grab bars in strategic locations, and enough space to maneuver a scooter. We discovered the need to ask about the accessibility of routes to dining and recreation facilities. Traveling to the tropics, we know to investigate facilities that Trish can use while I'm off scuba diving—whether the swimming pool is at ground level, with no stairs impeding access from our room, or whether the hotel has a deck facing the morning sun where Trish can read and enjoy a leisurely breakfast. We came to understand the complexities of utilizing other modes of travel, such as trains and trolleys, especially in foreign countries.

And we discovered a travel agency specializing in serving disabled travelers. We now sometimes use their services and information when traveling to unfamiliar places.

Those experiences give us confidence that we can handle—or, better yet, avoid—virtually any obstacles. The more we travel and the more we are challenged, the more we learn to adapt and overcome.

We sometimes get rude surprises despite our best efforts—lack of corner curb cuts even in major cities, airline personnel unfamiliar with electric scooters, or breakdown of the scooter itself. Thankfully, those events are rare and detract little from our otherwise positive experiences.

Most importantly, we have experienced astonishing kindness and assistance from many people in many places—free entry to museums, helpful flight attendants, assistance in accessing seemingly inaccessible buildings or restaurants, and a helping hand with a scooter whose battery has died..

We determined not to let Trish's mobility constraints interfere unduly with our activities. We have travelled together—Trish, the scooter, and I—to twenty countries and fifteen states. These travels provide the stories and experiences that fill this book, following us from the Arctic Ocean to Caribbean islands, from urban centers to remote glaciers and deserts. Each successive trip disclosed more things we could do together, more ways she could adapt to unusual conditions, and more ways I still could pursue activities of special interest to me.

We hope our travel successes will inspire other disabled, infirm, or merely aging individuals, as well as their partners and companions, to replicate our experiences or seek out ones of their own.

As we plan more trips, some places and experiences will remain off-limits for us due to topographic, structural, or other obstacles. Still, even with our constraints, we have gone to more places, including more remote and unusual ones, than almost anyone we know. And we have developed confidence that, wherever we go, we will have interesting experiences and find enjoyable things to do.

Friends and strangers alike often comment on how well we get around. We appreciate that and tell them there's almost no place we can't go—on two legs and three wheels.

# Chapter 1
# THE FIRST FALL

Trish on Palm Canyon Trail, Anza-Borrego

*Anza-Borrego Desert, May 2002*
*Travel…as exhilarating as falling in love.*
On a sunny spring morning, Trish and I picked our way along a sandy trail between rust-colored canyon walls in the heart of California's Anza-Borrego Desert. Without warning, her long legs crumpled. I thought she had lost her footing, maybe sprained an ankle.

I rushed to where she had fallen amid a cluster of weathered, pumpkin-sized rocks. A reddish scrape showed at the outside of her left knee, just below the hem of her tan shorts.

"Are you OK? Did you slip?" I asked.

"I'm fine, please help me up," she replied, sounding more annoyed than concerned.

We continued down the sloping path back toward the trailhead. I walked a few feet behind her. Her auburn hair hung in a loosely tied ponytail from beneath a white cap, and a daypack bounced on her back. I smiled and nodded as I watched her hips sway with each step. Only the soft sound of our footsteps disturbed the desert's quiet. I felt happy I brought her out here, as an important next step in our developing relationship.

A few minutes later, she fell again.

"I'm sorry," she said with a sigh. "It's the heat."

The heat? That seemed unlikely. I was puzzled, but also concerned for her. The April midday sun reflecting off the burnished rock slopes had begun warming the canyon earlier. But it didn't feel hot enough to cause heatstroke or anything else I knew of that would trigger these falls. Something else was amiss.

On our way in, we had followed the winding trail for two miles up a gradual slope flanked by car-sized boulders. Some showed smooth *morteros* on top, created long ago by Yaqui women grinding seeds and nuts. The trail led to an oasis of forty-foot-tall *Washingtonia* fan palms—the only native California palms—with a ten-foot waterfall that dropped into a shallow pool where hikers could cool their feet. The ephemeral stream running down the canyon had gone into hibernation for the season, disappearing beneath the tan, coarse sand, and evidenced only by slender desert willow trees and gnarled creosote bushes whose deep roots continued to receive its nourishment.

We scanned the canyon walls for bighorn sheep, the park's namesake *borregos*, which step down the steep slopes in search of water, but we saw none that day. Just before reaching the oasis, I turned and pointed up at a boulder jutting from the hillside and overhanging the trail at a point where it squeezed between rocks and trees.

"A couple of years ago, I was hiking here with a friend," I told Trish. "A bighorn ram stood up there motionless, like a statue, and looked down at us for several minutes. He had huge horns, a full curl. They looked way too heavy for his skinny legs to hold up. He just stared, and we stared back. Then he turned and ambled away. It was one of those rare close-up animal encounters, like coming face-to-face with a shark or a giant sea turtle in the ocean. You wish you knew what they were thinking."

"I know what you mean," she replied. "In the Rockies, I've come across deer and other animals. Most run off but, once in a while, you'll get one that will stop and stare, just like that ram."

As we neared the end of our hike, stepping carefully amid rocks strewn about by occasional flash floods, I could feel the temperature rising. I remembered what Trish said earlier about the heat and hoped she wouldn't have any more difficulty. The trailhead came into sight, and I spotted my forest green Explorer in the parking lot. Then, as we stepped down into a dry stream bed, Trish fell once more.

"Something's wrong!" I exclaimed. "Let's get you back to the car as quickly as we can." She nodded but this time said nothing.

We made it the rest of the way without further incident. Once in the car, Trish looked away, as if embarrassed. I didn't want to press her, but I wanted to understand what happened. I had hiked this trail a dozen times before with family and friends, often in hotter conditions, and never saw anyone react this way. Trish was an experienced hiker, so why, I wondered, was she having such difficulty? She would explain it in due time, I figured.

Trish and I had been dating for a few months, after meeting at a conference. She lived in San Diego and I in Los Angeles, but we soon began getting together most weekends. I had invited her to join me for this weekend at my favorite getaway place.

The community of Borrego Springs sits in a broad valley in the northern part of the 900-square-mile Anza-Borrego Desert State Park, a sprawling collection of mountains, washes, oases, trails, and streams, in the northeast corner of San Diego County. The park takes its name from 18th-century Spanish explorer Juan de Anza and from the elusive *borregos,*

I began exploring the park in the early 1980s. Growing up in Central Europe and New England, my exposure to nature concentrated on forests, mountains, and seacoasts. But I became fascinated with the deserts I saw in documentaries and western movies. That interest soared during a driving trip around the southwest soon after I moved to California to attend college in the mid-1960s.

A few years after my first visit to this desert park, I bought a home at the Borrego Air Ranch, a rustic airstrip community ten miles south of town, composed of a few dozen homes clustered along both sides of a 2400-foot, black asphalt runway. I flew a single-engine Piper Archer in those days, so this development held a special attraction.

I loved that the town, with just 3,500 year-round residents, changed little over the succeeding years. That kept me coming back and made me want to share this place with close friends. With no nearby freeway, it didn't experience the growth of the Palm Springs area on the other side of the Santa Rosa Mountains to the north. Small businesses along the single commercial street and a scattering of hotels sit almost dormant during the summer months, when temperatures stay well above 100 degrees. Winter brings an influx of tourists and "snowbird" refugees from colder locales. But the town's claim to fame, in years when the temperature and rainfall cooperate, rests on spectacular springtime bursts of wildflowers that carpet canyons and roadsides in displays of magenta, scarlet, and gold. The flowers had come and gone already this year, but the desert offered us lots of other attractions.

Back at the house, we sat in the shade of the patio overhang and relaxed after our hike. We sipped Tecate beers, in their trademark brown bottles with red-and-black labels, from a brewery just across the Mexican border.

For forty years, I've found this desert to be a magical place year-round. In my younger days, I even hiked isolated canyons during the intense heat of summer, feeling like I was sharing an experience with the onetime Native American occupants of the valley.

Once my relationship with Trish deepened, I wanted to share my special place with her. Now, still confused about what happened earlier in the canyon, I wondered if that would be possible. Perhaps sensing my unease, she turned serious.

"I've been waiting for the right time to tell you this, but things progressed between us before I had a chance. I have MS, multiple sclerosis. It was diagnosed about fifteen years ago, when I was in my mid-thirties. I have occasional symptoms, usually when I get overheated, but I've been pretty lucky."

Trish had my attention now. I didn't know much about MS, except that it could be a serious, disabling condition. I wanted to hear more, but felt a chill at what might come next.

After a long pause, she continued. "The problem is there's no way to know what will happen in the future. Odds are it will get worse at some point. How much and how soon, who knows? I have to live with that uncertainty. You may have to decide if you can live with it too."

I didn't want to react immediately. I had already experienced once before having a partner with serious health issues. My first wife, Joan, died of a heart attack after many years of illness and pain.

I put that aside and thought about what had attracted me to Trish. She was smart, attractive, and professionally accomplished, yes, but equally important was her love of travel. Like me, she had traveled extensively as a child with her family. During college, she spent a year studying in France and wandered all over Europe, from Bordeaux to Budapest to Dublin. Later, her work took her on memorable trips to Panama and Guatemala, and she roamed the Rockies as an avid fly fisher.

I looked up to see Trish furrowing her brow, pursing her lips, waiting for me to react.

"Yes, I understand," I said, trying hard not to sound too concerned. "Meanwhile, there's lots more we can do out here this weekend without getting you overheated again."

Trish gave a smile of relief. No difficult discussion to upend the weekend. That might come later.

"Let's drive to Font's Point for the sunset. It's a high spot named after a priest in one of the early Spanish expeditions through here. It has a spectacular view of the valley."

"Great," she replied with a nod. "Let's go."

As evening approached, we drove a back road that skirted the town. We then entered a broad, sandy wash leading four miles uphill and ending just before the point. Striations in the walls of the wash marked recent flash floods. Vehicle tracks swerved around islands of billowing *palo verde* trees. I drove this path for the first time ten years earlier in a regular street vehicle, repeatedly losing traction in the sand. A desire to explore the desert more led me to buy my first four-wheel-drive SUV.

Pleased to find few cars at the top of the wash, I parked and pulled a cooler from the back seat.

"What's in there?" Trish asked, smiling and raising an eyebrow.

"You'll see shortly. Are you OK to walk a little way?"

"Yes, it's cooler now. I shouldn't have any more trouble."

I led her up a steep, sandy slope to the viewpoint. From there, we looked fifty feet down on variegated badlands terrain eroded from deposits left eons earlier by overflows of the Colorado

River, now running a hundred miles further east. The late afternoon sun, preparing to drop behind the San Jacinto Mountains to our right, cast long shadows across the valley. To the left, the Salton Sea reflected the day's last rays.

"Now, I have a surprise," I said, pulling a bottle of champagne from the cooler. That drew a smile from Trish, and also from another couple standing nearby. I poured champagne into a pair of glasses, handed one to Trish, and held mine up in the manner of a toast.

"To my favorite place in nature," I began. "And to my favorite woman."

Trish's smile broadened. We sipped the first glass of champagne, then another. By that time, the sun had settled behind the mountains, leaving a bright yellow-orange glow over the peaks. In the twilight, I put my arms around Trish and gave her a long kiss.

"That was fabulous," Trish said as we coasted back down the wash. "What a beautiful, romantic spot."

"Yes, and I've got another surprise for you tomorrow."

Back at the house, we drank martinis made with Trish's favorite Chopin vodka, while I barbecued ribs on an outdoor charcoal grill. By then, the sky had darkened enough for stars to appear. Once we finished dinner, I turned off all the lights. We drew up chairs in the middle of the courtyard in front of the house. As our eyes adjusted to the dark, the sky overhead lit up like a magnificently decorated Christmas tree, confirming Borrego Springs' status as an International Dark Sky community. And the Milky Way showed how it earned its name, as if poured across the heavens from one horizon to another.

"This is spectacular," Trish said. "The only place I've seen a sky like this before was high up in the mountains."

The next morning, I awoke from a deep sleep to a rumble that built to a roar and rattled the house.

"Are we having an earthquake?" Trish yelled.

"No! It's that bomber I told you about!" I threw open the bedroom curtains in time to see a World War II-era B-25 fly by just twenty feet above the runway. Its twin radial engines sounded impossibly louder than any of the Air Ranch aircraft. The plane belonged to a friend of one of my neighbors. When the owner flew it from San Diego to airshows around Southern California, he sometimes buzzed the Air Ranch.

The pilot climbed enough to execute a U-turn and then streaked back the other way. In a departing gesture, he wagged the plane's wings before climbing again and disappearing over the desert to the east.

After this brief drama passed, we sat outside in the morning sun. Song birds chirped beneath the fronds of a palm in a corner of the yard, and a jackrabbit bounded past, visible for just seconds through a window in the garden wall. Otherwise, only the faint hum of an occasional car on the highway a half mile away interrupted the silence. A smoky aroma from the creosote bush by the gate scented the air.

"What a glorious morning," Trish announced. "I haven't felt this relaxed in a long time."

After a leisurely breakfast of *nopales* and eggs, along with a lot of coffee, we set out in the Explorer for the nearby community of Ocotillo Wells.

"Where are you taking me now?" Trish asked, her voice rising with excitement.

"Be patient. You mentioned you're interested in geology. Get ready to see some geology that will blow you away."

A cracked asphalt road took us past mobile home parks, business catering to RV travelers, and the locally popular Iron Door Bar. Like so many other desert communities, Ocotillo Wells was a refuge for people who didn't like city life or couldn't afford it.

The road eventually led south to the canyon known as Split Mountain. Three miles up a stone-strewn, sandy wash, we entered a hundred-foot-wide crack in the Vallecito range. The canyon walls exposed reddish-brown rock twisted and torn by intense heat and seismic forces eons before people came here. As I pulled over to get out of the way of speeding off-roaders, I recalled how I gasped the first time I came to this spot.

"This is a surprise!" Trish exclaimed, shaking her head and staring up at the hundred-foot rock face. "I almost can't believe what I'm seeing. It really reminds you of the kind of force nature can unleash!"

As we prepared to return home that afternoon, I asked Trish, "Well, did you enjoy this weekend?"

"I did," she replied. "I'm not as much of a desert rat as you, but I definitely understand the magical feeling you get in this place. I hope I'll be able to visit other magical places with you."

She paused for a moment, then continued in a lower voice. "It was a relief to be able to tell you about my MS, but I meant what I said. Before our relationship gets more serious, you really will have to make a hard decision. If you decide you can't live with the uncertainty, I'll be sorry, but I'll understand."

"I know, and I will think about it. But we don't need to deal with that right now. Let's just focus on how much we enjoyed being with each other this weekend." Despite the tightening in my gut, I wanted the weekend to end on a positive note.

As I drove back to Los Angeles, my thoughts swirled. What if Trish's condition worsened soon, or she became seriously disabled? Could I live with that? I didn't know the answer for sure, not yet. I did know, though, that I was too attracted to this wonderful woman to just walk away. For as long as possible, I thought, we could have great travel adventures together.

## Chapter 2
## AFTER THE GOLEM

Trish in Park, Prague

*Prague, October 2004*
Our first extended vacation together came soon after Trish's MS symptoms had begun to worsen. We planned a challenging driving trip through European cities and countries key to my personal background. The central piece of this adventure would be the Czech capital of Prague.

Prague combined the stately architecture and classic culture of Vienna with contemporary music, art, and cuisine in a way that had people comparing it to the level of excitement and creativity of Paris in the 1920s. It also was the ancestral home of my father's family. I had a memorable visit there with my daughter, Coralea, a few years earlier, so I looked forward to sharing it with Trish, as well.

Trish had heard something of my family history, but I saw this as an opportunity to immerse us both in that past, with roots going back more than five hundred years. Although neither of us spoke Czech, I knew from my previous visit that a combination of English and my faded German would suffice for most purposes.

When we began discussing the trip, Trish still walked with relative ease, just needing to pause and rest occasionally. But that changed over the months leading up to our departure. By then, she relied on a cane or my arm to support her in walking more than a few steps.

"I'm getting nervous. This is going to be a real test of our ability to keep traveling," Trish remarked as we scanned maps and guidebooks, making final plans for the fast-approaching trip.

"We'll make it work," I assured her with as much certainty as I could muster. I understood her concern, but I wanted her to feel comfortable about this upcoming adventure. If we could fly six thousand miles and then navigate some of Europe's oldest cities successfully, that would boost our confidence, Trish's especially, in our ability to take on more challenging travels.

Planning for the trip accelerated after a conversation Trish had with a manager at the Mercedes-Benz dealer where she had her car serviced.

"I was talking to Herbert about replacing my car, since it's eight years old," she told me over dinner. "I saw a brochure on his desk about Mercedes' European delivery program, so I asked him about it. It's a really good deal. You pick up a new car from the factory near Stuttgart. The price is lower than here, plus they throw in some financial incentives. You can drive the car in

Europe, then you turn it back in at the airport on your way home, and they ship it here for you at their expense."

"That sounds like a great idea. We'd have a comfortable car to drive over there, with no limits on where we could take it. And you'd have your new car when we get back."

She placed an order for a metallic silver-blue model 450 that looked sleek, yet reserved, in the dealer's showroom. The company soon provided a firm delivery date—a Friday in early October. That gave us a start date for planning the trip.

We arranged to spend our first few days in Europe, after picking up the car, touring historic towns in the Romantic Road region of Bavaria. Towns with unmistakably German names like Rothenburg, Dinkelsbühl, and Nőrdlingen, filled with half-timbered houses and surrounded by medieval walls. We then would embark on a grand circuit through Prague, Budapest, and Vienna, once the great capitals of the Austro-Hungarian Empire and now bursting with energy and culture of new generations.

A final stop would be my hometown of Braunau am Inn, north of Salzburg, including a visit to my friend, Karin Zinecker, the daughter of my now-deceased childhood nanny, Herma. I had been back to Braunau only twice since leaving Europe in the early 1960s and looked forward to returning. From there, it would be a short drive to the Munich airport to catch our flight home. But the centerpiece of this adventure would be Prague.

The trip did not begin auspiciously. High winds on the ground in Atlanta forced our Thursday flight from Los Angeles to divert just long enough that we missed the connections to Frankfurt and on to Stuttgart. That began a cascade of difficulties. By the time we arrived, a day later than planned, the Mercedes factory had closed for the weekend. Anticipating that, while still in Atlanta, we had canceled hotel reservations in Bavaria and reset our schedule to arrive in Prague according to plan.

As seasoned travelers, we knew to make the best of the situation and try turning it to our advantage. On the flight to Stuttgart, Trish had an inspiration.

"As soon as we get on the ground, I'm going to call Herbert back at the dealership and see how he can help us."

He was indeed helpful. At company expense, he arranged for us to pick up a rental car at the Stuttgart airport and leave it at the Mercedes plant in Sindelfingen the following Monday. We then telephoned Karin in Braunau to move up our visit with her.

Three hours later, we arrived in Braunau. I found my way over the Inn River bridge, past the medieval buildings surrounding the town square, and on to Karin's townhouse. Blond, pleasantly plump, and smiling, she greeted me with a hug and a kiss. Her husky father, Loisel, followed suit. I introduced them to Trish, whom they welcomed like a family member. Sadly, missing from the scene was Karin's mother, who had died the previous year.

"Braunau," I told Trish soon after we arrived, "will always be both my hometown and the place where I began the process of becoming American."

The town indeed figured prominently in my early life and in my identity. Although my first language was German, I began learning English here as my family interacted increasingly with my father's colleagues in the US Army Counterintelligence unit to which he was assigned during the postwar occupation. Some of them had families there, and I played with their children. By the time we moved to the much larger military base in nearby Linz, I was reasonably fluent in English. I also developed my first relationships there with adults outside my family. We had no family close by, most of my parents' relatives having been killed in the Holocaust and the few remaining ones living in the US. So I formed bonds with the local merchants whose shops I visited with my mother or Herma, the neighbors who regarded me as an American kid but appreciated that I could speak with them in German, and the counterintelligence agents who often gathered at our home.

We spent much of the next two days reminiscing at Karin's kitchen table. Trish spoke no German, but Karin was fluent in English and Loisel spoke enough to get by. After hearing details of our travel plans, particularly of driving a new Mercedes, Loisel cautioned us about the thriving traffic of stolen luxury cars in what he ominously referred to as "the east."

The rest of the time, Trish, Karin, and I wandered about the town, especially its historical center. We took it slowly so as not to tire Trish, but she remained upbeat and gave no sign of fatigue. That seemed like a good omen for the rest of the trip.

This quiet town of just 15,000 recently had become a favorite stop for cyclists touring along the Danube and Inn Rivers. I noticed kiosks providing maps and lodging information for those visitors, something entirely new since my years living there. Other than that, however, little had changed.

The town square, or Stadtplatz, fascinated Trish. Four-story buildings, all connected, filled with apartments over ground-floor businesses, ringed the square. Their stucco facades in pastel shades of green, blue, and tan, along with their ornate window frames, frescoes, and steep tile roofs, evoked the town's prosperous time as a trading center in the Middle Ages. The town museum, in a corner of the square, showcased a continuous history from its beginning as a Roman camp protecting trade routes, through wars and commerce, up to the present.

We lingered at an outdoor café at the edge of the square, sipping coffee beneath a crimson umbrella that provided shelter from the midday sun. Across the square, we viewed the town hall, or Rathaus, with its relief sculpture of 16th-century Mayor Hans Staininger, known for his floor-length beard. Then, as we approached St. Stephan's Church, Karin saw men she knew doing restoration work on the twenty-five-story spire. After introducing us, she asked if I could climb up into the spire. They agreed, and took me up a series of rickety ladders and shaky platforms to a height from which I could see the entire town, the surrounding countryside, and the German village of Simbach across the river. Once back down, I walked with Trish and Karin into the Gothic structure with its interior flying buttresses holding up granite walls rising a hundred feet to a vaulted ceiling. Columns bearing angels and apostles flanked the center aisle, leading to an altar decorated with gilded saints. All bore witness to Braunau's wealthy past.

I showed Trish the white stucco house my family lived in during our years there, a house whose wartime occupant, we were told, had been a German general. Feeling a profound sense of reconnecting to my childhood, I asked Trish to take a photo of me standing before the house.

From the ancient Roman parapet overlooking the Inn, I pointed out where a pontoon crossing built by US Army Engineers sat for years in my childhood. The current steel bridge later replaced one blown up in 1945 by retreating German troops.

Karin led us through the Torturm, a medieval stone tower and remnant of the original city walls. A gateway below it provided an entrance to the square. On the next block, we paused at a four-foot-tall, rough-hewn granite block inscribed with a somber message in German:

*"For peace, freedom and democracy. Never again fascism, millions of dead warn us."*

Those victims of fascism included many members of my own family. The memorial, known as the Remembrance Stone, stood before Braunau's most incongruous and controversial historical artifact—the birthplace of Adolf Hitler. The granite had come from a quarry at the nearby Mauthausen concentration camp site. I put my arm around Trish as I read the inscription to her and felt her shiver.

"I know you told me about this place," Trish said in a quiet voice as we stood before the pale-yellow former apartment building that had been converted to offices. "But it's still kind of eerie actually seeing it."

"Yes, when I was a child, this building cast kind of a pall over the community. People didn't mention it in conversation, and most people avoided walking by it. Thankfully, now it's more of a historical curiosity."

Monday morning came all too soon. We said our goodbyes and dashed back to the factory outside Stuttgart.

"It's gorgeous," Trish exclaimed at getting her first glimpse of her new car. After orienting us on it, and knowing of our plan to drive through Eastern Europe, the factory staff gave us special documents to prove Trish's ownership of the vehicle.

By the time we departed the factory, we had only enough daylight to go as far as Nuremberg. My parents had lived there just before my birth, while my father worked on the prosecutors' staff at the military war crimes tribunal. I hadn't been there since my childhood and had only vague memories of it. I wished now we had planned an extra day to spend seeing the historical sites and the Gothic architecture for which the city was famous.

As I drove, Trish scanned the internet on her phone in search of a hotel for the night. Rejecting the chain hotels along the highway, she found the Gasthaus Rottner, described as a former country inn, now renovated and modernized. A phone call disclosed they had a vacancy.

This stop turned into one of those fortuitous experiences that make travel exciting. While the guest rooms occupied a new, modern building, the original, timbered inn now housed a charming restaurant—a room holding a dozen tables, lined with antiques and pictures of country life, and topped by a ceiling of painted wood beams that looked strong enough to last several more centuries. As we devoured traditional Bavarian dishes — liver dumpling soup, roast pork, veal sausages, sweet dessert pancakes — the middle-aged proprietress approached. She must have overheard us, as she addressed us in English, asking about our travel plans and then regaling us with memories of years she spent living in California before returning to take over this family-owned establishment.

We rose early the next morning to begin the 200-mile drive to Prague. At the Czech border, Loisel's admonition was confirmed. While border guards accepted our US passports with a cursory glance, they scrutinized our auto ownership papers before waving us through the checkpoint. Today, with the Czech Republic being a party to the twenty-six nation Schengen Agreement that opened up movement within Europe, the border is invisible.

As we sped east along the motorway to Prague, I recognized names of towns from my father's stories and from my previous visit here. One name caught Trish's attention.

"Look," she exclaimed, pointing at the sign announcing the upcoming exit for Plzen. "That's the same as Pilsen, isn't it? Where pilsner beer originated? We've got to stop there and have a pilsner in Plzen."

From the exit ramp, we saw a neon sign rising high above a restaurant just off the highway, advertising Pilsner Urquell, a beer we often drank at home. Only thirty miles from the border, the staff all spoke German. We ordered mugs of beer, along with sandwiches of thick-sliced ham and sharp mustard on dense rye bread.

"This draft beer is so much better than what we get in bottles at home, even though it comes from the same brewery," Trish said after taking a taste. "We need to get a bar in San Diego to carry it on tap."

Once back on the road, with sixty miles to go, I said, "I'm amazed at how easy it is now crossing borders. You can't imagine how frustrating it was when we lived in Austria and Germany, so close to the Czech border, not to be able to cross over and visit my parents' birthplaces or other places important to our family. The Iron Curtain is gone now, so it's no longer a problem."

---

As evening came on, we left the motorway near the center of Prague and found ourselves on a thoroughfare crowded with cars and pedestrians. I could barely make out street signs in the dim light. Then, just when we needed it most, the car's GPS announced it could give no further directions. Momentarily stymied, we telephoned the Hotel Central, which we had selected for its Old Town location, in close proximity to the sights and neighborhoods we most wanted to explore. We explained our predicament to the manager, who chuckled. It didn't matter, he told us. We were just a few blocks away, but the labyrinth of one-way streets made using GPS impossible. He would send someone to assist us.

Within a few minutes, an English-speaking young man appeared and directed us to the hotel. I motioned to Trish to look up at the building's Art Nouveau façade, dating from the height of the Austro-Hungarian Empire, with its arched parapet, frescoes, and upper-story projections. Once she stepped out of the car and a porter removed our suitcases, the fellow who guided us there accompanied me to the hotel's parking lot. We took a dizzying series of turns, got back on the motorway, off again, and zipped down a few more streets, before arriving at the lot, fronting on another street but scarcely more than a block from the hotel.

"You should not try to drive here in the city," he cautioned me with a deadpan look. I nodded. We would be walking even more than I had expected.

I found Trish at the registration desk in the lobby. As I approached, the lively blond woman at the desk welcomed me in Czech and English. The hotel's interior retained its original splendor, with an open-brass-work elevator, Tiffany-style stained-glass windows, and marble decorations. However, in a stunning act of creativity, the owners had installed a dining room at a new open level suspended in the atrium above the lobby, as if floating in the air. Guest rooms, meanwhile, had been refurbished with contemporary furniture, polished wood paneling, soundproof windows, and wall-mounted flat-screen televisions. Trish's MS symptoms still being at an early stage, we didn't yet need an accessible room.

The next morning, after stuffing ourselves at a luxurious buffet of smoked fish, cold cuts, cheeses, eggs, breads, and coffee, we set out to explore the city. I felt exhilaration at being again in this city that played an important role in my family's past. I remembered a lot from my earlier visit and was eager to share it with Trish. But I knew this would be a different experience from the last time, when my daughter and I traipsed about, eager to see whatever lay around the next corner. Today, we would find out how ably Trish could negotiate the streets and plazas of Prague.

Reasonably well, it turned out. Just slower. With her right hand on her cane and her left arm holding onto me for better balance, she strolled at a leisurely but steady pace. I hoped she could sustain that. Nonetheless, I wanted to take it easy this first day and not wear her out.

The brisk morning air was already giving way to sunshine. We nonetheless carried sweaters and an umbrella in a shoulder bag, as the weather could change rapidly this time of year.

We started out walking west along Hybernska, into the heart of the Old Town neighborhood. The street took its name from the Irish (Hibernian) Franciscan monks who maintained a church and convent there in the early 1600s. This being a weekday, local residents thronged the street, bustling in and out of shops and offices. Despite the crowds, the wide, smooth sidewalks allowed us to move along at a comfortable speed.

"You're doing great," I told Trish. "Are you OK walking at this pace?"

"So far, so good. I'll let you know if I'm getting tired."

An easy two-blocks walk brought us to the Gothic, hundred-foot-tall Powder Tower, capped with a steep, black tile roof. It was built in the 15th century as a principal gate into the city and later was used to store gunpowder, hence its name.

A few blocks farther, we entered Old Town Square, the vast stone plaza people worldwide saw overflowing with demonstrators during news coverage of the Velvet Revolution that led to dismantling of the Communist regime in 1989. Now tourists and peaceful locals filled the square. A cacophony of voices in a score of languages echoed off the surrounding buildings. At the center of the square, dozens of young people, many in shirts bearing logos of American musicians or sports figures, sat around the base of the Jan Huss memorial, a ten-foot-tall, bronze statue atop a broad stone base of similar height. A progressive religious leader, Huss was burned at the stake as a heretic in 1415. His execution led to fifteen years of turmoil in the Hussite Wars and made Huss himself a permanent national symbol of resistance to oppression.

As we threaded our way through the crowds, we paused to look up at the stone edifice and twin towers of the Church of Our Lady Before Tyn, a prominent church here since the 14th century and still looming over all the surrounding buildings. The eight pointed black spires topping each of the church's towers looked like arrays of rockets preparing to launch. The odd name derived from the Tyn district behind the church, originally a marketplace in medieval days.

"Now I need a rest," Trish said as we neared the far side of the square. I glanced at my watch; her timing was perfect. We found a table at an outdoor café facing the square. There we drank coffee while waiting for the hourly performance of the three-story-tall, two-level astronomical clock built into the medieval Old Town Hall and decorated with religious icons. Its upper face displayed the time, as well as the positions of the sun and moon, while images on the lower face identified the month. On the hour, chimes sounded, and figures of the twelve apostles moved past windows above the upper face, as they had for nearly 500 years.

Refreshed and eager to explore further, we continued two more blocks to the Charles Bridge, the most ornate of the city's dozen bridges crossing the Vltava River. Statues of saints lined both sides of the stone pedestrian bridge. We worked our way among crowds perusing the work of artists and craftspeople lined up across the entire span.

From the middle of the bridge, I pointed to the imposing walls and spires of the Prague Castle on a hilltop across the river.

"That's where we're going this afternoon," I said.

Trish drew back her face and raised an eyebrow in disbelief.

"Don't worry," I continued, "You won't have to hike up that hill. We're signed up for a bus tour."

Back at Old Town Square, we bought rolls stuffed with white sausage and sauerkraut from a street vendor. We then found our tour group, gathering in front of a travel office just off the square. The guide, a forty-something university professor fluent in English and clad in a windbreaker and walking shoes, directed us onto the twenty-passenger bus while she began her commentary on Prague history and culture.

Trish needed a boost getting up the steps into the bus, where we found seats near the front.

"I am so relieved to be sitting down," she whispered to me. Maybe I had planned too much activity for this first day.

While the guide continued her commentary, the bus driver navigated narrow, mostly one-way streets out of the Old Town.

After crossing the river, the bus followed cobblestone ways through the Hradcany neighborhood up to the castle. By the time we pulled into the central courtyard, Trish was ready to get out and resume exploring. Perhaps out of deference to her and a couple of other slower walkers, our guide maintained a casual pace as she led us among the churches, fortresses, and halls filling the seventeen-acre site. From the easterly parapet, we had a panoramic view of the city and the distant countryside basking in the afternoon sun.

The next morning, as we consumed another hearty buffet breakfast to keep us fueled for our walks, I told Trish, "Today, I have a real surprise for you."

"I'm game, but yesterday took a lot out of me, so let's not overdo it."

I led her back toward Old Town Square, but then diverted to the right into Josefov, the historic Jewish neighborhood. We first came upon the Old-New Synagogue, the oldest active temple in Europe, dating from the 13th century. It replaced an even older temple that no longer stands, and was named to distinguish it from the nearby newer ones built later. Its façade, rising to a unique sawtooth-patterned stone roofline, towered over the street below and the adjoining cemetery.

With my help, Trish gingerly descended steps from street level down into the building. Candelabras hung from wrought iron frames against the far wall. The ark containing Torah scrolls sat at the base of a stone wall rising up fifty feet to an arched ceiling, interrupted only by a single round, stained-glass window.

"This is where my father had his *bar mitzvah*," I said. "There are several other, more ornate synagogues nearby, but this is the most historic one. It's the only one still used regularly for services."

"I'm surprised that everything is so intact, compared to what the Nazis did to buildings like this in other cities."

"Yes, they spared all this, but for a really horrible reason. Once they completed the Holocaust, they planned to make this district what they called a Museum of an Extinct Race. Now, it's preserved by the local community as the Prague Jewish Museum."

"That's pretty shocking. I never heard that before."

On that note, we left the synagogue and entered the wrought-iron gates of the cemetery. Lack of vacant land in Josefov made it necessary over the centuries to place graves atop one another, as many as twelve deep. Thousands of gravestones stood jammed together, many tipped at odd angles or leaning against their neighbors, partially sunk into the ground. With so many close together, their differences stood out: pointed, rounded, or scrolled peaks; freestanding or attached to crypts; plain with just inscriptions or decorated with religious images. Hebrew lettering on the oldest stones was weathered to the point of being barely legible. Moss or grass covered the ground in portions of the cemetery, while dead leaves from overhanging trees filled other spaces.

Trish had difficulty at the beginning here, as the tip of her cane sank into the gravel pathway. She persevered, but I needed to steady her from time to time.

I stopped and pointed to a light-brown gravestone, taller than most around it, sculpted with a lion and bunches of grapes, and backed by a structure resembling a miniature stone tent, signifying the grave of a rabbi or other important person. Pebbles covered flat portions of the crypt, reflecting a centuries-old Jewish tradition of placing such stones when visiting graves of relatives or friends. A plaque on a nearby wall highlighted the importance of the site. It gave me goosebumps, standing once again in front of a shrine that had great religious and historical significance to my family.

"This is the grave of Rabbi Judah Loew, my grandfather on my father's side twenty generations or so back. He was an important leader who met with the Austrian emperor to negotiate on behalf of the Jewish community here. His followers called him *Maharal*, meaning a highly respected teacher. He was a mystic in the philosophy of Kabbalah and the man who created a creature called the Golem. At least, that's the legend, that the rabbi created an animate being out of clay to protect Prague's Jewish community against the violent attacks that were common in those times. But he deactivated the creature later, when he became afraid of losing control of it, and stored its remains in the attic of the Old-New Synagogue."

"That's quite a story. It sounds kind of familiar."

"It should. Some say it was the inspiration for Mary Shelley's *Frankenstein*."

"I guess it isn't any more fanciful than most religious stories. Besides, I've always thought there's something a little mystical about you."

"More than you know. When I was here with Coralea, she went into a trance for several minutes standing by the grave. Afterward, she told me she was sure the rabbi sensed we were there."

We walked on among the other synagogues comprising parts of the Jewish Museum. We paused a long time to admire the Moorish architecture and intricate interior decorations of the Spanish Synagogue. The reconstructed Pinkas Synagogue, the second oldest after the Old-New Synagogue, was memorable for its interior inscription of names of the 80,000 Czech and Slovak Jews killed in the Holocaust, including many of my relatives. And at the neo-Gothic Maisel Synagogue, dating from the golden age of the Prague Jewish community in the late 16th century, we viewed a collection of local religious and cultural Judaica, from ancient silver candelabras to modern art works. Trish's scooter bumped over cobblestone streets between the buildings.

As we began meandering back toward our hotel, we came upon the Franz Kafka Café, an establishment frequented by the famous writer in his younger days and now bearing his name. We noticed a lot of empty tables—not a good sign—but we were there and felt hungry, so we took a chance and sat down. The disheveled and very surly waitress informed us the only food available was beef soup or a ham sandwich. We ordered one of each. After a long wait, and seeing a nearby couple who had arrived after us being served exactly what we had ordered, I called the server over. She informed us that "soup is finished," and presented us with the sandwich—plain ham on a very dry roll, in a plastic wrapper, a step below what we might find in a gas station mini-mart back home.

As we left the café, Trish shook her head and said, "That was like stepping through a time warp back to the Soviet era."

"I know. Hard to understand. It's the only place like that I've come across here."

Nearing the Powder Tower, we passed the Municipal House, an Art Nouveau concert hall that is home to the Prague Symphony Orchestra. An arched mosaic high above the entrance, flanked by stone sculpture groups, looked down on outdoor restaurants and the street scene of Republic Square. Trish stopped to view a poster listing upcoming concerts.

"Look!" she exclaimed. "There's a concert tonight. Let's check it out."

It turned out to be a performance in one of the smaller concert halls, but that suited us fine. We returned after having a nice beef goulash dinner at the hotel that more than made up for our earlier experience at the Kafka Café.

I held Trish's arm, helping her descend a flight of stairs to a wood-paneled room on the lower-level. The audience of 200 or so, a mix of young and old, formally and casually dressed, listened reverently to the performance of Dvořák classics, then applauded wildly at the end of each piece. Trish seemed so energized by the experience that she scarcely needed help in getting back to the hotel.

On our last day there, we left town to visit another family site. I had the hotel concierge mark on a street map the best route in and out of the city, but she still expressed concern over whether we would find our way, especially on our return.

Her directions succeeded in getting us on the motorway back toward Plzen. On my previous visit, my daughter and I hired a guide to help us find the village of Volenice, where my paternal great-grandparents had lived, and the cemetery in nearby Strakonice where they were buried. This time, I had better maps, as well as clear memories of the earlier search. Today, one can find descriptions and pictures of both on the internet.

As we drove from the motorway through rolling hills framed by dense, deep-green forests, I spied Volenice on a hilltop ahead, surrounded by farm fields. After winding our way up to the town, I parked next to the onetime family home, a two-story, gray stucco house opposite the towering town church with an eight-story steeple. That house was my father's birthplace. As on my previous visit, I wondered why one of the few Jewish families in the area would have lived in the house closest to the church.

The village consisted of fewer than a hundred homes, packed side by side along a handful of streets. Exterior walls of the outer ring of houses formed a perimeter for defense of the community. Coupled with the hilltop location, that apparently kept them safe for centuries. We walked around a bit while I reminisced aloud about my family history here, beginning when Hapsburg Empress Maria Theresa expelled the Jewish inhabitants of Prague in the mid-1800s.

Having found Volenice, I hoped I could find the cemetery again with equal ease. It did not appear on any maps. This took on special importance, as those graves represented the most direct link to my family heritage here. The last time, after a search like something out of an adventure novel led us there, I climbed a six-foot wall and located the graves. That search formed the opening of a book I later wrote about growing up in post-war Europe and then becoming an American.

Memory works when it needs to. I retraced my steps from five years earlier until we came upon the same wrought-iron gates and stone walls that blocked me then, hidden behind farmhouses off a rural road outside Strakonice. Trish joined me at the cemetery entrance. With a long sigh, I grasped and shook the locked gates, just as I had done on the earlier visit. This time, though, I satisfied myself by peering through the gates rather than climbing the wall. After Trish snapped a photo of me at the gates, I pointed out to her the five-foot-tall, grey granite slabs marking the graves, near the rear of the cemetery.

"I'm impressed," Trish said. "I can't believe you found your way back here. And I'm still amazed you and Coralea found this place the first time."

Armed with the concierge's directions and a bit of luck, we found our way back to the hotel. In the morning, we set off on the next phase of our trip, driving 325 miles to Budapest. Passing through Bratislava in Slovakia, we skirted the Austrian border, only forty miles from Vienna. I thought again about the frustration of being barred from crossing that border during the years my family lived in Europe after the war.

---

Budapest turned out to be just as challenging as Prague in finding our way and more challenging topographically. A kind hotel operator at the Hilton stayed on the phone with me for half an hour, guiding me to their ridge-top location on the Buda side of the Danube. The Pest side was relatively flat but too far away to reach on foot. Other than walking around the immediate neighborhood and to an evening concert at the nearby Matthias Church, we relied on tours and taxis to see the sprawling city.

A nearly hour-long taxi ride one evening took us to a restaurant in the countryside. A staffer at our hotel had recommended it for a cozy dinner of traditional Hungarian cuisine. Rain fell the entire way. I worried about getting back, but the driver assured me in broken German that he would wait for us.

Inside, the dim lights reflecting from the white plaster walls, the candles flickering on our table, and the violin music in the background all had me feeling especially romantic. After ordering our dinner of cold cherry soup and Székély goulash, we drank dark red Hungarian wine and chatted in soft tones about our most recent adventures.

Sitting opposite this beautiful woman with whom I'd been sharing a wonderful travel experience, I spontaneously reached across the table, took her hands in mine, and said, "I want to marry you." I had thought about this over the preceding weeks, unsure of how and when to bring it up, but that seemed like the perfect moment.

Trish fell back in her seat, then gave me a big smile. Without hesitation, she replied, "Sure, yes!"

After feeling a rush of relief and excitement, I stood to lean across the table and kiss her. Diners at nearby tables nodded approvingly in our direction.

The following evening in Budapest, we took a similarly romantic cruise on the Danube. I steadied Trish in boarding the open-deck riverboat as it rocked at its pier along the Pest waterfront. We hugged as the boat sailed beneath the brightly lit bridges connecting the two halves of the city. Our talk of marriage the previous evening cast a continuing glow over the rest of our stay. Three months later, during a New Year's trip to the Grand Canyon, I would seal our commitment by giving her a ring fashioned with diamonds from my late mother's engagement ring.

---

After three days in Budapest, we made the 150-mile drive to Vienna, a favorite city for me since childhood. Trish had visited once before, during her time studying in France thirty years earlier. Here, we walked as much as in Prague. The broad boulevards, lush parks, sidewalk cafes, and pedestrian malls all made this one of the most invitingly walkable cities in the world.

From our hotel on the Ring, at the edge of the Old City, we wandered to the iconic Stephansdom cathedral, which I remembered seeing the first time badly damaged by wartime bombing and artillery fire; through the lush gardens of the Stadtpark with its golden statue of composer Johann Strauss; and to the Demel pastry shop that was a favorite of my family. And, of course, we dined on the city's namesake Wiener schnitzel.

I was encouraged at seeing how well Trish maintained her pace. Whenever she needed a respite, we ducked into one of the many coffee houses for which Vienna is famous, where coffee is served in a dozen or more variations, and where one is welcome to sit for hours while reading newspapers, chatting with friends, or watching the street scene.

"I can see why you love this city," Trish said as we prepared to leave after three days. "It's not only interesting, it's really easy for me to get around. We've got to come back here the next time we're in Europe."

---

The last leg of our trip took us back to Braunau for an overnight visit with Karin and Loisel, and then on to the Munich airport.

There, in an astonishing act of faith, we followed the Mercedes factory instructions and turned over the car to a desk clerk at the Kempinski Hotel next to the terminal. Sure enough, the car appeared six weeks later at the dealership in San Diego.

The trip had its challenges. Not only was it the first time Trish and I traveled that long together, but we dealt for the first time while traveling with the limitations imposed by her MS symptoms.

Soon after our flight took off for home, Trish said, "I appreciated you being patient with me. I know I slowed you down from your usual fast walking pace. And it's likely to be harder the next time."

"It wasn't a problem," I replied. "Walking more slowly, I actually saw and experienced more along the way. This was a great trip. Whatever happens, I'm sure the next one will be just as good."

"I hope so, but it will have to be pretty special to top Rabbi Loew and the Golem."

# Chapter 3
# NO NEED FOR A SCOOTER UNDERWATER

Trish in Botanical Garden, Grand Cayman

*Roatan, December 2005*
*Grand Cayman, April 2009*

Trish had never strapped on a scuba tank before we took a winter holiday trip to Roatan in the Bay Islands of Honduras. It became a life-changing experience for her.

I had been traveling and diving in the Caribbean for many years, since a 1981 visit to the island of Cozumel off the Yucatan Peninsula in southern Mexico. Overwhelmed by the rainbow palette of fish and corals, as well as the experience of being in an entirely new environment, I took a scuba certification course as soon as I returned home. From then on, I regularly dove among sleek sea lions and leafy kelp forests around the Channel Islands along the Southern California coast and made an annual Caribbean pilgrimage, always to a different island.

I loved every island for its distinctive food, music, people, and nature. Jamaica's waterfalls, mountains, reggae music, and jerk chicken contrasted with Bonaire's flat terrain, cactus forests, and Dutch *rijsttafel*. And that was just on the surface. The underwater sights, topography, and wildlife varied just as much, from shallow gardens bounding with fish to corral-covered walls dropping hundreds of feet. What made Caribbean diving especially attractive was the warm water. I could dive at any depth in a thin, three-millimeter shorty wetsuit, rather than the full-length seven-millimeter suit I needed for protection in the frigid Pacific waters off California.

As soon as she turned fourteen, I enrolled my daughter in a scuba course. She had always been a water baby, and she took to diving as if coral reefs and kelp forests were her natural habitat.

Trish, Coralea, and I took our first Caribbean trip together to Grand Turk in the Turks and Caicos at the east end of the Bahamas island chain. Trish snorkeled while Coralea and I plunged into the depths of clear, warm waters and cavorted among turtles, rays, and wildly colored fish. Trish's view from the surface was fine, but couldn't compare with what Coralea and I described after our dives. So, when we planned our next tropical vacation, Trish was game to try scuba for the first time. But, by then, MS had hampered her mobility enough that she relied on a walker, so this would be a challenge.

We traveled to Roatan the day before Christmas. After we pre-boarded our flight in Los Angeles, the airline crew seated a stocky, twenty-something man across the aisle from us. His legs ended at the knees. I noticed the carry-on bag that the crew stowed for him in the overhead bin bore the emblem of a veterans' assistance organization. Once boarding concluded, Trish leaned over and engaged him in conversation. He had lost his legs to an insurgents' explosive device while deployed with the US Army in Iraq. An aid group sponsored this trip and arranged training for him with an adaptive diving program. He planned to scuba dive while on Roatan. That caught Trish's attention.

Turning back to me, she declared. "If he can do it, I certainly can."

Galvez International Airport on Roatan turned out to be less developed than we expected. Its single runway accommodated commercial jets, but lack of a taxiway required our pilot to turn the plane around right on the runway before proceeding to the terminal. Through the window to our left, we noticed no jetways. Rather, several men positioned a rolling stairway at the aircraft door.

"This is going to be difficult," she said. "I'm going to need help getting down those stairs."

Hearing this, the fellow across the aisle laughed and told her, "Don't worry. They'll be carrying me down. I'm sure they'll be happy to help you, too."

Sure enough, after the rest of the passengers had exited, I retrieved Trish's folding walker from a closet at the front of the cabin and helped her to the door. Then, as one of the ground crew kept her balanced, I grasped her ankles from the front and moved her legs down the stairway one step at a time.

Rental cars were unavailable. So, after retrieving our luggage, we located a van that would take us and a few others to our hotels. Before allowing the van to depart the airport, however, the brawny fellow apparently in charge of visitor transportation demanded a sizeable "tip" from each of us.

"Welcome to Roatan," I whispered to Trish. "That's what happens when tourists first swarm a place like this."

A twenty-minute ride on a smooth, two-lane road took us through dense jungle and past settlements of a few dozen colorfully painted houses, wiping away any bad initial impression of the island. At the Bay Islands Beach Resort, an entry drive lined with coconut palms led to a cluster of a half-dozen well-kept wood buildings nestled along a secluded beach near the northwest corner of the island. The proprietors welcomed us and led us to a nearby open-air bar covered with a thatched roof of palm fronds. After sharing glasses of rum punch with us, they got us settled into our home for the coming week.

I couldn't have been more pleased with what we found. Our room, one of four set side-by-side in a single-story building amid palms and hibiscus bushes, had all the necessary accessibility features for Trish's convenience. Outside, a smooth boardwalk connected all the resort's facilities—the bar, restaurant, guest rooms, dive shop, and pier. Clear, warm Caribbean waters sparkled like a gem-covered blanket in the afternoon sun.

"I want to get set up for diving this week," I told Trish. "I'm going over to the dive shop."

"Fine, you do that, and I'll explore this place some more," she replied. With that, she headed back down the boardwalk, pushing her walker with unusual energy.

With only about twenty guests, and not all of them divers, the resort's two thirty-foot dive boats easily accommodated everyone and would offer a variety of dive sites over the course of the week. I asked at the shop about the possibility of Trish getting basic instruction and trying scuba during our stay. The staff already had noticed her reliance on a walker. They assured me they were trained in working with disabled divers and would give her an unforgettable experience.

On returning, I found Trish standing along the boardwalk near the bar, peering through a screen into an eight-foot-high wood enclosure. She waved me over, then pointed inside, where a green parrot three feet in height sat on a pedestal. Its left wing drooped. A sign explained that resort staff had found the bird injured. Left outside, it would have starved or been killed by predators. Here, safe and well fed, it served as the resort mascot.

"Good news," I told Trish. "The dive shop says you can scuba with a guide whenever you're ready."

"Great, in a day or two," she replied in a subdued tone, with what looked like a forced smile.

"The bad news is that there's nothing happening in town now. No public events or celebrations around Christmas. The people here are very religious. They'll all be in church tonight and tomorrow."

I hadn't realized that the local population was mostly Hispanic and Catholic, having come over from the mainland in the couple hundred years that Honduras governed the Bay Islands. Early Spanish colonists had wiped out the original Indigenous population or transported them as slaves to other islands.

At the resort, on the other hand, vacation life went on as usual. Twinkling holiday lights and shiny foil decorations livened the bar and restaurant, and everyone seemed upbeat. We hung out at the bar well into the evening, listening to Latin-Caribbean music, consuming rum drinks, and chatting with couples from Texas and Michigan.

Coralea and I, along with several other guests, went diving the next day at a famous site called Spooky Channel, located within swimming distance of the beach. A crack in the offshore reef plunged from twenty-foot depth at the top down to ninety feet. That created a sensation of dropping into a canyon, in water so clear we could see all the way to the bottom. Schools of silvery fish cascaded down the walls, evading toothy barracudas. Neon, multicolored parrot fish nibbled at coral heads, as four-foot-long black groupers drifted by alongside us. Smaller tropical fish played in the sunbeams bouncing off the canyon walls, while an occasional olive-green moray eel peeked out from caves amid the coral.

The rest of the diving that week went equally well as we rode dive boats up and down the coast to the staff's favorite sites. The boats featured typical open-air arrangements, with rows of air tanks in racks behind seats along the sides at the rear, and a forward portion screened by a sun shade. A platform at the stern provided a step for entry into the water, and a pair of ladders extended down from there for return to the boat.

At Mary's Place, channels in the reef took us from a shallow plateau down nearly a hundred feet, amid rare black corals and bright blue sponges. The Halfmoon Bay and West End walls dropped thousands of feet into the offshore Cayman Trench. As a brisk current pulled us along, we flew across the face of the reef.

The weather remained sunny all week, with just an occasional afternoon rain shower. When it rained, we napped in our rooms or joined other guests at the bar for *pina coladas* made from fresh coconut pulp and local rum.

In between scuba dives, I snorkeled in the lagoon in front of the resort, part of a protected National Marine Park. With the aid of an inflated vest and extra-long fins to improve her propulsion, Trish joined me in following a snorkel trail with markers pointing out highlights of the lagoon's habitat and wildlife. Goldfish-sized fish in a dozen colors flitted about in the seagrass. Brown brain corrals grew on the scattered rocks. At one point, a pair of young green sea turtles lazily swam through.

One day, after a morning of diving, we took a taxi into the small nearby town of West End. Single-story wood buildings, many elevated on three-foot stilts and accessible by stairs, lined the dirt main street. With Trish using her walker, we inched our way through a throng of visitors. We bought fresh fruit drinks from an open-air, street-level stand and peered into shops selling wood carvings, pottery, and other local crafts. At a shop run by a particularly friendly woman, we bought a hand-painted ceramic tray—cobalt blue and decorated with flower petals—to place on our dining room table at home.

Another afternoon, a van from the resort took Trish, me, and half a dozen others to an iguana farm. On the way, we passed through the principal town of Coxen's Hole, where houses painted in bright shades of turquoise and pink, with fancy woodwork around doorways and verandas, gave the place more of a Caribbean feel.

The iguana farm took us by surprise. A thousand of the greenish creatures, as large as four feet in length, lay or crawled about everywhere—on the ground, in the trees, on the front porches of houses. With their wrinkled faces, scaly skin, and spiky dorsal crest, they looked like leftovers from the Jurassic era.

"Why do you raise them?" I asked the burly, gray-haired manager as he gave us a brief tour.

"Well, some people keep them as pets," he explained. "But mostly, people here like to eat them. They taste like chicken. We even call them 'chickens of the trees.'"

I knew he was right. Trish and I both had eaten iguana stew in Mexico. It did taste a lot like chicken, though more gamey.

On the way back, we detoured to a jungle-lined beach that was home to a community of Afro-Caribbean Garifuna. As our van pulled to a stop, a six-foot-tall, brown-skinned man approached us, apparently a greeter. He welcomed us in English, though with a strong accent different from that of the Spanish-speaking locals in town. He then gave a brief explanation of the settlement's origins.

"Our people were forced to move here from the Island of St. Vincent in the early 1800s. They were freed slaves who rebelled against the English colonial rulers. Few of us are left. Most of the community has scattered to other islands, some to America."

"The name of your people, Garifuna, what does it mean?" I asked.

"It comes from an African tribal name. Many of our ancestors were from the same region of Africa. They kept a lot of their language and culture. It's changed over time, but we still identify with them."

Every island has its own history, I thought. People here, like the ones in Jamaica or Trinidad or Cuba, were brought as slaves from various parts of Africa. Then, living on separate islands under different colonial powers, they developed unique histories and cultures, especially food and music. It was all foreign to my own culture, but I soaked it up, enjoying every interaction and experience.

"Why do you live here, on this isolated beach?" someone else asked.

"When the English brought us here, this was the place they made us live. For a long time, we stayed away from other settlements, for our safety. Now, we welcome visitors. We still like this place. It's been home for a long time."

He pointed to a nearby hut. "Over there you will find crafts that we make here. Please take a look."

Trish's walker couldn't negotiate the sandy soil, so we waited at the van while the others followed our host. They came back with an assortment of wood carvings of human faces, animal figures, and jungle scenes, all made there in the village.

We enjoyed the island explorations, but diving through Spooky Channel remained the highlight of the week. After hearing me talk about it, Trish grew excited when the dive guide said he would take her there. He gave her an orientation in the shallows, making sure she remained comfortable being underwater and breathing through a regulator. At that time, her legs still had enough strength for her to kick her way out to the reef with minimal assistance from the guide.

"Do you want me to go along?" I asked her, as we stood together at the end of the resort's fifty-foot, wood pier.

"No, I'm sure he'll take good care of me," she replied, gesturing toward the athletic-looking young man setting up her equipment. With that, she handed me her walker and put on her mask. With a little help from the guide, she stepped down a ladder into the water. She held onto the ladder while he slipped on her fins, strapped her into her buoyancy vest and tank, and placed the regulator in her mouth. With that, they were off for what I hoped would be a great experience.

I expected them to be down for a short time, so I was a bit alarmed when they didn't surface again for over a half hour. I scanned the water continually for bubbles. Then I saw two heads break the surface, and the guide gave the divers' "ok" sign, arcing his right arm up and around to the top of his head. I watched, smiling, as they swam back to where Coralea and I waited.

Once back at the pier, Trish flashed a huge smile as the guide and I helped her up the ladder and out of the water.

"It was amazing!" she blurted out. "He took me down to thirty feet. It was so clear. I couldn't believe all the fish."

That evening, over a dinner of grilled, locally caught grouper, Trish couldn't stop talking about her dive. "Now I understand why you like doing this so much. The fish, the coral, the light. It was like I was watching a movie, except I was right there in it." With each statement, her excitement grew, until she was almost hyperventilating.

"I'm really proud of you," I told her. "I know you were nervous, but it all worked out, even better than I expected." She smiled again and nodded. Coralea beamed at her.

She indeed overcame her apprehension and wound up having one of the most memorable experiences of her life. I hoped she could repeat that in another time and place.

---

Four years later, the Cayman Islands provided an equally memorable experience, especially for Trish. Scuba divers consider the Caymans, with their plunging undersea walls and lush fish life, among the top destinations in the Caribbean.

Trish and I booked a flight through Miami. We found what looked like a lovely boutique hotel, the Cobalt Coast Resort, on the north coast of Grand Cayman, largest of the three islands.

By this time, Trish's MS symptoms had worsened to where she relied on a mobility scooter. It seemed unlikely she would be able to enjoy another scuba dive, but I had a secret plan for an experience I hoped she would find even more memorable than her dive off Roatan.

On the flight down from Miami, the pilot pointed out the prominent island of Cuba, stretching far to the east. I had told Trish about my visit thirty years earlier with a lawyers' group during the brief time when the Carter administration permitted travel there. Maybe, I told Trish, political conditions would improve and we would be able to travel there again. Sadly, I learned later from a college professor friend who took groups to Cuba on educational exchanges that the island had limited provisions for the mobility-impaired.

On arrival at Owen Roberts International Airport in George Town, we rented a silver hatchback Hyundai—just large enough to carry us, our bags, and the scooter—and set off on the ten-mile drive to our hotel. We had acquired a lightweight blue scooter for Trish to use in the house, and also to take traveling. The car's low suspension would make loading and unloading the scooter easier, but would make it more difficult to help Trish in and out.

We traveled first along world-renowned, west-facing Seven Mile Beach. Then, as we neared our destination, I noted with surprise that the sandy beach gave way to a rocky shoreline along the north coast. No beach diving here, I figured.

An affable Dutch ex-pat owned and operated the Cobalt Coast Resort. The accommodations he provided for our eight-day stay met our needs—an accessible one-bedroom suite with a private shaded patio facing the ocean. The hotel's pool and sundeck lay just steps away, adjoining an outdoor dining area. And the hotel had created a sand beach above the rocks along its ocean frontage. A well-equipped dive shop operated on the grounds, with boats tied up at the resort's hundred-foot-long pier.

I went diving each morning, while Trish slept in and had a late breakfast. On my return, I typically found her lounging on a chaise by the pool or reading on the patio outside our room. What little rain we had fell at night and didn't interfere with our outdoor activities.

The diving proved to be every bit as impressive as I had heard and read. With scores of dive sites along the reefs ringing the island, we never encountered crowds. If another boat had moored at a site, we continued to the next one.

At the dive site known as Tarpon Alley, we followed a sloping channel out to the face of the reef, where we marveled at the wall extending as far as we could see, covered in olive-green plate corals and dropping thousands of feet into a cobalt abyss. Chain Reef, a series of rocky fingers extending downward to a sandy bottom, was more about wildlife, with ten-pound lobsters crawling along the bottom, brown-and-yellow Hawksbill turtles gliding past us, and four-foot-long turquoise parrotfish nibbling at the coral. At Eagle Ray Pass, we followed a sandy chute that plunged through a gap in the reef down to a hundred-foot depth. As we ascended along the outside of the reef, turtles and rays flew by so effortlessly, they made us jealous. In the shallows atop the reef lay a coral garden flush with striped sergeant majors, orange squirrelfish, dainty butterflyfish, spotted morays, and more.

But the peak experience came at recently discovered Ghost Mountain. A hundred-foot pinnacle resembling a gargantuan flower stem rose from the outer slope of the reef like an apparition and climbed to within forty feet of the surface. Blue sea fans and brown gorgonians waved from its crown amid purple and yellow vase sponges. Fish clustered around the top, as they do at every high point in the ocean. A five-foot grouper jolted me, pausing to stare into my mask lens for a few seconds before swimming away.

On my return from diving each day, we had a bite of lunch, typically sandwiches of freshly caught fish, at the excellent on-site restaurant. Then we spent most afternoons exploring. As in Jamaica, I adjusted to driving on the left side of the road in this former British colony.

The roughly L-shaped island had a main body twenty-five miles long, running east-west. At the west end, a peninsula extended twelve miles northward, culminating in the area around our hotel. The shallow North Sound Bay, open to the ocean, lay at the inside corner of the "L."

George Town, capital of the Caymans, turned out to be more urban than I expected. In recent years, it had become a financial hub of the region, a kind of Caribbean Switzerland — a cluster of office towers filled with law firms and accountants providing home to thousands of companies in need of a remote official address with little regulatory oversight. In sharp contrast, hotels, bars, and recreation facilities filled with vacationers lay close by. Both the business district and the tourist areas were generally accessible for Trish's scooter, with level entries or ramps at most buildings and curb cuts at corners. The island's flat topography and low elevation helped too.

Just south of the hotel, we encountered the amusingly named community of Hell. Its identity came from black algae encrusting a field of rugged limestone formations projecting from the earth, creating a scorched appearance. A gift shop sign declared "Welcome to Hell," and the post office featured "Postcards from Hell." I took a photo of Trish on her scooter next to the sign announcing the place name.

In nearby West Bay, we visited the Cayman Turtle Centre, where thousands of green sea turtles, from hatchlings to broad-shelled adults, swam in concrete ponds. Like the iguana farm on Roatan, this began as a commercial operation, breeding turtles to become soups and stews, since taking wild turtles was long prohibited. Now, though, it operated more as a research facility and tourist attraction.

One day, we drove out to the rural East End, where the island's highest point, known as The Mountain, reaches a grand elevation of forty feet. More impressive was the sixty-five-acre Queen Elizabeth II Botanic Park, a tropical garden as varied and colorful as any I've seen in the Caribbean. We wandered the dirt pathways among sage-colored fan palms, towering ironwood trees, bursts of white orchids, ruby-red ginger lilies, clusters of red-and-yellow birds of paradise, and hundreds more plants native to the island. Four-foot-long, bluish iguanas lounged in the sun along the paths.

As we paused to watch rare West Indian whistling ducks floating among water lilies and hyacinths in a pathside pond, Trish said. "This is my idea of a botanical garden. I didn't know these islands had so many kinds of plants and flowers. And I love the nice smooth paths. This will probably be the highlight of our visit here."

I just smiled and nodded. She had no idea what I still had planned for her.

We drove the island's circumferential road, following the coast all the way around to the north shore until it ended at a point marking the east side of the bay. We passed houses painted in pastel shades of blue or green, or white with turquoise trim, with steep tile roofs to shed occasional heavy rains. At day's end, we stopped at the Rum Point Club, a pink-and-blue beachside restaurant facing the mouth of the bay. From there, we watched a glorious red sunset while drinking Cayman Coladas, followed by a dinner of conch fritters and grilled snapper.

Eating at places favored by locals provided a pleasant sidelight to our explorations. I got some excellent recommendations from a maintenance man at our hotel. In small roadside establishments, we lunched or snacked on conch stew, fried mackerel, and jerk chicken, accompanied by bottles of golden, locally produced Caybrew beer. To our pleasant surprise, nearly all these restaurants had level entries, easy for Trish to negotiate. One even had a wheelchair ramp.

Some afternoons, we lay by the pool, reading and talking about our adventures. When Trish wanted to take a swim, I helped her down steps at the shallow end while she grasped the stainless-steel rail running down the middle. Once in the water, she was able to breaststroke short distances, kicking lightly. From our perch on the pool deck, we watched pleasure craft and inter-island freighters cruise by.

The surprise I saved for Trish came near the end of our stay, when the dive shop ran a weekly trip to the sandbar known as Stingray City. Located at the opening of North Sound Bay, in just twelve feet of water, it became a gathering place for rays drawn by scraps discarded by fishermen and treats fed them by divers. As soon as a boat moored over the sandy flats, the rays converged and prepared to interact with visitors. I experienced this once before, off Bora Bora in French Polynesia.

The evening before the dive, as we lingered over after-dinner drinks the at the resort's restaurant, I popped the surprise.

"Remember when we were planning this trip, and I talked about diving with stingrays?"

"Yeah, you got really excited."

"Well, it's happening tomorrow. And you're going to share the excitement. You're going to dive with me."

Trish looked down and pursed her lips. After a few seconds, she responded, "I don't know if I can do it. This isn't like Roatan. Back then, I could still walk a little. Now, how am I going to get on and off a boat?"

"Don't worry, I've worked it all out with the dive shop. Trust me, it'll be great."

A smile returned to her face. She shrugged, then looked right into my eyes.

"I do. I'll give it a try. It does sound exciting."

The crew and I helped Trish onto the boat at the hotel pier. Getting her in and out of the water at the dive site would be more complicated, but the dive master assured me they had done this before. On arriving, we saw a cluster of boats and a crowd of snorkelers at a shallower sandbar nearby. Since we came with scuba gear, our small group would have this preferred site to ourselves.

With the boat tied to a mooring buoy and the propeller stopped, divers entered the water in pairs, stepping off the starboard gunwale. Once the others were in and submerged, the crew dropped a ladder with flat rungs over the side, and assisted Trish in backing up to it and lifting her feet onto the top rung. While they gently lowered her by her arms from above, I moved her feet down the ladder a step at a time from below. She wore her mask and snorkel. When Trish reached chest-deep water, a dive master slipped a buoyancy vest and tank onto her back and put on her fins, as she replaced the snorkel with a regulator. The dive master then guided Trish to the bottom, where her colleague had positioned the other divers in a twenty-foot circle. I followed and came to a rest next to Trish, who gave me a thumbs-up sign.

Half a dozen light-brown stingrays, each three to four feet across, already had joined the divers. Another half dozen or so soon followed. They soared in and out of the circle, like birds catching updrafts, slowing occasionally to swoop up the front of a diver. That move took getting used to, as the wicked-looking barb at the end of the ray's two-foot tail stood out like a lance. But the rays showed no signs of aggressiveness. They loved having their velvety bellies stroked by divers' hands. At that shallow depth, we could stay and play with our marine friends without concern over our air supply.

I gestured to Trish and gave her an inquiring palms-up sign. She nodded several times and turned her attention back to the rays. I noticed a couple of them hovering around her for what seemed like several minutes. That struck me as unusual.

After nearly an hour on the bottom, the dive masters signaled us to return to the boat bobbing nearby. We reversed the previous procedure, with Trish slipping out of her gear in the water, then stepping up the ladder with my help below and the crew's above.

"Wow," Trish exclaimed once back on deck, grinning and clapping her hands. "I've never imagined anything like that, wild animals getting so close and even letting you touch them."

"Yes, I've had fun experiences before with rays, sea lions, turtles, even sharks. Interactions with animals like that in the water are some of the greatest joys of diving. That's a big part of what keeps me coming back to the ocean."

"Not only that. I felt so free down there. I moved around on my own without needing my scooter."

The dive master who guided her down interjected, "Wasn't that something, how some of the rays hung around you? We've seen that before with disabled divers, where rays seem drawn to them, even where there's no visual cue about being disabled."

Trish gasped at that. "How cool! They sensed it and acted like it's something positive. So different from the way most people react."

Flying home the next day, Trish talked more about the Stingray City dive. "Now I wish I'd taken up diving when I was younger, before MS set in. Hopefully, I can still do easy dives like this once in a while on vacation."

"You might even get certified. There are organizations that work with disabled divers."

Whether or not she ever took the certification training, I was pleased that my surprise turned out so well, and that she would have this indelible memory of our latest Caribbean trip, with more to come.

# Chapter 4
# IT DOESN'T GET ANY LOWER

Trish at Zabriskie Point, Death Valley

*Death Valley, December 2006*
It took considerable persuasion for Trish to acknowledge the beauty and grandeur of the desert. She enjoyed living on the coast in San Diego and spending time-off in the mountain town of Idyllwild. So, when I suggested in late 2006 that we go to Death Valley for New Year's Eve, she gave me one of those "Are you insane?" looks, squinting, scrunching up her face, and drawing her head back as if avoiding a lunging predator.

"Death Valley," I repeated, nodding as if certain there could be no finer place to enjoy the holiday season. "I've been there a half dozen times over the years. It's stunningly beautiful. Just get past the name."

"The last time you were there, was that the time you told me about, when it was so hot, your airplane almost wouldn't take off? Like it was 120?"

"Well, 117, but it was mid-summer. In December, it'll be chilly at night but clear and balmy in the daytime. It shouldn't bother your MS symptoms at all."

"Then why is it called Death Valley?" she challenged me, still with a note of sarcasm.

"It's just hype. During the California gold rush, a group on their way to the goldfields got stranded there and one of them died. Someone got dramatic and tacked that name on it."

Trish knew I liked the desert as much as she liked the mountains. Nothing wrong with the mountains. I had grown up vacationing in the Austrian and Swiss Alps, and I liked Idyllwild too. But I fell in love with the desert soon after moving to California and exploring the Southwest. The vast landscapes, stark vegetation, and sheer solitude astonished me, like seeing the Mona Lisa or the Statue of Liberty for the first time.

Death Valley remained the Holy Grail of desert worshipers. On my first visit, in the summer of 1972, I lay on my sleeping bag in the campground at ominously named Furnace Creek, looked up at a black, moonless sky studded with billions of stars, and listened to a chorus of coyotes howling from the surrounding hills. I felt as if I had stepped into one of the western movies I adored watching as a child. I had this 5,000-square-mile national park almost to myself. The only other visitors I encountered were a few French and German tourists who came here to experience something that epitomized the American West for them.

"We spent last New Year's Eve at the Grand Canyon," I reminded Trish. "We drove across a lot of desert to get there, and you thought it was beautiful."

"Where would we stay? I don't want to be stuck in some windblown motel."

"The Furnace Creek Inn. It's one of those grand national park lodges. Not quite like the Ahwahnee at Yosemite, but as nice as El Tovar at the Grand Canyon. We can splurge again for a holiday trip."

"Alright," she conceded with a sigh. "Show me their website."

We viewed on-line photographs of the neo-Spanish-style inn perched on a ridge overlooking the heart of Death Valley, with the Furnace Creek oasis in the foreground and jagged mountain peaks in the distance. Trish soon reversed her attitude.

"You're right," she said. "It is nice. The view from the terrace is very cool. And the restaurant looks great. OK, I'm in. Let's make a reservation."

Almost easier said than done. Three months in advance, the Inn's website showed it as fully booked through the holiday season. But we knew from experience to call anyway.

"We need an accessible room," I told the reservations agent. "Do you, by any chance, have one left?" They did, their very last room. Our hotel karma held up once again.

Since this would be Trish's first visit to Death Valley, I looked forward to showing her the sights. I drove my Explorer with a built-in lift in the rear for her mobility scooter. At that time, she still managed with a walker at home and in the office, but used the scooter anywhere that involved covering greater distances or sloping terrain.

We began our 350-mile trek from San Diego on the morning of December 29th, soaring up Interstate 15 in bright sunshine to the north side of the San Gabriel Mountains and into the high desert. Spiky Joshua trees soon surrounded us.

"Those things must have been the inspiration for the trees in Dr. Seuss books," Trish said with a laugh.

We left the freeway and took old US Highway 395 as far as the former mining towns of Randsburg and Johannesburg, dusty rural settlements bearing little resemblance to their South

African namesakes. From there on, our route of travel followed local roads of sunbaked asphalt. In the late afternoon, we passed through Trona, a mining company town filled with dead trees. I recalled a law school classmate who had grown up there talking about the company shutting off water during a bitter labor strike many years earlier.

When I stopped in Trona for gas, Trish wanted to use the restroom, so I unloaded her scooter. But, unlike the McDonald's where we stopped earlier in the day, the toilet at this service station was not functionally accessible—a common problem, especially in small towns. With a shrug, the attendant told us the town had no other public restrooms.

"I guess I'll have to hold it," Trish said, shaking her head. "Just please stay off bumpy roads."

I knew this wouldn't be easy for her. I honored her request, taking a longer but smoother route, and she held on until we reached our destination.

In the early evening, we crossed over a modest pass through the Panamint Range and coasted down into Death Valley. In the distance, the lights of Furnace Creek glowed like a navigational beacon. Trish looked apprehensive, but I felt like I was returning to a familiar former home. I rolled down my window and let the desert night air permeate my shirt and soak into my skin like a warm, clean fog.

A smiling, middle-aged man sporting a forest-green vest greeted us at the Inn's reception desk and gave us a quick orientation. Our room came with the usual accessibility features—grab bars and roll-in shower in the bathroom, wider doorways and aisles. Our patio overlooked a palm-filled garden sloping down the hillside. Hungry after our long trip, but feeling too grubby for the Inn's dining room, we opted instead to drive a mile back down the hill to the steakhouse at the more casual Furnace Creek Ranch.

After dinner, we took a closer look at the Inn. The lobby and reception area, paneled in dark wood, had the aura of a private club or an ageless resort harking back to a grander era. We ordered vodka tonics from the lobby bar and wandered out on the front deck, where I dropped into a chair next to Trish's scooter. The fringed umbrellas of fronds on forty-foot palms rustled in a light wind and reflected a half moon shining through a clear sky. This place certainly was classier than the campground and the motel down the hill where I spent previous visits, but the night sky, the desert breeze, and the silhouetted mountains evoked the same familiar feelings.

"Just gorgeous," Trish said, leaning into me and squeezing my arm.

In the morning, after a breakfast of omelets and coffee, I began playing tour guide. Although the park extends about eighty miles both north and south from there, most of the accessible features lie within easy reach of the National Park Visitor Center and the Furnace Creek amenities. The Park draws most visitors in the cool winter months, but the crowds thin out during the year-end holiday season.

We started out with a winding three-mile drive to Zabriskie Point, a promontory overlooking a landscape of ridgelines sculpted by wind and water. It provided the key location for a 1970 romantic film of the same name. Where the narrow road running a hundred yards to the top once was open to cars, a sign now directed drivers to a nearby parking lot. It made an exception for cars with handicapped placards, but pedestrians swarmed the road and the slope looked manageable, so we parked, unloaded the scooter, and made our way up to the point.

As many times as I have seen that view, it always captivates me. Trish gasped, momentarily breathless.

"It's not exactly the Grand Canyon or Half Dome," she said, "But it's still awesome. I'm so glad you convinced me to come here."

With that, she gestured toward the prominent rock formation known as Manly Beacon, named after the explorer who led the stranded miners out of the valley in 1849. It pointed upward like a dagger amid the ridges and steep-walled arroyos, all glowing golden in the morning sun. I followed Trish as she rode along the inside of a two-foot-high rock wall surrounding the point. She gasped again and pointed at a trio of hikers following a ridgeline trail.

"Oh my god!" she exclaimed. "Those people look so small. The terrain is so much bigger than it looked at first."

We returned to the highway and continued a few more miles before turning off on a cracked secondary road. That took us upward into the Amargosa Range lining the east side of the valley, through a landscape of cacti and abandoned mines, to Dante's View. Like many natural features here, it bore a name associated with heat or hell.

No need to unload the scooter here. With no one else around, we had an unobstructed view from the car. The valley spread right and left to the horizon, with the barren salt flats in the middle shimmering below us. By contrast, on my last visit, a rare season of heavy rains had created a lake down there and stimulated long-stemmed wildflowers to bloom everywhere. Telescope Peak, at 11,000 feet, dominated the Panamint Range on the other side, and the Funeral Mountains stood behind us. The landscape rising on all sides from the valley floor consisted of sun-bleached rock in shades of white, tan, and brown.

As we wound our way back to the highway, Trish asked, "Where to now? How about somewhere we can get out and look around?"

"I've got just the place. Especially knowing your fondness for Old West relics."

At the north end of the valley, in the oasis of Grapevine Canyon, sits Death Valley Ranch, otherwise known as Scotty's Castle. Built a century ago as a retreat for a San Francisco businessman enchanted by the desert, the rambling, Spanish-style, white stucco mansion topped by towers and turrets now is owned and operated by the National Park Service. It received its nickname after Death Valley Scotty, a prospector and con-man whom the original owner was staking, claimed the home was his, built with profits from an actually non-existent gold mine.

We managed to gain access for the scooter, but furnishings and visitors crowded the interior, so we settled for a limited view. The dark woodwork, intricate tiles, and airy design of the house, along with the on-site power plant and gardens, all seemed incongruous in the middle of the desert.

We found the nearby Ubehebe volcanic crater more interesting. A half mile across and over 500 feet deep, the crater formed thousands of years ago when hot magma hit groundwater along a fault line, causing a steam explosion. Today, trails skirt the rim and descend into the crater. Despite the steepness of the pebble-strewn trail, we reached the crater rim and strolled along it a way, awed by the striated yellow and orange interior slopes. Hikers near the bottom looked like slow-moving bugs. Although the sun had grown intense by winter standards, a steady breeze kept us comfortable.

Then came a decision point. Another thirty miles away, down a washboard dirt road, sat one of Death Valley's most astonishing features, a dry lake known as the Racetrack. Rocks weighing hundreds of pounds litter the lake bed, with furrows tracing their movement across the ground. After a century of guessing how this occurs, geologists documented winter rains covering the lakebed and freezing overnight, and then wind pushing hard enough to nudge the rocks.

"Will we actually see rocks move?" Trish asked in a tone tinged with sarcasm.

"Doubtful. They move too little at a time for your eyes to notice."

She considered this for a moment, then declared, "I'm not riding two hours on a bumpy road to see some rocks sitting on the ground. Let's head back."

"No problem. I can show you pictures of it on-line." I had visited the Racetrack years earlier and found the phenomenon interesting, but I had no appetite either to repeat that long, bone-jarring drive.

We made one more stop. Near the point where we entered the valley the previous evening lay the sand dunes that comprise one of the lasting impressions of this place. Nowhere else in the park do winds combine to amass such volumes of sand and form it into undulating, ever-changing dunes. Sometimes the dunes acquire endless rows of inch-high ridges. Other times, they smooth out or form peaks. Early and late in the day, when the sun is low in the sky, the dunes become a maze of moving shadows. Every time I've seen them, they've looked different, sometimes from one day to the next or even from morning to afternoon.

The Park Service doesn't restrict access to the dunes, but also doesn't provide boardwalks over them. Trish perched on her scooter and settled for admiring the dunes from the adjacent parking area. Meanwhile, I took a brief walk across the dunes to experience once again this unusual environment. My shoes sank into the sand, slipped down the sides of dunes, and left a temporary record of my passing through. Scores of visitors traipsed by me, obliterating the intricate patterns carved by the wind. Creosote bushes with tiny, dark green leaves sank roots deep enough to find water beneath the dunes and gave off a smoky smell unique to the desert.

That evening, after a quick, early dinner, we drove to Death Valley Junction, at a higher elevation just east of the national park, to visit the Amargosa Opera House. A refurbished adobe structure attached to a motel, it began as a social hall for workers at the old Pacific Coast Borax Company. Since 1967, former New

York ballerina Marta Becket had been presenting one-woman musical and dance recitals here to something of a cult following. I had read about her, but hadn't made a point of visiting her venue until an artist friend in Los Angeles urged me to do so the next time I came out here.

We called before leaving home and received assurance the performance space was accessible. Just knock at the door, the friendly man on the phone instructed, and he would let us in ahead of the crowd. By the time we arrived, a group of mostly twenty-somethings already had gathered. We nudged our way to the entrance, ignoring glares from several patrons who had been shivering and waiting for some time in the frigid night air. I saw no point in trying to explain to them why we needed special consideration. Someday, when they were older or maybe infirm, they would get it.

The manager let us in as promised and guided us to front seats close to a radiant heater. Murals depicting a vast theater audience covered the walls, creating an illusion of a much larger room. A bare stage, occupied by just a chair, stood in front.

Once the audience filled the hundred or so seats, the room lights dimmed. Marta emerged, clad in a knee-length, long-sleeved black dress, and still lean from her years of dancing. She edged onto the stage, greeted the crowd in a quiet voice, and launched into her performance. Now in her eighties, she could no longer dance as she had for decades. Instead, she remained seated most of the time, while singing classic operatic tunes and telling stories for two hours. Even at this age, Marta brought such energy and passion to this exhibition that we couldn't take our eyes off her.

I leaned over at one point and whispered to Trish, "Isn't this fantastic?"

"Beyond fantastic," she replied. "It's surreal, finding this out here in the middle of nowhere. No one at home will believe us describing this."

Several years later, we read Marta had died, still there at her adopted home in Death Valley Junction. We felt fortunate to have seen her perform at least once.

When we travel, we enjoy doing most things together, but I also look for opportunities to do more physically challenging things on my own, like scuba diving on a tropical island or climbing to a high viewpoint overlooking a city. That also gives Trish some alone time to read or just relax.

So, the next morning, while Trish slept late, I drove to nearby Golden Canyon to hike the four-mile loop trail through the badlands below Zabriskie Point. The narrow trail took me past the base of Manly Beacon, which looked even more imposing close up. No vegetation grew on the dry, eroded sediment along the trail. I passed and greeted just two other hikers, both going in the opposite direction. Otherwise, I heard no sounds other than an occasional buzzing insect. Being alone in this gorgeous yet desolate setting brought on the spirituality that often floods my mind in the desert, where nothing distracts me and I am immersed in surroundings that might not have changed in millennia.

By the time I finished the loop, the day was warming. I needed to return to the Inn and pick up Trish to resume our explorations.

Part of the valley's salt pan consists of interlocking, rock-hard, hexagonal salt columns running deep into the earth. Wind and rain have worn the exposed tops into pointed, twisted shapes. No wonder it's called the Devil's Golf Course. We drove south to the gravel turnoff leading a half mile into this field that I consider one of the desert's most astonishing features. Trish rode her scooter to the edge of the turnaround to get a close look at the salt crystals.

"Nature must love this hexagon pattern," she remarked. "It's just like the basalt columns of cooled lava at Devils Postpile up in the Sierras and Giant's Causeway in Northern Ireland."

Our next stop was Death Valley's most famous and most visited site—Badwater, the lowest point in North America at 282 feet below sea level, along the rim of a onetime inland sea. It lies at the base of the Amargosa Range, almost directly below Dante's View that we visited the previous day. By now, the sun was high in the sky and reflected off the white valley floor.

We found an accessible parking space in the crowded lot and followed a paved path down to the salt flats that extended for miles. A wooden walkway spanned the wetland around a salty spring and ended at the vast crystalline flat. The firm ground surface supported Trish's scooter as we continued another hundred yards. I tasted minute bits of salt kicked up by the wind.

Heading back to the car, I pointed to a sign painted high on the cliff face.

"See that?" I asked Trish. "That's sea level, way up there."

"Wow," she replied. "I guess it doesn't get any lower than this.

"Nope. I have such a vivid memory of the first time I flew into the Furnace Creek airstrip, watching my altimeter drop below zero on the way in and then passing that marker as I climbed out on the way home."

On the way back to Furnace Creek, we turned off at Artist's Drive, a nine-mile, one-way road through badlands where oxidized minerals in volcanic deposits had turned the canyon walls into an array of pale reds, greens, and purples. We stopped and got out at the most vividly colored site, known as Artist's Palette. Trish rode along a canyon edge and snapped photos with her cellphone camera.

I pointed out a dirt road into the Timbisha Shoshone village, a Native American reservation surrounded by the national park. We then made a final stop that day at the Harmony Borax Works, just north of Furnace Creek. This weathered, historic site contains the last remnants of the borax mining and refining operations that began in the 1880s, sending their product by mule-drawn wagon a hundred sixty miles across the desert to the railhead in Mojave. The white material scraped off the valley floor was in high demand for industrial and agricultural uses in the late 19th century.

Unlike Badwater, this site attracts few visitors. We had it all to ourselves that afternoon. A pedestrian pathway took us past a string of weathered wood transport wagons weighing four tons each and built to carry more than thirty tons of borax. The paved path then wound up and around a twenty-foot-long cast iron boiler surrounded by adobe brick ruins, remains of the borax refining operation. Nearby lay foundations of long-gone buildings that housed workers and offices.

As dusk approached, we reloaded the car and dashed back to the Inn. That night was New Year's Eve. The festivities would begin soon.

We dressed for the occasion. Trish wore a ball gown with a gold bodice and flowing white skirt. I opted for a dark grey suit, rose silk shirt, and grey tie spotted with red dots. We drew a few looks and smiles as we entered the dining room, especially with Trish's dress sweeping alongside her scooter.

Hotel staff had prepped the room for the celebratory evening. Tables held white linens and full place settings. Strands of ribbons hung from the dark-brown wood ceiling beams, and a tasteful number of balloons rose from scattered tables. A six-piece band softly played smooth jazz from beyond a dance floor at the far end of the room, as aromas of the meal to come wafted from the kitchen.

The dining room hostess led us to a table set for eight. We were the first to arrive. I helped Trish transfer to one end seat, stowed the scooter in the nearest corner, and took the seat to her left. Our tablemates soon drifted in — a retired couple from Ohio on their first visit to California, a twenty-something couple from Newport Beach, and a tall couple from Russia. The Russians particularly drew our attention. The woman wore a dress even more formal than Trish's, with billowing lace and scores of rhinestones, while her husband's black suit bore what looked like an official medallion on his right breast. All were congenial and talkative. The evening flew by as we ate our way through salads, filet mignon or roast chicken entrees, and crème brulé, all accompanied by copious amounts of wine.

As dinner finished, the band picked up the tempo and couples ventured onto the parquet dance floor. Trish stood and grasped her chair back for balance while I held her and we swayed together to the music. It all made for another memorable New Year's Eve.

Just before midnight, servers poured a champaign toast into tall flutes. At the stroke of twelve, the band broke into "Auld Lang Syne." We toasted, and I gave Trish a kiss and a long hug before leading her back to our room.

The morning sun announced New Year's Day by peeking in through the heavy hotel room curtains, as if letting us know it was time to conclude our visit. We fueled ourselves for the drive home with a late breakfast of fried eggs, pancakes drenched in prickly pear syrup, and lots of coffee.

"I'm sorry we're leaving," Trish confessed as we loaded the car. "This place is fascinating. I'd come back here." I smiled but didn't say a word.

We departed Death Valley by the same route we came in on. This time, though, soon after passing Stove Pipe Wells at the edge of the valley, I turned south on Emigrant Canyon Road, a partly paved, partly dirt road that meandered among long-abandoned mining claims and jeep tracks into the Panamint Range. I told Trish only afterward that this was the back road on which my Explorer broke down on the previous visit, leaving me and my daughter to be rescued by a pair of French tourists.

After rejoining the highway back to Trona, we took a final detour to visit the ghost town of Ballarat. Named after a city in

Australia, it began in the late 1800s as a supply center for mines in the Panamint Range. When the mines played out, the town died. We parked and explored a bit. I followed Trish as she rode her scooter past a historical marker, rusted pieces of mining equipment, and ramshackle remains of wood and stone structures. We found one person living there, operating a convenience store at the edge of what remained of the town.

Back on the highway, bound for San Diego, Trish rhapsodized further about the unique place we had just left and how accessible it turned out to be for her.

"We'll come back," I assured her. "Next time, we'll visit other ghost towns, explore dirt roads up some of the canyons, maybe visit the Shoshone reservation."

"Yes, I like exploring with you," she replied, "but I'd also be happy to spend time by the pool, soaking up sun and drinking vodka tonics." She paused, then said with a smile, "You know, just like the old-time prospectors."

# Chapter 5
# A TALE OF TWO WINTERS

Trish and Cary at General Sherman Tree, Sequoia

*Yosemite National Park, December 2007*
*Sequoia National Park, December 2016*
In the fall of 2007, soon after wildfires ravaged parts of San Diego County, Trish and I sought a cooler, greener place to spend the upcoming winter holidays. Yosemite National Park, not impacted then by drought or wildfires, conjured up wonderful memories from previous trips we each had taken there. And a visit to Yosemite would be especially memorable if we stayed at

the Ahwahnee, the stone and timber lodge set in the heart of Yosemite Valley, surrounded by waterfalls tumbling hundreds of feet down glacier-chiseled cliffs. We had spent many memorable New Year's Eves far from home, often at lodges in national parks or other locations surrounded by spectacular natural settings, so the Ahwahnee seemed a perfect fit.

I had visited Yosemite in the winter a few years earlier with my daughter. That time, we stayed at the Yosemite Lodge, a pleasant but more conventional hotel. For this visit, though, we wanted something more special. Our hotel karma held up again. The Ahwahnee had an accessible room available for our desired dates.

After departing San Diego early on December 29th, a 400-mile drive took us along the Southern California coast, through the urban sprawl of Los Angeles, over Tejon Pass in the Tehachapi Mountains, up the agricultural San Joaquin Valley, and finally into the foothills of the Sierra Nevada. By the time we entered the park, we were above the snow line, but we found the road well-plowed, and I had heavy-duty tires on my four-wheel-drive SUV, with chains in a box under the rear seat just in case.

Once in the park, we wound our way for thirty-five miles through dense Ponderosa pine forests dripping with recently fallen snow. I frowned at seeing the road to Glacier Point, a view spot overlooking Yosemite Valley, closed for the winter. Too bad. Trish hadn't been up there, and I had hoped to share with her one of the park's most panoramic accessible views. But another one lay a short distance ahead.

The mile-long Wawona Tunnel, dug through a mountain seventy years earlier, serves as the main road access to Yosemite Valley. We emerged from the tunnel at the west end of the valley and pulled into a viewing lot. From there, we caught the reflections of sunset on the monolith of El Capitan to the left, shimmering Bridal Veil Falls to the right, and snow-capped Half Dome in the distance towering over it all. Not a building in sight.

I imagined John Muir and President Teddy Roosevelt standing there a century earlier, experiencing the same majesty of what would become one of America's first national parks.

"It's always beautiful here," Trish observed with a sigh. "But there's something special about it this time of year. It's the perfect image of a winter wonderland."

Entering the atrium of the Ahwahnee raised our spirits even more, as we surveyed the thirty-foot-high windows looking out at the forest and up at the valley walls. Clusters of cushioned seats invited visitors to linger before fireplaces large enough to walk into. The Yosemite Park and Curry Company, the first parkwide concessionaire back in the 1920s, had endowed us with a structure and a place as memorable as any monument or cathedral.

Our room turned out to be accessible as promised and spacious enough for Trish's scooter to maneuver, but in a poor location. Long roof eaves obscured the view and blocked sunlight.

"I get so tired of accessible rooms being put in the least desirable places in hotels, especially at these prices," Trish said in an irritated tone. "I'd rather take a regular room, if they have one with a better view."

They did. After hearing Trish's complaint on the phone, the manager offered us an equally spacious room with a great view toward the towering granite escarpments. No accessible features, but we would manage. We learned long ago to carry portable grab bars with suction cups to attach to bathroom and shower walls precisely for occasions like this.

Dinner in the Ahwahnee dining room is one of the great pleasures of visiting there. The cathedral ceiling beams that look like they could support a mountain, floor-to-ceiling windows, blazing chandeliers, and a sea of neatly arranged dinner tables elicit a mix of excitement and serenity. We drank a couple of dry

Chopin martinis, then shared dinners of pan-fried brook trout and roast venison.

I reached across the table and took Trish's hands. Her face lit up like the glow from the overhead candles.

"A beautiful lady in a beautiful place," I said with an easy smile. "What more could I want?"

For the next few days, we alternated between wandering the snowy landscape and luxuriating at the Ahwahnee. Inside or outside, we marveled at how different Yosemite Valley looked, adorned with a snowy blanket—an already gorgeous setting made even more so.

On a clear morning, we walked a mile to the base of Yosemite Falls. Sunshine glittered on the snowy surroundings like millions of tiny diamonds, while overhanging pine boughs exuded their distinctive sweet scent. Trish's scooter rolled along the cleared, paved trails without difficulty.

Yosemite Falls dwindles late in the year, but the upper fall still carried an impressive flow, a wide ribbon emerging from a hanging valley and tumbling fourteen hundred feet down to the lower sets of falls. I had hiked the steep, winding trail to the top of the falls one spring, when Yosemite Creek roared like a freight train as it sent a torrent of snowmelt crashing down into the valley.

Wider but shorter at three hundred feet, Vernal Falls also impressed, like a miniature Niagara. We rode a park shuttle bus with a wheelchair lift from the hotel to the nature center at the trailhead. The paved trail here was not as well cleared but, with me pushing, Trish made it a mile or so to the bridge over the Merced River that offers a straight-on view of the falls. Descending was more treacherous, as the scooter skidded on icy patches while I held onto the rear.

"Are you OK?" Trish asked, after I grunted from the effort of keeping it under control.

"It's fine. Good thing I learned to maneuver on snow and ice back in New England."

A passing hiker called out, "Hey, can you put skis on that thing? Might make it easier to control." A good thought, but not doable. We had looked into attaching some form of tracks to the rear wheels, but settled for keeping solid rubber tires with deep treads.

On returning to the hotel, again by shuttle, I needed to change from boots to shoes.

"Go on," Trish said. "I'll be warming up in front of that stone fireplace over there."

I returned to find her conversing with a middle-aged couple, also from the San Diego area—a captain in one of the local fire departments and his schoolteacher girlfriend. Slim, mustached, and balding, he had been the commander on-site in fighting one of the major recent wildfires, the ones we had come up here to forget about. I had studied and written about wildfires, so I found it interesting to hear his take on what had transpired at home.

"These fires almost always start in the backcountry," he explained, "Power lines spark or people do something careless. But they spread really quickly into developed areas and become hard to control. Homes built right at the top of slopes, palm trees with dry fronds hanging on them, roofs with open attic vents— these things all help fire jump from house to house, especially in windy conditions."

He took a long sip of his drink and shook his head, then continued, "I hope folks learn from these last fires to change the way we develop, but I'm not optimistic. After every fire, they just want to go right back in and rebuild their homes in the same places."

"I understand," I responded. "I've worked with developers and talked with them about this. They keep building in these fire-prone areas because that's where there's land available and because so many home buyers like that feeling of living close to nature."

We shared drinks and conversation with them for an hour until they excused themselves to prepare for dinner. As they rose to leave, the fire captain handed me his business card and made me an offer.

"You seem to understand this stuff. When you get home, call me. I'll give you a tour of the last fire area and show you exactly what I was talking about."

"You're on," I replied. Weeks later, I would follow up and take the tour he had promised.

On the way back to our room, I said to Trish, "That's one of the things I love about traveling, meeting interesting people along the way and learning new things from them."

Another day, we followed a well-cleared trail along the Merced River flowing down the valley floor. Ahead of us, on the north side of the valley, the exfoliated rock formations known as the Royal Arches dominated the landscape like granite rainbows soaring a thousand feet up a cliff face. Turning to the east, we gazed a long time at Half Dome, known worldwide as the symbol of Yosemite. Its flat northwest face, formed by weathering and glacial sheering over millennia, turned auburn in the afternoon sun sweeping down the valley. I understood how early explorers doubted any person would ever reach that promontory.

"I've been wanting to get to the top of that since my first visit here," I told Trish.

"That sounds like a bucket list item. You should do it."

"I will." I said it with confidence, but it would be another five years before I got the necessary permit and returned to hike eight miles up the John Muir Trail and then climb four hundred feet up the arced backside of the mile-high dome.

The trail to Mirror Lake, at the far east end of the valley, was less used and not as well cleared. Though it sloped upward a bit, it remained smooth enough that the scooter's wheels handled the light coating of snow and a few icy patches, again with my occasional pushes. On this windless day, the glassy lake surface reflected the image of Half Dome like a mirror. A handful of other visitors joined us in admiring the view.

An older couple wandered over and peered at the scooter. "I'm surprised to see that here," the woman said to Trish, "and that you can get around on it in all this snow and ice. If gives me hope we can keep traveling to interesting places, even when we can't walk anymore."

"Yes," Trish responded. "You wouldn't believe the places I've been able to ride on this."

The Ahwahnee dining room on New Year's Eve was awash in holiday décor, the chatter of hundreds of guests, and an abundance of good cheer. We shared a round, linen-covered table with three other couples, all lively conversationalists. Vodka tonics led to Caesar salad and crab bisque. Filet mignon followed, accompanied by substantial volumes of Cabernet Sauvignon. A band at the front of the room played upbeat jazz, as a few couples danced. Soon after midnight, we retreated to our room to celebrate the new year more privately.

We awoke late on New Year's Day to bright sun streaming in, reflected off the snow and rocks. The dining room's expansive breakfast buffet was just the thing to facilitate recovery from the previous evening's festivities. We loaded up on omelets, smoked fish, carved roast beef, and fruit salad.

Then, time for one more stroll before packing up. Melting snow created puddles along the trails. Trish's scooter handled that fine, while I had to step around them. Sun glinted off a narrow waterfall on the opposite side of the valley, as fireplace smoke wafted up from scattered chimneys.

We crossed a stone bridge over the river and wandered westward along a snowy meadow until we got a clear view of El Capitan, the monolith that draws rock climbers from around the world. Even now, in midwinter, we spotted a few making their way 3,000 feet up the seemingly vertical face. I told Trish about a friend who had climbed it with several others, then parachuted off the top, for a television documentary.

With the car loaded, we backtracked our way to the park's south entrance. Sunshine had melted most of the snow from the road. Just short of the park boundary, I made a final stop at the Mariposa Grove, the largest of three Sequoia groves in the park. We wandered among hundreds of the gnarled giants, including some of the largest known, dating back as much as 2,500 years.

As we descended into the San Joaquin Valley and began our trek back to San Diego, we remained silent for a long time.

"This place is so magical," Trish finally said. "We need to come back here more often, but not too often. I don't want it to lose its magic."

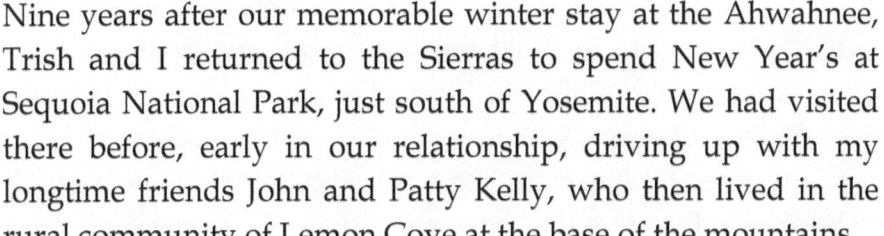

Nine years after our memorable winter stay at the Ahwahnee, Trish and I returned to the Sierras to spend New Year's at Sequoia National Park, just south of Yosemite. We had visited there before, early in our relationship, driving up with my longtime friends John and Patty Kelly, who then lived in the rural community of Lemon Cove at the base of the mountains.

That first time, Trish did not yet experience limits to her mobility from MS. We hiked among the grove of trees hundreds of feet tall in Giant Forest and clambered up four hundred steps to the viewpoint of Morro Rock. A picture of us at the railing there, windblown on an autumn afternoon with monumental Sierra peaks in the distance behind us, sits on our living room mantle—an inspiration to keep traveling to places of natural beauty.

This place illustrated dramatically the reasons for creating the national parks. Deep in the woods, we came upon stumps wider across than the length of a car—remnants from the pre-park days when lumberjacks freely cut down these unique specimens to build homes and furniture. Historical exhibits in the park showed century-old photos of workers standing atop cut trees, smiling and proud of their accomplishments in bringing down something so much larger and more majestic than themselves.

For our 2016 holiday adventures, we planned to stay three nights at Wuksachi Lodge in the heart of the park, then drive back down into the San Joaquin Valley to spend New Year's Eve with John and Patty, now living in nearby Visalia.

I recalled from a December visit many years earlier that the park, much of it located two miles or so in elevation, collected lots of winter snow, with some roads and trails impassable. My SUV would do fine, but Trish's scooter was another matter. We had yet to see how well it would perform in winter conditions that likely would be far more demanding than what we experienced at Yosemite.

Trish was game to try. We booked an accessible room at the lodge, after confirming that the restaurant and other facilities were equally accessible. We also checked out the pathways, exhibits, and other park features that looked scooter-friendly.

Our route of travel from home was similar to the one we took to Yosemite. Due to a late start, we arrived at the park entrance after dark. I knew from experience how snowmelt freezes rapidly as the temperature drops, potentially creating hazardous driving conditions on the winding road. Sure enough, signs notified visitors of a requirement for tire chains. With four-wheel drive and deep-tread tires on the car, and not wanting to try installing chains in the dark, I took a chance and proceeded. Thankfully, we encountered few cars and little ice on our fifteen-mile drive to Wuksachi Lodge.

The heavy timbers and stone pylons of the lodge entrance gave it a classic national park feel, even if not on the scale of Yosemite's Ahwahnee. Guest rooms turned out to be in a cluster of two-story, wood-clad buildings a couple hundred yards away on a hillside above the parking lot. We found a handicapped space at the far end of the lot. Aisles had been cleared, but mounds of snow remained behind and between cars, as well as at the entrance to the pedestrian ramp leading up the hill. I gave Trish a push onto the pathway and up to our room, then went back for our luggage.

"This is going to be a lot harder than Yosemite," Trish remarked, with a shake of her head, when I returned to the room. "I'm kind of nervous. I hope they keep the walkways cleared."

"Well, we knew there would be snow. It's not too far to the lodge for meals, and we can catch shuttle buses from there to get around the park."

Our first trip back to the lodge exposed our excessive optimism. The two-block walkway was cleared of fresh snow but, as with the roads, snow which softened or melted in the daytime froze at night. That left a collage of rough surfaces—bumps, ridges, and cracks—and slick patches, something of an obstacle course.

"This is bumpier than a European cobblestone street!" Trish exclaimed. "Hold on to the scooter. I don't want to tip over."

"I should have anticipated this better," I replied in frustration. "I dealt with these kinds of conditions for years in New England. But then I didn't have to think about getting around on a scooter."

The lodge provided a reward for our efforts. The dining room and the menu couldn't compare to the Ahwahnee, but ceiling-height windows provided views into a dense forest of snow-covered evergreens, moonlight glinting off ice crystals—the kind of wilderness feeling we had hoped to find.

By the time we returned to the lodge the following morning, the sun had softened the icy coating on the walkway, allowing Trish a smoother ride. After breakfast, we waited with a few others at the nearby shuttle stop. Sunshine masked the chilly wind, but the wait for a shuttle seemed endless. When it arrived, the driver explained that traffic was held up while a tow truck assisted an auto that had skidded off the road. He lowered a hydraulic lift from a door at the side of the bus and loaded Trish and her scooter before allowing others to board. A group of German-speaking tourists stared at this entire process, pointing and talking in excited tones, perhaps never before having seen a scooter like Trish's. We have grown accustomed to reactions like this, whether in cities or wilderness.

From the lodge, the shuttle ran in only one direction—south, back the way we entered the park the previous evening. Four-foot-deep snow drifts blocked the road north toward the Sequoias in Grant Grove. We rode the shuttle instead to Giant Forest, where dozens of trees as tall as thirty-story buildings had so impressed me on prior visits. While deep snow made much of the Congress Trail through the grove impassible for us, the trees towering over the landscape still left us breathless. And we found a path cleared to the 3,000-year-old General Sherman Tree, believed to be the largest living thing in the world.

"The first time I saw this, I was so astonished, I stood there for the longest time staring up at it," I told Trish. "People must have thought I was in a trance."

"I can see why," she replied, staring up herself at the snaggled crown two hundred seventy-five feet above us and branches as thick as barrels. The tree's roots had ruptured the walkway surrounding its thirty-six-foot-wide base, so I needed to give Trish an occasional push over ridges the size of roadway speed bumps.

After perusing the museum at the edge of the grove, we looked for a shuttle back to the lodge. By now, the sky had clouded over and we could feel the temperature dropping as rapidly as a cone falling from a Sequoia.

"Thank goodness," Trish exclaimed at seeing a shuttle approach. But her relief proved premature. With apologies, the driver informed us his lift was out of order. Another shuttle would be along soon, he promised. So we shivered for another twenty minutes until a shuttle with a working lift arrived.

After returning to the lodge thoroughly chilled, we opted to spend the rest of the afternoon in the bar drinking Irish coffee. The forest scenery outside the picture windows brought back memories of walking about my small Massachusetts town after a fresh snowfall, like the setting of a Robert Frost poem.

We needed to hurry back to our room and change clothes before dinner. So that Trish could avoid the bumpy, icy walkway, we followed the street around to the lot where our car was parked. That put us at the base of the path up the hill. To our astonishment, another guest, apparently not wanting to walk any distance, had parked their car in such a way as to block access to the path. A scooter, a wheelchair, a baby carriage, even a person pulling a large suitcase could not pass.

We stopped and stared at this seemingly insurmountable obstacle. More than just frustration, I felt furious at this utter lack of consideration. A call on my cell phone to the lodge desk, giving them the license number of the offending vehicle, yielded a promise to locate the owner, but that would take time. I looked around, seeking an alternative to taking a long, roundabout way to a point where we could intersect the walkway from the lodge. At a corner of the parking lot, a short but steep slope led to the midway point of the blocked path.

"Ride over there," I told Trish, as I pointed to the possible route. "Get a running start, and I'll push. I think we can get up to the path from there."

She gave me one of those looks that parents give a child who has proposed something crazy while lacking the experience to realize how crazy it is. But she followed my request anyway. After lining up toward the slope, she gunned the scooter on a patch of bare asphalt. As she hit the snowy slope, I pushed hard from behind and dug my boots into the ground like I was helping get a car out of a mudhole. In a few seconds, to my pleasant surprise, we made it onto the path.

Trish reached up to give me a hug. "My hero," she exclaimed, cocking her head and smiling.

"I love rescuing maidens in distress," I replied, leaning in to her.

Having learned from that experience, we took the shorter but icier walkway to the lodge for dinner and again returning to our room afterward. By that time, the offending car had been moved.

Our last day there, we decided not to chance the shuttle again. After spending the morning strolling the area around the lodge, we loaded the car and drove to nearby Lodgepole Village to check out the Visitors Center and buy some souvenirs. With snow blocking the road northward to other Sequoia groves, we headed back south toward the park entrance.

Near Giant Forest, we paused at a snow-blanketed meadow with an inviting trail, but found the snow and ice on the trail impassable for the scooter. To finish our visit, we parked at Giant Forest and walked as far up the trail as the scooter could make it, to get a last close-up view of the massive trees. I stared up at them for a long time, thinking about how many of them had been growing there for over 2,000 years, but knowing that their days might be numbered on account of a changing climate and increasingly vicious wildfires. In just the next few years, much of that would come to pass, killing thousands of trees that previously survived for so many centuries.

I wanted to get down the mountain before the road iced up, so we continued toward our friends' home in Visalia. There, we got bad news. John had just come down with the flu and was too sick to do more than say hello and goodbye. Given Trish's MS-compromised immune system, I knew better than to press for even a brief visit under the circumstances.

Too late to go back to the park, we started on our way home, expecting to reach San Diego before midnight. Unless the weather blocked us. A radio report predicted heavy snowfall in the Tehachapi Mountains, possibly closing Tejon Pass on I-5 north of Los Angeles. Sure enough, as we drove through Bakersfield and approached the mountains, the snowfall began, first a fluttering of powder but soon dense flakes that the windshield wipers labored to clear. Thankfully, we passed the crest and started down into the LA Basin before the Highway Patrol closed the freeway.

I then had an inspired thought. On my cell phone, I called our friends, Charlie and Laura Schoor, in Los Angeles, wondering what they were doing for New Year's Eve. It was our good luck to catch them at home preparing for a small dinner party. They happily added us to the group and invited us to spend the night there before driving home in the morning. Their house didn't have an accessible entrance, but the portable ramp we carry in the car solved that. So it was that we unexpectedly spent New Year's Eve in Los Angeles, regaling our dinner companions with our adventures in the snowy wilds of Sequoia National Park.

———•———

Despite the difficulties we encountered, our experiences in Sequoia, as in Yosemite years earlier, reinforced our conviction that we could travel with the scooter nearly anywhere, even in inhospitable conditions. And they reminded us of the need to remain flexible in our travel plans when those conditions arise, as they so often do.

## Chapter 6
## FIRST SCOOTER TO THE ARCTIC OCEAN

Trish and Cary at the Arctic Ocean, Prudhoe Bay, Alaska

*Alaska, June 2008*
Dawn came early on our first morning in Alaska. By the time our alarm sounded at six a.m. and we drew back the blackout curtains in our hotel room, it had already been light for almost two hours. Sunshine from a cloudless sky cast a golden glow over the otherwise plain buildings of downtown Anchorage and reflected off snowy peaks in the distance.

Groggy but excited, Trish and I pulled on our jeans, sweaters, and boots. Then, dragging our two oversized suitcases and a pair of shoulder bags, I followed Trish on her blue mobility scooter downstairs to join our companions for the start of a two-week adventure.

We began planning this trip six months earlier. We both had long wanted to see Alaska. I hoped we hadn't waited too long. Trish's MS symptoms were worsening, making it necessary for her to rely on a mobility scooter most of the time. Our initial idea was just to take a cruise down the Alaskan coast, hoping for views of wildlife and spectacular scenery, especially Glacier Bay with its calving glaciers. The Holland America line caught our eye, with its mid-size ships catering to a more mature clientele. No need to endure hordes of drunken, twenty-something partyers. Then we noticed we could couple the cruise with a week-long land tour into the interior of Alaska and up to the north coast.

"That's it!" Trish declared. "I really want to go all the way to the Arctic Ocean."

I had my doubts. Over the previous three years, her legs had become increasingly unresponsive. Her reliance on a scooter limited us somewhat in our choice of destinations, and it put a greater burden on me to deal with logistical issues along the way. But we loved traveling together and were determined to take it to the limits. So, when a cruise line representative assured us that they could accommodate Trish and her scooter on all phases of the trip, we booked our land-and-sea adventure.

A five-hour flight took us from Los Angeles to Anchorage. On Alaska Airlines, of course. Boarding in LA, we followed our usual ritual of Trish riding her scooter to the airplane door, then turning it over to the gate crew to be stowed below with baggage, and hoping the airline would deliver it to us intact at the other end of the flight. We always sought seats at the front, to minimize how far Trish would need to go, taking small steps while holding onto me or airplane seatbacks.

By the time we got off the plane, retrieved the scooter, and collected the luggage, our anticipation began building. After checking in at the hotel, we located our tour group milling about in a wood-paneled conference room off the lobby. We discovered an eclectic bunch, from confident, seasoned travelers to folks out of their home state for the first time. Mostly couples, and a range of ages from the twenties to the sixties. They all had in common one important feature that I thought boded well for the coming week: they had self-selected to embark on this inland adventure rather than settling for just the usual ocean cruise.

Our trip leader stepped forward and introduced herself. I had expected to see someone like the former Alaska wilderness guide I knew back home, a slender, dark-haired, serious environmentalist. Cathy, by contrast, turned out to be a stocky blonde with a perpetual smile, a fountain of energy, an enthusiastic chaperone who would spend the next week gently herding us like a great sheepdog.

Cathy welcomed us and gave us a brief orientation. In the morning, we would travel north by train to Denali National Park for a two-night stay. Then, again by train, on to Fairbanks in the middle of the state. From there, a two-day bus ride on the unpaved Dalton Highway the rest of the way to the Arctic Ocean, with an overnight stop at the settlement of Coldfoot. Our destination, north of the Arctic Circle, would be the charmingly named Deadhorse oil camp on Prudhoe Bay.

With the orientation behind us, Trish and I headed out to explore downtown Anchorage. We always enjoy our first stroll around a new place, though Anchorage turned out to be quite ordinary in appearance, filled with boxy commercial buildings. At seven in the evening, we found the streets largely empty. It wouldn't be dark until close to midnight and, even then, more like twilight. The city was quite accessible, with curb cuts at most corners and ramps into stores and restaurants.

After wandering into a local department store, we came upon a stuffed, shaggy Alaskan brown bear, or peninsula grizzly, standing eight feet tall on its hind legs, inside a glass case. Its front paws displayed wicked-looking, four-inch claws and its mouth stretched agape as in its final roar.

At a nearby outdoor café, under a still bright sky at nine in the evening, we enjoyed our first dinner of Alaskan salmon actually in Alaska. Despite it being mid-summer, we had wisely brought jackets, as the evening air soon turned chilly. Wild salmon is Trish's favorite food. We joke that she is personally depleting the world supply. But these fish, grilled on reddish cedar planks, tasted better than any of the hundred or more we had eaten at home.

Over dinner, Trish expressed concern about how well the tour could accommodate her needs. That still concerned me too. On our return to the hotel, we found Cathy buzzing about the lobby, making arrangements for the next day. She admitted she hadn't previously had a disabled visitor on a scooter along in her half-dozen years of leading Alaska tours, but she was confident we would have no trouble.

"Don't worry," she assured us. "I've been thinking about it. Your lodging and dining accommodations all will be accessible. The double-decked passenger car on the train has an elevator between the seating on the upper level and the dining facilities on the lower. And you two can have the first-row seats on the tour bus after that. We'll stow the scooter in the baggage compartment underneath."

Trish still enjoyed enough mobility then to mount a few steps into a bus, albeit slowly and with a little help, so this all seemed doable. With renewed confidence, we queued up in the morning with our fellow travelers. At the downtown train station, we boarded our designated railroad car and reached our seats on the glass-domed upper level without incident. The train crew stowed Trish's scooter near the elevator on the lower level, and she made it the short distance from the elevator to her seat with my help and a cane. We then sat back in comfortable, well-upholstered seats and prepared to begin our adventure.

Under a sunny sky, the first phase of the train ride took us along a gleaming arm of Cook Inlet, the broad bay connecting Anchorage to the Gulf of Alaska. We soon crossed an iron railroad bridge over the shallow delta of the Knik River. The snow-covered profile of Mt. Susitna, known locally as the Sleeping Lady, filled the western horizon.

Ninety minutes out of Anchorage, we passed the town of Wasilla, which had become known nationwide as the hometown of vice-presidential candidate Sarah Palin. It appeared to be just a nondescript collection of small houses, a distant bedroom community for Anchorage.

After that, as wilderness surrounded us, it seemed more like we were in Alaska. Virgin evergreen forest spilled out in all directions, interrupted only by the roaring Susitna River and occasional tunnels through rocky mountainsides. Alaska's Route 3, known as the Parks Highway, ran somewhere nearby but remained invisible to us.

Our group occupied the entire upper deck of the car, so people soon began striking up conversations, getting to know our fellow travelers. Recognizing Trish's limitations, many thoughtfully came to us and introduced themselves—a retired couple from New York hooked on adventure travel, a twenty-something lesbian couple on their first trip together, a vivacious school teacher from Boston and her much quieter husband.

While Trish admired the view from her window seat on the upper deck, I made frequent jaunts down to the outside platform at the rear of our car to photograph the scenery rushing by. The chilly wind and clicking of the train wheels gave me more of a sense of adventure than sitting inside. Over the next six hours, I took dozens of pictures, unable to get enough of the vastness of the place, with no roads, vehicles, or even people in sight. We might have been taken back a century in time to the early days of the Alaska Railroad.

As we passed the remote town of Talkeetna, a boomtown in the long-ago Klondike gold rush, we got our first unobstructed views of Denali, the tallest peak in North America at 20,000 feet. It stood out from the surrounding mountains like Everest does in the Himalayas. Travelers flew with their cameras to the west-facing windows and snapped away.

By late afternoon, we arrived at the rail station in the northeast corner of Denali National Park, facing six million acres of forest bisected by a single gravel road. Sunshine glinted off Denali's glaciers, drawing our collective gaze. The pungent aroma of dense spruce forest rolled over us and we breathed in the freshest air I had experienced in as long as I could recall.

Tired from the train ride, we checked into the nearby lodge in Denali Park Village, a wood-and-stone structure close to the rail station but at the edge of the park wilderness. Also hungry, we then headed to the log cabin restaurant across the road for a caribou burger and local draft beer before retiring. So far, everywhere we went was wheelchair-accessible.

But soon a calamity almost struck. As the scooter bounced along the tree-lined trail from the restaurant back to the lodge, Trish's purse fell from where it had sat behind her feet on the platform. It contained not only her wallet and cell phone, but also several important medicines. We backtracked and searched but had no luck finding it. We returned to the lodge, intending to ask the manager to post an inquiry about it. To our surprise and glee, sitting on the manager's desk was the missing purse, just turned in by a guest who had found it on the trail, probably moments before we went back to search. We took that as a good omen for all that lay ahead. And Trish carried her purse more securely, strapped around her neck, from then on.

The next morning, we boarded what appeared to be a converted city bus to foray into the park. A lift at the rear of the bus raised Trish's scooter up to passenger level and we settled into a nearby bench seat.

A few miles up the Denali Park Road, we spied a dozen caribou grazing in a meadow, looking like grayish, oversized reindeer. As we approached, they bolted across the road and into the woods on the other side. Except for one, which halted in the middle of the road, tipped back its long, rounded antlers, and stared at us. In a classic standoff, we couldn't pass on the narrow road and the caribou wouldn't move. The driver told us he experienced this often. The animal eventually would get out of the way. After a few minutes, as the driver predicted and to our amusement, the caribou seemed to shrug, averted its gaze, and plodded off into the forest.

Soon after, the bus halted at the roadside to allow us to photograph Denali. We had all just clambered back on when the driver abruptly closed the door and ordered us in a whisper to close all windows. In a moment, we saw why. An adult male grizzly, nearly as big as the bear in the glass case in Anchorage, approached from behind us and ambled by within ten feet of the bus.

I had seen bears in New England and in the Sierras, but none as large or as ominous-looking as this furry brown behemoth. At least three feet tall at the shoulders and more than six feet long, with a distinctive hump behind his head, he must have weighed at least 500 pounds. He looked straight ahead, down the length of his prominent nose, paying us no notice.

No one spoke. We all focused on what we knew was a rare, close-up wildlife encounter. Only the clicks of camera shutters pierced the silence.

We followed the grizzly's movement, powerful as a battering ram, as his muscular haunches propelled him down the road and out of sight. Only then did the driver speak.

"We don't often see them up close like that. You were very lucky. The wind was blowing our way, so he didn't smell us or he would have gone off into the woods. And the bus didn't bother him. Predators like that are concerned mainly with what they can kill or what could kill them. The bus isn't either of those. As you saw, he just ignored us, didn't even look directly at us."

Our encounter with the grizzly dominated my thoughts the rest of the day. Even closer views of Denali and long views down the rippling Savage and Sanctuary Rivers seemed less vivid. Although we had a barrier between us and the bear, it reminded me of similar experiences I'd had swimming among large sharks while scuba diving, like being an intruder in a predator's environment and trusting they would not react.

The following morning, we resumed our train trip to Fairbanks, the end of the line. The four-hour ride took us through a gap in the Alaska Range, following the Nenana River as it rushed northward with its load of snowmelt. Green-black, undisturbed forests surrounded us again most of the way. But our minds had already begun focusing on the next phase of the journey, beyond where the paved highway and the railroad ended.

After arriving at our hotel in Fairbanks, we discovered that our suitcases, along with a few others, had missed the train. Fortunately, we had kept all of Trish's medicines and our other personal items with us, crammed into a shoulder bag and purse. After a frantic phone call by Cathy, followed by a few anxious hours, the suitcases showed up on a later train that night.

In the morning, we boarded our cobalt-blue tour bus for the two-day drive to Deadhorse. Trish had expressed concern over how comfortable the bus would be on this lengthy ride. But her concern evaporated as soon as she saw it was a genuine touring bus, with well-spaced plush seats elevated over a spacious luggage compartment, a pair of restrooms, and three-foot-high windows for easy viewing.

We would travel on the Dalton Highway, the unpaved road built for construction of the Trans-Alaska Pipeline in the late 1970s to carry oil from wells on the north coast down to the port of Valdez on the south coast. As Cathy had promised, Trish and

I got front-row seats so that she wouldn't have to make her way painstakingly down the aisle getting on or off. That gave us excellent views and photo opportunities out the windows spanning the entire front of the bus.

The bus driver was taken aback by Trish's battery-powered scooter. He hadn't needed to deal with one before.

"It's going to bounce around in the baggage compartment," he worried. "I can't be responsible for what happens to it."

"Don't worry," I replied. "We've gone a lot of places with that scooter. It traveled here from California in an airplane luggage compartment. We'll take responsibility." That mollified him. We loaded the scooter, locked the wheels, and hoped for the best. Trish's walker went in there too.

Getting on and off the bus still took some effort for Trish. While she held the doorway railings for balance, I grasped her ankles and helped lift her feet on the stairs, one at a time. We usually got off first and back on last. I initially noticed a few impatient looks among our bus-mates, but that soon passed. They could see her struggling to go as quickly as possible. They even began coaxing her along in a friendly way.

We made our first stop on the outskirts of Fairbanks, at a visitor center for the pipeline. We hadn't been fans of building this 800-mile conveyance, four feet in diameter, resting on thousands of above-ground piers, and running through previously pristine wilderness. Still, we couldn't help being impressed by the exhibits and the project from an engineering and construction standpoint.

Eighty miles north of Fairbanks, we left the paved road. We would travel the next 400 miles on a dirt road now used mainly by trucks transporting equipment and supplies to the oil fields. The well-graded road was wide enough for two semi-trailer trucks to pass. This was the highway later made famous on the television reality show *Ice Road Truckers*, for which my son Brett would be the editor for a time.

This being summer, the road and the surrounding countryside were free of snow for much of the trip. The dense evergreens had already transformed into stunted boreal spruce forest or taiga, the northernmost forest environment. That gave way to broad valleys of arctic tundra, ground cover in mixed shades of brown, green, and orange, clinging to rocky terrain in this locale of little rainfall and short seasons of sunshine. Other than an occasional southbound truck, a few travelers in campers, and of course, the road itself, the ever-present pipeline was the only reminder of civilization as we knew it.

"I've always been impressed with the wide-open spaces in the Southwest," Trish said. "But this is so much bigger, just spectacular."

At first, the passengers behind us remained quiet, taking in this jaw-dropping scenery. Gradually, we all loosened up and resumed chatting, exchanging comments about what we were experiencing and what lay ahead.

Around midday, we came to the Yukon River, where a half-mile-long bridge on concrete piers took us over Alaska's greatest waterway, flowing two thousand miles from deep in the Rockies to the Bering Sea. During the gold rush of the late 1800s, it was the principal travel route across Alaska and the Yukon Territory. Once across, we stopped for lunch at the Yukon River Camp, a truck stop with a restaurant and gift shop in a set of brown, attached mobile homes. Only a couple of long-haul trucks and a camper sat in the parking lot, so the café staff reacted with excitement at our arrival. The stop also gave us an opportunity to walk down to the river bank, where snowmelt kept the brownish water surging throughout the summer and sent icy spray at anyone getting close.

Two hundred miles out of Fairbanks, the bus pulled off the highway. An eight-foot-tall sign announced we had reached the Arctic Circle, at latitude sixty-six degrees, thirty-two minutes. While the driver swept road dust off the bus windows, we all wandered over to the sign, just to experience being this far north for the first time. Trish stood up from her scooter, and Cathy photographed us smiling before the sign.

Another sixty miles up the road, we arrived at Coldfoot, so named after the many would-be treasure hunters and explorers who gave in to the cold at this point and returned home rather than continue into the imposing mountains ahead. The community consisted of just a café, gas station, and hotel, mainly serving truckers. And, for tourists, the US Forest Service operated a one-room visitor center. Truckers themselves had put up wooden buildings, now replaced by pre-fab structures, around a roadside food stand. Saloons, stores, and gambling halls of earlier mining days had long disappeared, along with the miners. The year-round population now was down to just a dozen.

The Slate Creek Inn, bearing the community's original name (but later euphemistically renamed the Inn at Coldfoot) and originally serving as housing for workers building the pipeline, was unlike any hotel we had seen before. Permafrost made the earth rock-hard in winter, but the surface softened in summer, so structures had to be set on piers above ground level. The hotel consisted of a row of double-wide mobile homes on a hillside, with the front one serving as a lobby and the rest divided into guestrooms. A ramp by the front steps allowed Trish to ride to the entrance. The wood-paneled rooms contained just a pair of twin beds and a sink. A common bathroom was down the central hallway.

Tish summed up our reaction, saying, "Nothing fancy, but what would we expect at a truck stop north of the Arctic Circle?

We crossed the parking lot to the café, happy at not having to deal with the snow or mud that would be there most of the year. Seated in the half of the café open to non-truckers, we stuffed ourselves with Coldfoot burgers and local pilsner beer.

The sparse hotel accommodations were enough for us to have a good night's sleep, followed by a breakfast of omelets and coffee at the café. Then, back on the bus for the final leg of our ride.

North of Coldfoot, the terrain rose toward the Brooks Range. We could see its snow-covered peaks not far off. The road passed through a long valley separating Kabuk National Park to the west and Gates of the Arctic National Park to the east. Steep, icy slopes soared in both directions.

As the bus climbed the curving road nearly five thousand feet up to Atigun Pass, I sensed we were approaching a high point of the trip, literally and figuratively. This range forms the northernmost segment of the Continental Divide. We disembarked at the top of the pass to take in the mountain terrain and marvel at how early travelers made it across without the benefit of a road. Feeling adventurous, Trish used her walker here rather than unloading the scooter. Slopes above us remained deep in snow, even in June. We were too taken by the scenery to notice the chilly air. Below us, the highway snaked down into a valley bracketed by peaks that stood like rows of sentinels.

We watched a group of travelers unload half a dozen bicycles from a van and begin riding down the far side of the pass. From their smiles and excited chatter, we guessed this would be the peak moment of the trip for them, something they had come hundreds, maybe thousands of miles to experience.

When the bus pulled off at an overlook a short time later, we all gasped. The fabled Alaska North Slope stretched out before us, a plain reaching from the foot of the Brooks Range to the Arctic Ocean another sixty miles away. Herds of caribou dotted the plain, foraging all summer before making their annual migration south for the winter. A network of rivers and streams threaded their way from the mountains to the sea. Far off, our destination of Deadhorse stood out from the natural surroundings like a dark ship on a distant ocean horizon.

"Now I'm really getting excited," Trish whispered to me. "Arctic Ocean, here we come!"

At the overlook, I seized the opportunity for a walk out on the tundra. My friend back home, the former wilderness guide, had urged me to try this, assuring me it would be a unique experience. Layers upon layers of lichen and ground cover, interspersed with grassy tussocks and a few shrubs, formed a thick blanket over the frozen earth. It felt like strolling across a massive sponge, yielding slightly to my steps and rebounding as I moved on.

As we continued toward Deadhorse, an oncoming trucker waved us to a stop. He had seen a wolf close to the road a mile back, a rare sight. Sure enough, a few minutes later, I caught the first glimpse of the wolf, still wandering close to the other side of the road. Its whitish front and darker grey haunches stood out from the surrounding vegetation.

"Wolf!" I yelled, loud enough to be heard throughout the bus. The driver pulled over. We all stared and took photos before the animal ran off. But the wolf continued to wander on a course parallel to the road, as if posing for an occasional photo-op, then darted off across the tundra. As with the grizzly back in Denali, I felt privileged to see an apex predator like this in its own environment. Wolves inhabit most rural areas of Alaska, but Cathy told us she hadn't previously seen one so close up in all her tours.

The bright-blue Arctic Caribou Inn at Prudhoe Bay was a glorified version of the hotel at Coldfoot. The sparsely furnished, two-bed rooms had individual baths, and common areas were carpeted and well-lit. It served mainly as short-term lodging for oil field visitors. Larger, multi-story buildings housed workers there for several-months stays. All the structures stood on piers atop the permafrost.

While most of our companions retired to their rooms to rest, Trish and I set out to explore. Snow and ice on the ground offered little traction for her scooter wheels, but we managed by moving between hard-packed areas and bare pavement. The parkas we brought came in handy here, as the daytime temperature in June remained in the 40s and a chilly wind blew off the bay. We followed a road along nearby wetlands. From there, a raised peninsula stretched out into the bay, populated with structures the size of our tour bus that housed scores of oil wells.

Back at the pipeline visitor center outside Fairbanks, a docent had mentioned that oil flows were dropping as the North Slope wells produced less. That jeopardized the pipeline itself, as it would freeze and warp during the winter if too little liquid flowed through it. I understood the oil companies' concern over the future of this costly piece of infrastructure, but it distressed me to hear about plans to open new oil fields further out in the Arctic Ocean. The spill from the tanker Exxon Valdez running aground on the south coast of Alaska twenty years earlier was bad enough. In this even colder, more fragile environment, an oil spill of any size would be devastating.

By evening, cooking aromas floated down the hotel hallways. Dinner that night consisted of "reindeer stew," actually caribou. Quite tasty, much like venison. I suspected that was a frequent menu item. We sat with several oil field workers and chatted with them about life here near the top of the world. Most had worked other oilfields, from Texas to the Middle East. They told us the isolation took getting used to, but it paid well for several months at a time and enabled them to afford a comfortable life for themselves and their families back home. It amused them that tourists would pay to travel here.

Hotel guests and staff alike found Trish's scooter fascinating. They hadn't seen one before. The North Slope was inhospitable to anyone with a physical handicap. Probably the same in other oil camps. Some oil field workers inspected the scooter closely, curious about the mechanics and electronics of it. We, on the other hand, found it curious that the little scooter was so interesting to men who routinely worked with massive machinery.

The following day, we toured the area by bus, beginning with the oil fields. Then, circling inland around the town, we spied a herd of musk oxen out on the tundra, looking like something yanked from a National Geographic spread on the Arctic. Two massive, grey-brown males with forward-curving horns charged each other and collided head-on, then backed off and repeated this contest several times, for herd leadership or maybe for a mate. Finally, the bus drove us to a pebbly beach near town. Shallow water gave way to wetlands and then the open ocean, where ice floes the size of automobiles drifted by.

Smiling and suddenly finding extra strength, Trish dismounted from the bus with little assistance and mounted her scooter. We got within twenty feet of the water before the scooter's wheels sank too deep into the sand and gravel to go any farther.

"This whole trip, I've been wanting to reach the Arctic Ocean," she cried plaintively. "I can't stop here."

"I can fix that," I replied.

I walked to the ocean's edge, scooped up frigid water in my hands and brought it to her. If she couldn't quite get to the ocean, the ocean would come to her. Before the water all drained out of my cupped hands, Trish dipped a few fingers into it and patted her face, as if to get the full effect of the near-freezing liquid. A few of our companions standing nearby cheered for her.

"Thank you," she said, giving me a big smile and then a kiss. "That was great. That makes the trip here complete."

With our land tour coming to a close, we were scheduled to fly back to Anchorage the next morning and then embark on the cruise portion of the trip. Before going to bed, I spoke with Cathy about how excited Trish was about the whole adventure, but especially about reaching the Arctic Ocean. Cathy mentioned it to the hotel manager, who came up with an idea to celebrate that.

After breakfast the next morning, as we prepared to load the bus for a short drive to the airport, Cathy asked Trish and me to accompany her to the manager's office, saying there was some item of business we needed to take care of. Trish commented that this seemed odd, but followed her down the hallway and into the hotel office with me in tow. There, we found several of the hotel staff and a few of our traveling companions.

"We have something for you," the manager said. He took from his desk a printed sheet of paper, the kind used for employee recognition certificates, and handed it to Trish. Her name appeared near the top. Large, hand-drawn, capital letters across the middle read "FIRST SCOOTER TO THE ARCTIC OCEAN."

Trish broke into a broad smile and small tears formed in her eyes. At that, the whole group applauded.

"Thank you all," Trish declared, squeezing my arm. "What a great finish. I hope the cruise is even half as good."

## Chapter 7
## CRUISING COLD AND HOT

Trish and Cary aboard Elation, San Diego

*Alaska, June 2008*
*Baja California, December 2009*

Our inland tour of Alaska, from Anchorage in the south to Deadhorse on the Arctic Ocean, turned out to be so memorable that we almost forgot about the cruise that was to follow, the voyage that had been our original motivation for traveling to Alaska. This would be our first cruising experience, and we were eager to see how Trish's scooter would adapt to shipboard life.

Waiting at Prudhoe Airport, I dashed into the gift shop for a last-minute souvenir. I bought a white t-shirt with a graphic showing a baleful-looking polar bear balancing on a miniscule ice floe and asking, "Who says climate change isn't real?" That drew a loud laugh from my environmental consultant spouse.

The two-hour flight from Deadhorse to Anchorage felt anticlimactic. As she gazed out the airplane window at the prominent, icy peak of Denali, Trish mused, "That's a great view, but it isn't nearly as cool as all the wildlife and scenery we saw up close from the train and the bus. That was a real adventure."

I nodded in agreement. I kept reviewing in my mind images of a grizzly bear ambling past our bus, a wolf staring at us from the roadside, caribou herds roaming the tundra, crossing the roaring Yukon River, and our first view of the North Slope from Atigun Pass.

Unlike our visit a week earlier, we found Anchorage enveloped in a gloomy overcast that filtered much of the late-night sun. Early in the morning, amid a chilly wind and misting rain, we joined our tourmates on another bus for the 120-mile drive to Seward. There, the Holland America ship *Volendam* awaited us.

The tour guide again reserved front row seats for us, allowing Trish to sit right after struggling up the half-dozen steps. Before boarding, I made sure her mobility scooter was securely stowed in the luggage compartment.

Seward lies directly south of Anchorage, but mountains and water block the way. The bus soared along the two-lane, undivided Seward Highway, Alaska Highway 1. For the first sixty miles, we followed a branch of Cook Inlet off the Gulf of Alaska. From our vantage point on the right side of the bus, we stared across the water at snowy peaks of the Kenai Peninsula. Where the bus turned southward into the mountains midway to Seward, we glimpsed the face of the Portage Glacier, a preview of things to come on the cruise. The rest of the drive took us down a thirty-mile-long valley flanked by ice-encrusted mountains, along a stretch of the Kenai River and several lakes, and finally down a second valley into Seward. As Resurrection Bay came into sight, the clouds lifted and midday sun bathed the waterfront. *Volendam* sat alone at an asphalt-paved pier large enough to accommodate at least four ships.

We exited the bus at the head of the pier and made our way into the cavernous cruise ship terminal. Check-in was fast and painless, with no paperwork, since we already had been guests of the cruise line for a week.

Out on the pier, back in cool, salty air, I sized up *Volendam*. It looked to be about three-fourths the length of *USS Saratoga*, the aircraft carrier I served on nearly thirty years earlier. A medium-size vessel by cruise ship standards, it would carry about 1,400 passengers plus a crew of 600. *Saratoga*, by contrast, carried a crew of over 5,000 plus dozens of aircraft and thousands of munitions, but then, it provided more basic living quarters and no promenade decks, casino, or swimming pool. *Volendam's* dark blue hull, standard for Holland America vessels, stood out against the lighter blue, cloud-streaked sky. On the ocean side, puffins looking like cartoon characters, with their chubby, black bodies and bright orange bills, dove off the pier after fish.

"My scooter made it all the way to the Arctic Ocean and back," Trish said with a laugh as we approached the ship. "I guess it'll manage on there."

With that, she led me up the gangway onto the floating city that would be home for the next five days. With just a whiff of nostalgia, I realized I was boarding a ship for the first time since that long-ago time in the Navy, a ship larger than the Catalina Island ferry, anyway. Trish had never before been aboard a full-size, ocean-going ship. On lanyards around our necks hung rectangular passes bearing our photographs, that would allow us to board and disembark, as well as incur expenses aboard ship.

Signs directed us to elevators up to the open-air Lido deck. There, we could relax, drink a glass of auburn-colored, draft Alaskan Amber, and take in the ocean and mountain views, while crew delivered luggage to our cabins. I couldn't remember ever having a beer so refreshing. Like our fellow travelers from the inland tour, the rest of the passengers tended to be middle-aged but enthusiastic, with no obvious young hard-partyers.

We had reserved an accessible stateroom, one of only five. We made a point of getting one near the stern, far from the noise of the activity centers, and on the port side, facing the coast as we traveled south. It turned out to be nearly as accommodating as an equivalent hotel room, with aisles wide enough for Trish's scooter, a roll-in shower with accessible controls, and strategically mounted grab bars. More accommodating, actually, than many hotel rooms we have occupied over the years.

After we unpacked and then stowed our luggage under the queen-size bed, the stateroom seemed almost spacious. Best of all, we had a private veranda, allowing us to sightsee without having to maneuver our way to the upper observation decks. A wise choice, as the elevators would be in perpetual use by older or infirm passengers, often resulting in long waits.

We found the ship delightfully accessible. Passageways and promenades plenty wide for two-way traffic. Restaurants, lounges, foyers, and other common areas spacious and unobstructed. Accessible restrooms on each deck. Staff in the main dining room consistently finding us seating with enough space for me to help Trish transfer to a chair and then park the scooter nearby.

We would have preferred a smaller ship, one with even fewer passengers and a more intimate ambience, but our research made clear that such smaller ships were far less accessible. And, while *Volendam* was not exactly intimate, it provided a far cozier ambience than the mega-liners, some four times as heavy and carrying upwards of 6,000 passengers. So this ship struck a nice balance.

Many cruise passengers regard unlimited food, including expansive buffets, as the high point of a voyage. We appreciated the quantity and quality of the dining options, but our interest centered more on the shipboard environment and the non-stop coastal views of snow-capped peaks, deep-green primeval forests, and rugged shoreline.

In the cocktail lounge on the Promenade deck below our stateroom or at the outdoor bar on the Lido deck above, we regularly encountered newfound friends from the land tour. Traveling with people, especially in a closed space like a bus or train, creates immediate bridges of mutual experience, even if they don't last beyond the end of the trip.

As we left the lounge the first day, after sharing drinks with half a dozen of our traveling companions, Trish remarked, "We're usually very private people, but all this social interaction is making the trip pretty enjoyable, more than I expected."

After a pause, she added, "As long as we can retreat to our stateroom when we feel like it."

On departing Seward, the ship skirted the Resurrection Peninsula, summer home to thousands of Peregrine falcons that travel to the tip of South America in the winter months. Flocks of the blue-grey birds with three-foot wingspans soared around nests high up on red-brown rocky cliffs overlooking the bay.

Mid-afternoon, the public address system announced a mandatory lifeboat drill. In a chilly breeze, passengers lined up on outside decks, next to the lifeboat stations identified on our ship passes. Loudspeakers instructed us on the procedures to be followed in the event of, say, striking an iceberg or running aground on uncharted rocks.

After taking this all in, I leaned down and said to Trish, "We can probably manage getting you into a lifeboat in an emergency, but I'm afraid your scooter would go down with the ship."

We generally avoided the ship's entertainment—lounge singers, casino gambling, and various classes. This evening, though, still wide awake from the excitement of being underway, we took in a screening of the film *The Bucket List* before retiring.

As we returned to our stateroom, Trish suggested, "We should make up our own bucket list. You know, places we want to travel to. This trip definitely would have gone on my list."

We awoke the next morning to a view out our window of a rocky, heavily wooded coastline. After ordering cappuccinos and croissants from room service, we donned heavy sweaters and sat out on the veranda. Midway through breakfast, we both gasped at a female moose and calf emerging from the trees. The cow looked at least six feet in height at the shoulder. Like the grizzly bear that walked past our bus a week earlier in Denali, the moose appeared oblivious to the passing ship. After a few moments, they melted back into the greenery.

As the ship maneuvered, I realized there was land on both sides of us. That meant we had turned north up the Sitakaday Narrows leading to Glacier Bay. Our excitement began to build when we began seeing chunks of ice floating by. Seals hauled out on occasional flatter ice floes, looking at a distance like brownish splotches on an otherwise pristine white background. And groups of them lounged on rock outcroppings along the shore.

When the ship's captain announced over the intercom that we were bearing left, up the west arm of the bay, we knew it was time to make our way up to the Lido deck for an unobstructed view of the highlight that drew us all to this cruise. We donned heavy jackets and gloves, then waited to allow the crowd to thin out at the elevator lobby.

Dense spruce forests hugged the shoreline, interrupted by occasional waterfalls cascading down from ice-covered ridges. We soon found ourselves nearing the hundred-foot-high face of Margerie Glacier, the largest of the tidewater glaciers there. Jagged protrusions and deep crevasses laced the surface of the rugged glacier that reached miles back into the mountains. Trish pulled her scooter up to a vantage point at the rail, while I stood behind her taking photos.

*Volendam* halted at what seemed at first like an unnecessary distance from the ice fall. It then began a slow rotation, providing circumferential views to the hundreds of passengers on all sides. A smaller touring boat, carrying just a few dozen passengers, dodged floating ice to get a closer look. A half dozen kayakers ventured even closer. Too close, I thought. Then came a cross between a roar and a crack, loud as a dynamite explosion, as the glacier calved a hunk of ice forty feet high, sending it tumbling into the bay and sending equally impressive swells in all directions. For a moment, I feared it would swamp the kayakers, possibly even the smaller boat, but they all rode it out.

Turning and looking up at me, Trish commented dryly, "I guess that's why the ship doesn't get any closer."

For the next hour, as the ship continued rotating, more calves broke off the glacier face, which moves at a rate of a dozen or so feet per day. Each ice fall was announced by another explosive sound and followed by a twenty-foot splash in the ice-strewn water. By this time, the tour boat and the kayakers all had moved to a safer distance. Then, as a blanket of clouds descended on the bay and sunset came on, the ship's engines rumbled, and we began moving to our next destination.

We were surprised the next morning to find the ship already tied up at a wooden pier on the Chilkoot Inlet, in front of the village of Haines. The only other craft at the pier was a catamaran that ferried passengers further up the bay to the onetime mining town of Scagway. Despite a grey cloud cover, it looked to be a dry, temperate day. We forewent parkas and opted instead for dark blue fleece pullovers for our shore activities.

We knew this small town of fewer than 2,000 residents, backed by snowy mountains. was a jumping-off point for hiking, boating, fishing, and other outdoor activities. Our challenge aboard ship was finding an activity that Trish could take part in. An agent at the tour desk suggested a visit by motorboat to the nearby Chilkat Bald Eagle Preserve, where hundreds of eagles nested and fished along the Chilkat River. Trish was skeptical.

"How am I going to transfer from my scooter to a boat that's rocking at the dock? I don't want to fall, and I definitely don't want to fall into a freezing river."

She relented after the smiling, eager-to-help agent assured her other disabled visitors had done this. A white van from the touring company met us at the gangway on the pier. A burly, bearded driver helped her up into the van and out again when we reached the river dock. Along the way, he briefed us on the eagle preserve and what we should expect to see.

At the dock, Trish hesitated once more as she eyed the steel motorboat, just large enough to hold us, two other couples, and a guide.

"I still don't see how I'm going to get into that boat," she declared.

"No problem," the guide told her. "Ride out to the end of the dock and we'll help you in. And don't worry about your scooter. We'll park it in the hut over there."

She gave me a quick glance and a grimace, but then complied with the instruction. After she stood up from the scooter, the driver and another equally burly fellow held her arms as she inched forward and stepped out from the dock into the boat. Once seated, she flashed a smile as I dropped onto the bench next to her.

For the next hour, we motored first upstream and then downstream on the smoothly flowing river through the eagle preserve. Sure enough, within ten minutes, we encountered the first eagle, its dark brown body gliding down to the water ahead of us on an eight-foot wing span to snatch a squirming salmon from the chilly water. From then on, we saw scores of eagles, perched on tree limbs overhanging the river, soaring along the river alone or in pairs, and seated in nests that looked like jumbles of twigs in nearby trees. Each sighting elicited a chorus of "oohs" and "aahs" from our little group, along with steady camera clicks.

Back at the dock, Trish happily allowed our hosts to help her back out of the boat and onto her waiting scooter.

"That was so cool!" Trish gushed, without waiting to be asked. I smiled and nodded in agreement. With that, she ducked into the gift shop to buy a tan baseball cap with the eagle preserve logo at the front, a piece of memorabilia she still wears and treasures.

The van dropped us off short of the pier so we could take in something of the town. Built on terrain sloping upward from the shore, its handful of smooth paved streets allowed easy travel for Trish's scooter. In a park along the waterfront, a fifteen-foot totem pole, composed of a stack of animal figures painted in red, white, and black, stared at nearby houses. When the ship's horn blew, we strolled back to the pier. With the tide out, the gangway had dropped almost level with the top of the pier.

The day's adventure left us feeling hungry. That evening, while the ship steamed toward Juneau, we looked forward to a big dinner. We wound up seated opposite a quiet, fiftyish Italian immigrant and his much younger, much more gregarious American wife. As we savored our Alaskan salmon, she regaled us with stories of her even-better ways of cooking salmon, while her husband smiled as one might at a precocious child. By the third glass of wine, she became even livelier, telling all within earshot how she and her husband were matched up by relatives concerned she hadn't yet found a husband. Back home, we would have found her annoying, but here her stories provided an amusing finish to a long day.

Arriving by sea at Juneau, the Alaskan capital on the state's southerly panhandle, we learned that the only other way to get there is by air, as no roads penetrate the mountains and glaciers ringing the city. Steep slopes topped by the Mendenhall Glacier rise up behind downtown, limiting development to a narrow strip along the coastal waterway. No wonder the population remains at fewer than 35,000.

All of that made for a gorgeous setting, despite the town itself looking too much like so many other cruise ship ports that have surrendered to the tourist industry. On a clear day like the one we were fortunate to have there, the sun glistened on the channel, eagles rode updrafts over the mountainsides, cable cars soared up Mt. Roberts, and seaplanes floated down to landings along the waterfront.

We steered clear of the concentration of tourist shops close to the cruise ship piers, instead taking in the views up at the surrounding peaks or across the water to Douglas Island. Later, at the Juneau Raptor Center, we watched staff aid eagles and hawks recovering from fights, gunshots, or other calamities, before returning them to the wild.

At day's end, the ship departed for Ketchikan, our last port of call. This small town of 8,000 lies on Revillagigedo Island, just off the mainland, at the southern end of the Alaska panhandle. A prominent welcoming sign proclaimed the town to be the "Salmon Capital of the World." Equally important for us, it had a historic downtown amid scenery rivaling Juneau's.

Ketchikan had two especially notable features, both scooter-accessible. Creek Street, actually a nine-block-long boardwalk built on pilings along Ketchikan Creek, served the red-light district of town in the Gold Rush days. Today the row of restored buildings supports a tasteful collection of shops, restaurants, and homes. We wandered in and out of several shops, buying some Alaskan Native cooking implements at one. The boardwalk creaked beneath us, and I had visions of Trish and her scooter tumbling down into the frigid, rushing whitewater, but all went well.

"This must have been a wild place in the old days," I said, as we passed the Dolly's House Museum.

"Yeah, I bet you would have spent lots of time here," Trish replied with a smile and a wink.

Ketchikan holds the world's largest collection of totem poles. In Totem Bight State Park at the north end of town, we paused again and again to admire totem poles carved from cedar logs, bearing figures of bears, eagles, and other wildlife in a dozen vivid, even fanciful colors. We were more familiar with the crafts of Southwest Native tribes, but couldn't help but be impressed by the imagination and workmanship that went into creating these cultural masterpieces. In between, I snapped photos of crimson rhododendron blooms and other lush, colorful plants. Trish, who is more knowledgeable than I am about flora and fauna, exclaimed, "I never expected to see plants like this at such a northern latitude."

The ship's horn brought an end to the final day of our adventure. We celebrated that evening with dinner in the Pinnacle Grill, the on-board steakhouse. The hostess arranged a table with enough space around it for me to assist Trish to her seat and then park the scooter alongside us. I indulged in a well-aged Porterhouse, medium rare, while Trish stuck with her favorite rack of lamb, all accompanied by a bottle of excellent Oregon pinot noir.

Over dinner, we talked about our most memorable experiences on both this cruise and the preceding land adventure to the North Slope. We had seen some highlights of

Alaska, but realized so much more of the state remained to be explored.

"I'm up for coming back," Trish said. "It turned out to be easier traveling with the scooter up here than I expected. I'd like to see more of the interior, maybe some of it by bush plane."

"Me too. I'd also like to see more of the coast. They have a great ferry system. It would be fun to get on and off, staying in any one place as long as we want."

The following morning, we disembarked at the Vancouver cruise ship terminal, a blocks-long structure topped by a series of faux sails. After a brief wait, an accessible cab took us to the airport for our flight home to San Diego. We haven't made it back to Alaska yet, as other destinations and unforeseen circumstances keep delaying us, but we will.

•———•

The positive experience of our Alaskan cruise opened us to the possibility of cruising again. A year later, as we discussed where to spend the upcoming holidays, I spotted a newspaper ad for an end-of-the-year Carnival cruise from San Diego down the coast of Baja California.

The ship would leave San Diego on December 31st and sail south to Cabo San Lucas at the tip of Baja, spending New Year's Eve at sea. We would have a full day at sea in each direction and return home on January 3rd.

"It sounds like fun," Trish opined as I read her the itinerary. "Even if it draws more of a party crowd than the Alaska cruise."

The timing, itinerary, and cost all appealed to us. We again opted for a stateroom at the stern, this time at the very stern, with a balcony just large enough for a couple of lounge chairs and a round table. Though a little smaller than our room on *Volendam*, it seemed fine for three nights at sea.

Preparations for this cruise proved simpler than our experience in Alaska. The warm climate and the brief trip duration required fewer and less bulky clothes.

Our departure from San Diego couldn't have been more convenient. We arranged a wheelchair-accessible shuttle for the five-mile ride from our home to the waterfront. At the cruise ship pier, we prepared to join a line that snaked out the terminal's door. Just then, a cruise line representative, seeing Trish on her scooter, intercepted us and escorted us past the line, straight to an express check-in desk inside. We had downloaded and completed the cruise line paperwork in advance. So, after taking our photos, checking our passports, and issuing us onboard ID tags, the staff directed us out onto the pier, to the gangway of Carnival's *Elation*.

Larger than *Volendam*, able to carry over 2,500 passengers, the ship presented a blindingly white steel wall along the pier, topped by a fire-engine-red smokestack with swept-back wings. Once again, we waited with other passengers on an open upper deck while staff delivered luggage to our staterooms. The surrounding crowd confirmed our expectation that this cruise would be heavily populated by youthful, party-oriented passengers. Most were in their twenties and thirties, and socialized easily with those around them, in contrast to the somewhat older, more reserved passengers on the previous cruise.

"I guess a New Year's cruise is bound to attract a wilder crowd," Trish remarked with a laugh. "Hopefully, not too wild!"

Trish's scooter at once drew attention, as the only mobility device we saw aboard ship. Again, a reflection of most passengers being younger and able-bodied. Several stopped to look at the scooter and ask about it, most commenting that they wanted to tell an older friend or relative. Trish answered their questions good-naturedly, though I knew she tired of those inquiries.

As the ship cast off and began a slow passage out of San Diego Bay, we caught a panoramic view of high-rise downtown buildings backed by mountains, with the retired aircraft carrier-turned-museum *USS Midway* in the foreground. The arched span of the Coronado Bridge rose behind us, and the imposing ridgeline of Point Loma framed the west side of the channel. By the time we passed Ballast Point at the mouth of the bay, a salty breeze had picked up and a cloudless, crimson sunset filled the view across the open ocean.

As the evening lights of Tijuana appeared, Trish declared, "It's New Year's Eve. I want a drink."

We headed down to a bar on the Lido deck. By now, we had discovered that elevators here were not nearly as crowded as those on *Volendam*. Younger passengers, more fit and in more of a hurry, didn't mind using the stairs. On the other hand, they roamed the ship's corridors at high speed and in tight groups, making it difficult for Trish to negotiate her way through the crowds. It didn't help that they kept their eyes fixed straight ahead, with no thought they might run into someone at a lower level, like a person on a scooter or wheelchair, perhaps even a child.

In the bar, tequila flowed into hundreds of margarita glasses, dance music blared, and bar patrons became as boisterous as teenagers at a beach party. There appeared to be lots of singles looking to meet other singles, all lubricating their libidos to speed the process.

"Takes you back, doesn't it?" I asked Trish.

"Yeah. Not that I want to relive those years, but there are some fun memories."

"No reason we can't make new ones. Isn't that why we're here?"

With that, we ordered another round of margaritas.

By then, it was time to prepare for dinner. We overdressed, it turned out. I wore grey slacks, a blue blazer, and a red-and-blue striped silk tie over a white shirt. Trish opted for a white cotton pantsuit set off with a Navajo turquoise pendant and matching bracelet. Our tablemates, like people at tables around us, tended toward khakis and tropical shirts — nice but way more casual.

As the evening progressed, wine bottles emptied and the room's sound level increased. By midnight, the crowd was ready to sing the traditional Auld Lang Syne before filtering back out to various bars.

*Elation* and its hungover passengers spent the next day steaming down the 800-mile coastline of Baja California. With many of our shipmates still sleeping off the previous night's celebration, we glided through the buffet line and enjoyed our breakfast in a quiet dining room. We then found plenty of available lounge chairs by the Olympic-sized pool on the Veranda deck. After helping Trish off her scooter onto a chair, I plunged into the nearly empty pool to swim a few laps.

I noticed for the first time families with children, also up early. The kids delighted in climbing to the top of a winding, two-story-high water slide and careening down into the pool. I couldn't resist joining them.

By midday, the atmosphere changed. Large numbers of passengers, still droopy-eyed and staggering a bit, emerged to join us around the pool. Many set about trying to prove that the best remedy for a hangover is another drink, or several. As in the bar the previous evening, couples congregated in certain areas and singles in others, with the latter again doing their best to pair off. The process went more slowly here, perhaps because bikinis and swimming trunks revealed the not-so-complimentary aspects of their flirting wearers. After a couple of hours, when the poolside party became too boisterous, we retreated to our stateroom patio.

Suppertime tamped down the partying a little, but we noted lots of empty seats in the high-ceilinged dining room. Not everyone had paused to get some nutrition. A fortyish couple from the Midwest, on their first visit to Mexico, joined us. When they discovered we were from California and had traveled in Mexico, they peppered us with questions about what they regarded as a very exotic place. They sounded astonished but relieved to hear that our destination city would be filled with English-speakers and that most businesses accepted American currency.

After excusing ourselves, we searched for a suitable location for a nightcap. In a cocktail lounge, we nestled into a booth and listened to an excellent folk-rock singer-guitarist reminiscent of my friend, John Kelly, who serenaded us at our wedding reception two years earlier. The room's décor still reflected the just-passed holiday season, as the musician sat flanked by the complementary lights of a well-decorated Christmas tree and a five-foot-tall electric Hanukah menorah.

By morning, the ship had anchored off Cabo San Lucas, once a quiet fishing village but now a bustling tourist mecca of 80,000. The shallow harbor made it necessary to ferry passengers in by tender rather than disembarking at a pier. Our pre-cruise research had told us that Trish's scooter could not get into a launch or onto a pier at this port. Since we both had visited Cabo before, when it was a less-developed destination, we didn't feel we would miss anything.

We watched from our balcony as a stream of boats delivered loads of passengers to the harbor, then returned for more. That allowed us a quieter day aboard ship, as most passengers left to party and shop in town. We again sunned ourselves by the uncrowded swimming pool and enjoyed the uninterrupted attention of the wait staff, who seemed much more affable that day. At lunchtime, the expansive buffet was devoid of the usual lines.

"It practically feels like we're on a private yacht," Trish commented, as we enjoyed our lunch in blissful quiet.

"I agree. If we take another cruise, we should think about staying aboard like this in any port that doesn't excite us."

From an upper deck, we took in the familiar views of desert hills overlooking the town and the jagged rock formations leading to the iconic El Arco stone arch at Land's End, marking separation of the Sea of Cortez from the Pacific Ocean. Motorboats roared across the bay, towing parasailers suspended from multi-colored parachutes. In the late afternoon, the local fleet of fishing boats hung with nets returned to port. We were shocked, though, at the rows of six-story condominium and timeshare developments lining the shore, far more than on our previous visits.

As evening approached, the ship's horn alerted passengers to return to the pier and be shuttled back aboard. By the time *Elation* weighed anchor and began steaming northward, the onboard party was back in full swing. We lingered on a high, open deck to watch an orange sun sink into the blue-green sea.

The next morning, as *Elation* followed the Baja coast, I awoke early. After retrieving coffee and croissants from the breakfast buffet, I stood at the balcony rail and stared at the churning wake from the ship's twin twenty-foot-wide propellers. I smiled to myself at the memory of finding similar relaxation on the fantail of *USS Saratoga* decades earlier, drinking coffee, smoking cigarettes, and watching the ship's wake streaming off toward the horizon.

As I settled into a chair on our balcony and scanned the desert-like coastline, an object the size of a city bus rose from the waves two hundred yards aft of the ship, then dropped back with a monumental splash. It happened too fast for me to realize what I had seen. Then it happened again. This time, though, I recognized it as a breaching whale. Grey whales migrate annually from north Pacific waters to give birth in tranquil Baja lagoons. Consequently, whale watching is a popular entertainment along the Southern California and Baja coasts, where the forty-ton creatures swim close enough to be seen from small boats or even from shore.

I rushed back into the cabin and tried to wake Trish to share this sight. To no avail. She mumbled for me to leave her alone and fell back asleep. I grabbed my camera and sped back to the balcony, afraid I might miss more of this display. On the contrary, now I saw two whales, possibly more, repeatedly launching themselves out of the glistening sea, then crashing back. I watched and photographed them until the ship had moved so far north that the whales looked like minnows.

"You missed quite a show," I told Trish later, as I shared the photos with her.

Back by the pool, we found partying at a new crescendo. Our shipmates appeared determined to empty the *Elation's* liquor lockers before returning to San Diego. As we threaded our way through the crowd toward lounge chairs at the far end of the pool, I saw a fellow ahead of us talking loudly and gesturing wildly with both arms. Large-bodied but chubby, like a onetime athlete gone to seed, and decked out in loud-patterned swimming trunks, baseball cap, and wraparound sun glasses, he appeared a caricature of his fellow partiers. I doubted he saw Trish seated on her scooter well below his eye level. His left hand, holding a lit cigarette, swung toward her face. I reached forward and grabbed his wrist. He gave me a shocked, angry look, but then, maybe recognizing at least for a moment the accident he had nearly caused, he pivoted away and resumed the uproarious dialogue with his drinking buddies.

*Elation* arrived back in San Diego on a bright Sunday morning. The water glittered among scores of sailboats taking advantage of the gathering breeze. In what seemed like no time at all, we disembarked, located our shuttle van, and sped around the bay to our home. From our front deck, we could see the ship moored at its pier across the water, it's white hull shining, preparing to receive another load of vacationers.

"So, what do you think of that experience?" I asked Trish as I handed her a homemade margarita to celebrate our return.

"I'm glad we went. I always enjoy going somewhere around the holidays. And it makes we want to go to Mexico again, for a real visit."

But that was not to be, at least not soon. For years to come, tight security, crime, and long lines at the border would deter us from driving south to once-favorite beach towns of Rosarito and San Felipe. And drug gang violence made visits deeper into the country, including scuba diving havens in Yucatan, even less attractive. We hope this will pass. Meanwhile, we find other tropical places to explore in the Caribbean and Pacific. Maybe we'll take a cruise there some day.

# Chapter 8
# LET'S TAKE A ROAD TRIP

Trish at Molera State Park, Big Sur

*Big Sur, December 2008*
On a lazy October afternoon, as we sat in our living room drinking wine and viewing photos from our trip to Alaska four months earlier, Trish wondered about our next destination.

"We've been going to places like national parks for New Year's. Yosemite last year and the Grand Canyon the year before," she said. "It's getting a little late, but we should plan something special again."

"Yes, I've been thinking about that too. I don't want to fly anywhere during the holidays. Let's take another road trip to someplace pretty, someplace we haven't been before or haven't visited in a while."

"Sure, just keep one thing in mind. My MS has gotten worse since our last long drive. My legs will feel really weak after sitting for so many hours, even if we break up the drive. I'll have trouble getting in and out of the car or getting on and off my scooter. You'll have to help me more than usual."

I nodded. That had already occurred to me. I knew a road trip would be challenging, but I didn't want that to stop us from going somewhere.

As we continued sipping Cabernet and tossing around possibilities, I got an idea.

"How about driving up to Big Sur? Neither of us has been there in a long time, and we've never been there together."

"Great, but it's a long drive from here."

"It is. We could stop off someplace else nice on the way up and the way back."

I retrieved a California road map from my car and spread it out on the coffee table.

"It's a little more than 200 miles to Santa Barbara, another hundred to San Luis Obispo," I said, pointing to the route on the map. "That's all freeway. Then about a hundred more on Highway 1 to Big Sur. That's a lot slower. Without stops, and with no traffic, at least eight hours total. Realistically, probably more like ten, plus any stops. A shorter distance than our drive to the Grand Canyon, but at least as long time-wise, and harder driving. If we split it up, where would you like to stop overnight along the way?"

"I know. Let's stop in Los Olivos going up. We can visit a couple of wineries, stay overnight, and then drive on to Big Sur the next day."

We had recently seen the film *Sideways*, set in the picturesque vineyard communities of the Santa Ynez Valley, north of Santa Barbara. That sounded good to me.

"And Santa Barbara would be a nice stop on the way back," she added.

---

We left San Diego on a cool but sunny Monday morning, with Trish's scooter loaded in the rear of my Explorer, connected to the built-in lift. We wanted to start early enough to get through the Los Angeles area after the morning rush but before traffic thickened at midday. Holiday traffic actually turned out to be light, even on the often-overwhelmed Ventura Freeway northward out of LA.

As we passed La Conchita and Carpinteria, beyond Ventura on US 101, the ocean sparkled off to our left, while coastal bluffs rose hundreds of feet to our right.

"I used to drive to Santa Barbara a lot to see friends when I was in college," Trish said. "This stretch was always my favorite part of the drive. It's hardly changed at all."

In Santa Barbara, we left the freeway and turned north, following speedy San Marcos Pass Road up into the Santa Ynez Mountains rising 5,000 feet above the city. Near the top of the pass, I pulled over at the historic Cold Spring Tavern, a onetime stagecoach stop nestled amid towering California live oaks.

As expected, after almost five hours on the road, Trish needed my help to get out of the car, even using a support brace that attached to the door post. She grimaced as she dropped onto the scooter, but then coasted up the ramp at the entrance of the wood-and-stone structure and made her way to a table inside.

"I love the Old West ambience of places like this," she said, gazing around at the dark wood-paneled walls, the gray stone fireplace, and the abundant memorabilia from the building's original use. After a lunch of Santa Maria tri-tip barbecue, the signature dish of the Central Coast region, we resumed our drive.

Thirty minutes later, we arrived at the Fess Parker Wine Country Inn, owned by the former actor who achieved film fame as Davy Crockett. With twenty guest rooms, the white clapboard-sided inn provided a cozy getaway in the small town of Los Olivos, surrounded by the vineyards for which the area had become famous.

"Cool room," Trish opined as she surveyed our accessible lodging for the night, with its king bed, wide aisles, fireplace, and view of nearby vineyards. "I'd come back here."

After washing up and resting awhile, Trish felt more energetic. We strolled down Grand Avenue, passing the shops of several local wineries in the few blocks of downtown. Trish being more of an oenophile, I waited for her to make a choice. She soon pointed to a vine-covered shop near the town's central traffic circle, and declared, "Let's try that one."

By the time we sampled a flight of pinot noirs and merlots, we were hungry for dinner.

"What's your favorite place to eat here?" Trish asked the bearded, thirtyish fellow behind the bar.

"Right there," he said, pointing across the street to an oak-and-glass, one-story building housing the Los Olivos Wine Merchant and Cafe. "Every place here is good, but I recommend that one. It's not fancy, but the food is excellent."

Heeding his advice, we crossed over and got seated quickly for an early dinner. The roomy interior allowed us to park the scooter at the side of our table. A wine shop, with racks of bottles lining the far wall, shared the space with the restaurant. Aromas drifting out from the kitchen assured us the fellow at the winery had given us a great suggestion.

Trish eyed the wine list like the proverbial kid in a candy store. Meanwhile, the young man waiting on us returned. He chatted with us about the town and the vineyards before taking our orders.

"Please recommend a wine," she implored him. "I'm having roast chicken, and my husband wants the short ribs."

He suggested a local pinot noir. We enjoyed it so much that we asked him after dinner to get us a bottle from the adjacent shop to take with us. As she looked over our prize, Trish saw a problem.

"We don't have a corkscrew," she lamented to the server.

He glanced to both sides, then slipped his hand into an apron pocket and removed a professional-quality corkscrew and foil cutter. "Don't mention where you got it," he whispered with a sly smile as he placed it under Trish's napkin on the table. That earned him a generous tip.

With our treasures in hand, we exited into the cool evening air and ambled back up the street to the inn. Holiday lights glowed from building facades and from a fifteen-foot-tall Christmas tree in the Grand Avenue roundabout.

After rejoining the freeway the next morning, we sped sixty miles to the college town of San Luis Obispo before turning onto California Highway 1, the scenic coast road that would take us the rest of the way. My excitement built as I recalled past drives on this route and pictured what lay ahead.

At San Simeon, just north of Hearst Castle, I pulled off the road on the seaward side to give Trish a surprise. After she put up with a bouncy scooter ride across a gravel parking area, we looked over a wood railing at the beach below. Scores of elephant seals lolled about the sand and in the shallows. Sixteen-foot-long bulls, weighing as much as four tons, roared and pushed at one another, while smaller cows watched to see which of their suitors would prevail.

"Males acting tough to impress the females, with sex hopefully to follow," Trish observed. "Reminds me of college parties."

The next sixty miles are among the most scenic drives in America, if not the world. Highway 1 undulates along the rocky coast, a ribbon hanging on the edge of the mountains, threatening to drop into the raging surf a hundred feet down. The iconic, arched Bixby Bridge straddling Big Creek signals arrival at the Big Sur section of coast.

"I still remember the first time I drove through here forty years ago," I said. "The sight of this bridge took my breath away. It still does."

I pulled over at Hurricane Point, just short of the bridge. We got out to savor the view of the bridge and the jagged coastline beyond it. A friendly couple sharing the experience offered to take a photo of us with the bridge in the background. Trish stood and held onto me to keep her balance just long enough for a quick picture.

We passed the weathered wood sign marking the entrance to Esalen Institute, the sixty-year-old cliffside retreat center known for its programs promoting human potential. Next came the Henry Miller Memorial Library, both a library and an arts center in the former home of the late, celebrated writer.

Soon after that, we turned off the highway at Pfeiffer Big Sur State Park and followed a narrow road through the forest to the Big Sur Lodge. Our accessible cabin sat a hundred yards from the main lodge building, surrounded by towering coast redwoods, incense cedars, and ponderosa pines. Minutes earlier, we had been driving in bright sunshine along the ocean. But here a cool, heavy mist, almost a fog, lay like a blanket across the forest floor, while dense tree crowns filtered sunrays struggling to reach down to the base of massive trunks.

After riding in the car all day, Trish's legs were like spaghetti. I raised her from the edge of the passenger seat and held her up until she gained her footing outside the car, then eased her down onto the waiting scooter.

The cabin was more basic than we expected, like a budget motel room. A far cry from the inn back in Los Olivos, but comfortable enough and fully accessible, with a ramp at the entrance and plenty of room inside for Trish to move around on her scooter.

"Let's take a walk," Trish suggested as soon as we unpacked. We spent the next hour winding through the forest on a network of pathways, some paved, some smooth dirt, but all scooter-friendly. Pungent evergreen aromas swirled around us, while mist settled on our heads and clothing. Only an occasional car motor disturbed the silence of the forest.

Feeling chilled, we made our way to the lodge, in search of the bar and restaurant. We sat before a fireplace in the wood-paneled lounge and sipped Irish coffee until we felt warm and restored. Through the wall of windows, we watched as dusk settled into the forest outside while we dined on roast salmon and steak frites. Afterward, back in the lounge, an elderly couple sitting near us expressed interest in Trish's scooter.

"I'll need one of those all too soon," the woman said. "Does it take you everywhere you need to go?"

"Pretty much," Trish replied. "I use it at home, shopping, at work. And it lets me travel almost everywhere."

"With an occasional push from me," I added.

We rose early the next morning, excited about exploring the area after so many years. As we devoured breakfast burritos and coffee at the lodge restaurant, I spread out a map showing the various parks and other local sights.

"There was a wildfire in the mountains here a few months ago," I reminded Trish. "From what I saw on-line, some parks are still impacted. Trails might be closed. We'll see."

We began by driving south in sunshine, back toward the Bixby Bridge, until we came to Julia Pfeiffer Burns State Park, named for a member of a pioneering family that settled in the area in the late 1800s. The parking lot was empty at that time of morning. I hoped to take Trish up the Overlook Trail for views of the coast and of McWay Falls tumbling eighty feet down a granite cliff into the ocean.

We got out of the Explorer amid redwoods and firs that stood precariously on steep slopes. Soon after leaving the parking area, we came upon a sign informing us the trail was closed ahead. The recent wildfire had burned a wood bridge over the creek feeding the waterfall.

"Well, that's disappointing," Trish said with a long sigh. "And it's the only accessible trail here. Let's go on to one of the other parks."

Shortly after beginning our drive northward, we noticed a dozen cars stopped on the ocean side of the road and a cluster of people looking out from the seaside cliff.

"Whatever all those people are finding so interesting, let's check it out," I said, wheeling the car across the road and into a dirt parking area.

We had just gotten out of the car when Trish spotted the attraction that had drawn all those other visitors. "Omigod, condors!" she yelled.

Sure enough, above us and out over the ocean, half a dozen of the endangered black birds circled and rode updrafts on their ten-foot wingspans. We joined the cluster of people at the cliff edge, following the condors' swooping maneuvers and snapping photos of this unexpected spectacle.

"They must fly over here from Pinnacles National Park," I told Trish. "It's their best remaining habitat, just thirty miles inland from here."

As quickly as some birds disappeared from sight over the ridgeline behind us, more appeared.

"This is so exciting," Trish declared, beaming. "They are so rare, only a few hundred left. I never thought I'd see even one in the wild, let along dozens. This makes coming here extra special."

After a half hour, the excitement wore off enough that we resumed exploring. I had another surprise for Trish. Just up the road from the condor view, we came to Nepenthe, the cliffside restaurant that has been a favorite Big Sur dining spot for a half century. It being a pleasantly warm day, we asked to be seated on the broad deck overlooking the ocean. Over sandwiches and beer, we gazed at the dazzling views of surf crashing on coastal rocks and of forest foliage still turning shades of red and yellow.

"I'm so glad we came up here," Trish said. "I almost forgot how magical this stretch of coast is."

"Yes. And the condors. I didn't expect that. What a treat!"

Our next stop, Andrew Molera State Park, was far more hospitable than the earlier park. We wandered well-maintained trails through woodlands and up to an ocean viewpoint. Recent rains had left some trails too muddy for the scooter to pass, but most of the park remained accessible.

Sunshine lit up mature sycamores with their mottled, peeling bark. Some had already dropped serrated, golden-brown leaves that carpeted the trails and crunched beneath the scooter's wheels.

After we had toured the park's interior for about two hours, I told Trish, "This is lovely, but it's time to leave. We need to get back and change for dinner."

New Year's Eve turned out to be a low-key affair. We had made a dinner reservation at the Big Sur River Inn, a stone building dating from the 1930s alongside the river. That proved to be unnecessary, as the pine-paneled dining room was barely half full. But our salmon and roast chicken dinners, accompanied by a bottle of red wine from a vineyard in nearby Monterey, were excellent.

"I'm surprised there isn't more of a crowd," Trish commented to the young woman serving us. "It's so quiet for New Year's Eve."

"This is typical," she replied. "We're not a big holiday destination, and local folks tend to stay off the roads on nights like this."

We lingered a while, staring through the picture windows at the redwoods clustered outside, barely visible in the dark. By the time we finished our bottle of wine, we noticed all the other diners had departed. At that, we returned to the lodge for a nightcap to close out the year.

New Year's Day dawned cool and bright. We checked out early and drove fifteen minutes south to have breakfast at Deetjen's Big Sur Inn. This vine-covered collection of cottages and cabins had been hosting adventurous visitors since the 1930s, when a dirt wagon road provided the only access to this area. I wished we could have stayed there, but their one accessible room had already been taken by the time we thought to make reservations.

Deetjen's seemed like a fitting place for our last meal before leaving Big Sur. Despite the dining room being a bit crowded, the staff made way for Trish's scooter. The interior décor, resembling an English country inn, provided the perfect backdrop for a breakfast of eggs benedict, muffins, and tea.

"We have a long drive ahead of us," I told Trish as she took the last bite of a cranberry muffin spread with orange jam. "We need to go." She agreed.

We backtracked our route up here, only this time bypassing the Santa Ynez Valley. Instead, we continued on to Santa Barbara, to spend the night at the Harbor View Inn on the beach at the foot of the State Street shopping and restaurant district.

Trish exited the car with ease here, as if rejuvenated by the last few days.

The inn's accessible rooms all faced an interior courtyard, so we had opted for a standard room with a balcony looking out at the beach. Arriving mid-afternoon, we had time for a leisurely stroll along the East Beach promenade before dusk, followed by a seafood dinner on nearby, hundred-year-old Stearns Wharf. Trish's scooter bounced along the uneven timbers of the historic working wharf all the way to the Harbor Restaurant, as squawking sea gulls floated above us.

"This is like a cobblestone street in Prague or Vienna," Trish grumbled, though good-naturedly.

We returned to San Diego the next day. As we sped down I-5, nearing home, Trish said to me, "That was really a long drive. It took more out of me than I expected. I'm glad you were doing the driving. But Big Sur was great!"

"It seems to me the trip energized you. You got stronger as we went. You think we should plan another road trip?"

"Sure. To go to a place like Big Sur, I'd put up with that drive again, every minute of it."

# Chapter 9
# FINDING RELIGION IN THE CARIBBEAN

Trish at Waterfront, Willemstad

*Curacao, September 2010*

Under a cloud-flecked autumn sky, Trish and I flew into Hato Airport on the north coast of Curacao. Out the airplane window, we saw a green land mass far off to our left across an emerald blue channel.

"That's the coast of Venezuela," I said, feeling surprised and excited. We both had traveled in Mexico and Central America, but this was our first view of South America.

A ten-hour, overnight journey from San Diego, including a plane change in Houston, had brought us to this nearly southernmost point in the Caribbean. We had visited the nearby island of Bonaire two years earlier. Another year we would go to Aruba, the third of the "ABC Islands" that once comprised the southern group of the Netherlands Antilles. Two things brought us here—excellent scuba diving and an interest in further experiencing the blend of Dutch, Caribbean, and Latin American cultures.

This was our fourth trip together to the Caribbean, my tenth in all, rarely visiting any island more than once. So many islands, so little time. Each presented unique culture, sights, food, and music. Since English is one of several languages spoken on all the ABC Islands, our experience on Bonaire gave us confidence that we would get along fine.

Thankfully, this was not one of those island airports without jetways. Ones where Trish, seated in an aisle wheelchair, had to be lowered to the ground by a hydraulic lift or carried down the passenger stairs by a gang of airport workers.

As we exited the airport terminal, the Caribbean welcomed us with a soft, warm breeze, like a lover's kiss. That moment is always my favorite part of arriving in the tropics.

A taxi carried us over a low ridgeline and into the capital city of Willemstad. On the downgrade, we got a sweeping view of the harbor in Saint Anna Bay. Cruise ships, cargo carriers, and pleasure craft lined the wharves surrounding the deep-water port. We spied the town's famous floating bridge near the mouth of the harbor channel. Instead of a drawbridge, this one-of-a-kind span, hinged at one end, swung ninety degrees on motor-driven pontoons, allowing maritime traffic to pass. Further up the channel, a steel highway bridge arched two hundred feet above the harbor.

We had booked a room at the Avila Beach Hotel, a modern, mid-rise establishment a mile and a half east of downtown. As always, we asked for an accessible room to accommodate Trish and her scooter. But, as so often happens, we found the accessible rooms to be in an undesirable location, in this case facing a parking lot rather than the ocean. Trish called the desk and told them we would prefer a view room, even if it was not accessible. That meant giving up some convenient features, but Trish considered that a fair tradeoff. Besides, we had our detachable grab bars for the bathroom, and I could help her with anything else.

To our relief, the very cheery woman on the phone complied with Trish's request. We soon settled into our home for the week, relaxing on the balcony, sipping local diNos Pilsner beers, and gazing at the sparkling ocean reflecting the afternoon sun, like gems leaping from one wave to another.

We followed our typical routine for tropical vacations. I would go diving on alternate mornings, while Trish slept late, immersed herself in a new novel, and ate a late breakfast in the room or on the hotel patio. Once I returned from diving, we would have lunch and either relax at the pool or take a walk. On non-diving days, we explored the rest of the island.

I wished Trish could share the diving experience with me. For forty years, it has been an important part of my life, providing mental relaxation and spiritual cleansing. Early in our relationship, she expressed interest in getting trained. Her experiences diving into an ocean canyon off Roatan and among sting rays in Grand Cayman, both times aided by guides, reinforced that desire. Since then, however, MS had further weakened her legs to where she no longer felt comfortable donning scuba gear and going underwater.

The first morning, I awoke early, gathered my dive gear, and gulped down some yoghurt and fruit we had bought the previous evening at a nearby convenience store. I lightly stroked Trish's shoulder and gave her a goodbye kiss.

"Have a good time," she murmured, barely awake. "Watch out for sharks." With that, she rolled over and fell back asleep.

A van from the Ocean Encounters dive shop picked me up outside the hotel and drove me and a few others to a pier two miles further from town. There, a dozen of us boarded a white, forty-foot power boat for a short ride to the dive sites.

Our initial dive was on a sunken freighter, the 165-foot-long *Superior Producer*, perched on a white sand bottom at a depth of a hundred feet. In clear water, the sight of a full-sized ship sitting upright on the sea bottom was surreal. With its entire mass visible at once, its twin propellers immobilized, the openings to the cargo hold yawning like cavern mouths, and the bridge sitting empty atop the superstructure, it seemed like a giant toy resting on the bottom of a swimming pool. And, like all wrecks, it acted as a magnet for sea life. Corals, anemones, and sea fans attached themselves to any available surface, creating a palette of colors and textures. Schools of blue-striped grunts and reddish snappers clustered in the hold, inside the bridge, under the stern—anywhere they could find shelter from the currents and from predators. An occasional grey reef shark or silvery barracuda swam by in search of an easy meal.

The rest of my dives that week were on undersea walls, where a reef top at twenty to thirty feet sloped down or dropped off hundreds of feet into an abyss. I always gasped at the first view of the bottom dropping away beneath me. At these sites—with fanciful names like Rolling Stone, Hole 5, and Mushroom Forest—orange and blue tubular sponges stuck out from the wall, stacks of plate coral encrusted the reef's face, and brown gorgonians waved their fingers in the current. Olive-green moray eels emerged from narrow caves, ready to sink their stiletto teeth into passing fish or into divers whose fingers probed too close. Clusters of spotted eagle rays soared by, keeping a safe distance from us. And an occasional sea turtle, four feet long and ungainly on land, flew past like a great armored bird.

The top of the reef looked like an aquarium, with turquoise parrotfish nibbling at coral heads, bright red squirrelfish hiding beneath outstretched elkhorn coral, and pairs of phosphorescent angelfish flitting about among green-gold brain coral, dancing sea fans, and wide-mouthed barrel sponges. I marveled at the variety of shapes and colors, and snapped away with my underwater camera in the clear surroundings. Trish always enjoys seeing photos from this part of my dives. We would screen them on her laptop later while eating lunch.

On the second day, Trish and I began our on-shore exploration of the island. The distance from the downtown waterfront hadn't seemed far while riding in the taxi on our arrival, so we decided to walk. Regrettably, we had failed to notice the virtual absence of ramps at street corners other than in the neighborhood surrounding our hotel. Without them, and with only occasional driveways, Trish couldn't ride her scooter on the sidewalks.

By the time this trend became apparent, we had already covered several blocks. I shook my head in frustration and turned to Trish.

"I don't see any taxis. Do you want to go back to the hotel?" I asked.

"No, we've come this far. I want to keep exploring."

I was game to continue, if she was. We made our way along the busy street toward downtown, with me scouting ahead in search of curb cuts, while Trish took shelter between parked cars.

"There's no one coming, and I see a driveway halfway down the block," I told her. "Let's make a dash for it." With that, she pulled out from her temporary refuge and sped toward the next opportunity to get out of the street.

That became our pattern for the remaining mile or so. But some blocks had no curb cuts, forcing us to remain in the street. Passing drivers honked their car horns at us, as if annoyed that we were intruding on their space.

Nearing downtown, Trish stopped, turned to me, shook her head, and blurted out, "What's wrong with them? Doesn't anyone here use a wheelchair?" I fully shared her frustration. We hadn't encountered such a wheelchair-unfriendly streetscape in any previous travels, not on other islands or in other cities.

The waterfront itself had more welcoming features — wheelchair ramps at corners, wide sidewalks, well-marked crosswalks. We guessed the city had modernized that area to accommodate cruise ship passengers. It certainly wasn't for the benefit of island residents. During our entire stay on Curacao, we didn't see another disabled person riding a wheelchair or scooter. They must have been there, but not out and about. Who could blame them, when the public rights-of-way were like an obstacle course?

After completing that gauntlet, we found ourselves at one end of the floating bridge reaching over five hundred feet across the harbor, connecting the two sides of the capital. As we watched pedestrians, many pushing bicycles, walk across on its wooden planks, a siren blared, giving warning that the bridge would move shortly. Entrance gates then closed at both ends. As soon as the last walkers finished crossing, motors whirred, propellers spun, and the structure separated from the dock in front of us and rotated on its hinged far end.

Fifteen minutes later, after several boats passed and the bridge returned to its home position, the siren sounded again, the rolling gates reopened, and pedestrians again swarmed across in both directions. This time, we joined them, making our way beneath an arcade of overhead light stanchions. The sixteen pontoons supporting the structure rose and fell gently, like being on a boat moored at a dock. Trish's scooter drew stares from others crossing, though here on the bridge most people smiled. Hers was the only type of motorized vehicle allowed to cross.

"This is more like it!" Trish yelled back to me as she sped through the crowd, sounding as excited as an eight-year-old on her first bicycle ride.

I had crossed pontoon bridges before. In my hometown in Austria, US Army engineers built one across the Inn River to provide a connection to Germany. In Frankfurt, a similar but longer one crossed the broad Main River. But those were temporary structures, put in place only until steel bridges destroyed during the recent war could be replaced. And, other than bobbing on their pontoons, they sat fixed in place. The one here, known as the Queen Emma Bridge, was built over a hundred years earlier. With only slight updating, this ingenious example of Dutch civil engineering had been in operation ever since.

From the westerly Otrobanda district, we looked back at a row of classic, high-peaked Dutch buildings lining the opposite side of the waterfront. Their bright blue, yellow, and orange facades added a Caribbean touch to the harbor. We entered the square Rif Fort, built in the early 1800s to guard entry to the bay but now repurposed as a shopping mall.

"I'd like to see the view from the parapets," I said, pointing to a steep flight of stone steps leading to the top of the wall.

"Go ahead," Trish replied. "I'll browse through these shops." She knows there will be places she can't reach and doesn't mind if I want to check them out, as long as she has another diversion available to her.

I made a quick run to the top. Peering over the parapet walls, I saw the port in one direction and the ocean in the other—the same views early Dutch sentries would have had as they kept a lookout for French or English invaders. Enveloped by a salty ocean smell, I took photos in both directions to share with Trish later.

After crossing back to the Punda district on the easterly side, we set off to explore further. Foremost in our minds was to locate the Mikvé Israel-Emanuel Synagogue, the oldest Jewish temple in continuous use in the Western Hemisphere. The next day would be the eve of Yom Kippur, and we hoped to attend services there. I'm not religiously observant, but this seemed like a unique cultural experience not to be missed. And, while Trish was raised very Catholic, she became intrigued by Jewish culture and rituals.

We found the synagogue just a few blocks from the waterfront. Its mustard-colored, stucco exterior, peaked roofline, and rows of arched upper-story windows blended in with the design of surrounding buildings, except that the ground-floor outside walls were pierced only by a few doorways. A stern-looking guard at the narrow entrance informed us the building was closed that day, but we would be welcome to return for services the following evening. I found it disappointing and sad that, even here, such security was needed.

We next went in search of a restaurant. After eating dinner at the hotel the previous two evenings, we were ready for local cuisine. In keeping with the street scene, few restaurants were accessible. Most had at least one sizeable step up from the sidewalk at their entrance. After a brief search, we found a pleasant-looking restaurant at the waterfront with outdoor seating at sidewalk level. We shared plates of red snapper sauteed in a spicy Creole sauce and grilled chicken with mango chutney. For contrast, we accompanied that with Heineken beers and finished with a plate of Dutch cheeses.

After dinner, we walked along the wharves, enjoying the views of buildings and the floating bridge under bright night lights. On subsequent evenings, we called ahead to restaurants to confirm their accessibility.

From our first pedestrian experience, we knew to take a taxi to the synagogue the next day. The hotel found us a van that could carry Trish's scooter in the rear. At the temple, the security guard seemed to remember us, smiling and waving us in. We followed a stream of worshippers down a corridor lined with display cases holding mementos of the congregation's history dating back to the arrival of Spanish and Portuguese refugees in the mid-1600s. Knowing that we weren't regular members of the congregation, numerous people welcomed us and thanked us for coming.

The photographs we had seen on-line did not prepare us for the splendor of the temple's sanctuary, modeled after the congregation's prior home in Amsterdam, where they had found refuge after fleeing Spain. All the woodwork appeared to be dark mahogany. Rows of pews covered with red cushions lined both sides, as well as an upper balcony level. Forty-foot columns supported the massive wood beams holding the roof. Six brass chandeliers hung from the ceiling, each with twenty curved arms holding candles that danced inside glass lamps. An ornately carved ark containing the Torah scrolls rose twenty feet at one end. The rabbi's pulpit stood in a balcony forward of the ark, above the level of the seated worshippers, similar to what I recalled seeing in European Gothic cathedrals. White plaster walls set off the rest of the design.

More surprising was the sand floor. As in several other Caribbean synagogues built by Iberian immigrants, it mimicked a device used back in Spain and Portugal to absorb the sounds of prayer and thereby avoid discovery by authorities during the years of the Inquisition. Coincidentally, it also served as a reminder of the biblical Jews' wandering in the desert after escaping Egypt. With all of that symbolism, I could see why this house of worship had remained active for so long, even in a place with relatively few congregants.

Trish's scooter typically does not perform well on sand, as the wheels sink in and get stuck. Fortunately, this sand was only a couple of inches deep and underlain by a hard surface. With a light push from me, she was able to navigate her way in.

We were not prepared for the heat inside. The centuries-old building remained without air conditioning. Electric fans three feet in diameter were stationed about the interior, but they merely kept the temperature in what felt like the mid-90s. Recalling how Trish's MS symptoms would flare up in the desert back home, I feared the heat here would have a similar effect. Fortunately, a helpful usher steered us to a spot at the end of a pew, right below one of the fans, where we found it warm but tolerable.

Despite the advanced age of much of the congregation, we didn't see anyone else using a wheelchair or scooter. Just a few people with canes or walkers. MS is less common in the central latitudes, where high vitamin D levels resulting from year-round sunshine appear to have a preventive effect.

A final surprise came in the service itself. I had expected that a high holiday service at an orthodox synagogue here would be mostly in Hebrew and perhaps partly in Dutch. Instead, the prayer book, the rabbi's sermon, even the hymns, alternated between Hebrew and English, with English dominating. It all brought back childhood memories of attending similar services with my family.

Perhaps in deference to the heat, the service was abbreviated compared to ones I had experienced at home. Afterward, we waited while the crowd cleared out of the sanctuary, allowing Trish a clearer path for her scooter. That also gave us an opportunity to check out the architecture and furnishings in greater detail. I closed my eyes and imagined myself in this place four hundred years earlier, among people who had found refuge here in the same way my family did in coming to America.

As we exited, several people again thanked us for attending. Some commented on the scooter, something they apparently hadn't seen before on this island.

For the last few days of our visit, we rented a Toyota Scion, a boxy silver sedan not much larger than a VW bug, but with the great advantages of having a rear hatch and fold-down back seat that allowed me to load Trish's scooter. We drove the island's circumferential road, stopping to view hillsides dotted with cactus, waves breaking over coastal rocks, ruins of a colonial fort, and a cemetery of crypts built like small, colorful houses.

Near the northern end of the island, we stopped for lunch at Jaanchie's, a popular establishment in a white, red-roofed building situated at the very edge of the road. Seated outdoors in a garden filled with flowering plants and populated by colorful songbirds, it felt the most like the Caribbean of anywhere we had been on this island. After refreshing ourselves with a couple of Heinekens, Trish went for sauteed fish, while I ordered the house specialty, iguana stew.

Another day, after driving into downtown, we sat outdoors in a dockside café and watched the tankers, tugs, and ferries ply the harbor. An oil refinery, a sprawling tank farm, a pair of tanker ships, and a floating drilling platform in the distance reminded us how large a part the oil industry played in the local economy. I recalled a Dutch friend in California telling me about his father working down here for Royal Dutch Shell in the years after World War II.

Our last day in Curacao, we wandered back streets without sidewalks, pausing in amusement at a relief sculpture of a six-foot-long, bright green iguana on the side of a commercial building. At a canal off the bay, we came upon Willemstad's famous floating market. From rows of dockside stands set up in front of scores of small boats, merchants sold produce brought over from Venezuela. Shaded stalls brimmed with luscious-looking mangos, bananas, and papayas, as well as a variety of fresh vegetables, none of which grow in the sandy soil of the island. Some stalls offered freshly caught fish, mostly snappers, spread out on ice-covered tables. Aromas from this cornucopia flooded the wharf area. Meanwhile, sellers and buyers called out in Dutch, English, Spanish, and the local Papiamentu dialect.

On our flight home, Trish and I agreed Curacao hadn't been an easy island to visit, with its general lack of attention to accessibility. Years later, I was happy to read on the island's tourism website that much of downtown Willemstad has been made accessible, and that a company now rents wheelchairs and mobility scooters.

Notwithstanding the accessibility issues, we viewed the trip as a success. I got in several wonderful days of diving. And we enjoyed the multi-cultural ambience, even though we didn't have as much of an opportunity to immerse ourselves in the music and cuisine as we did on some other islands.

The standout event, though, was our evening at the synagogue. From the overhead candelabras and the sand floor to the history emanating from the building, that experience provided me with a kinship — cultural and even spiritual — that I have found in few places, and never before in the Caribbean. That Trish could share the experience with me made it even more special.

## Chapter 10
### WE'LL ALWAYS HAVE PARIS

Trish outside Musee d'Orsay, Paris

*Paris, May 2011*

When Trish announced her desire to return to France, and especially to Paris, I demurred at first, out of concern that the places she wanted to visit likely would be inaccessible to her on a mobility scooter. She had fond memories from the year she spent studying at the University of Bordeaux and hitchhiking around the country in the mid-1970s. In her student days, however, she was fully ambulatory.

While I recalled pleasant experiences traveling in France as a child with my family, my one visit to Paris as an adult was awful, due to the disdain shown by the Parisians I encountered for anyone not fluent in their language. But that was twenty-five years earlier and conditions might have improved, so I cautiously agreed. After all, I reasoned, Trish remained fluent in French, so we should be able to make our way. But we needed to check on accessibility before making plans.

Our initial research threw up red flags. Today, Paris' tourist bureau has a program to promote accessibility. But in 2011, despite national laws requiring accommodation of disabled persons in public settings, the internet and tourism brochures provided scant useful information. Even then, we made troubling discoveries: for instance, that the Paris Metro lacked elevators at many stations, rendering much of the subway system inaccessible.

Hesitant to go it on our own, we turned to Sage Traveling, an agency specializing in assisting disabled travelers. They assured us of the accessibility of most of the Paris landmarks and found us an accessible room at a centrally located boutique hotel in the Latin Quarter, close by the Luxembourg Gardens.

Our arrival at Charles de Gaulle Airport in Paris proved less than auspicious. After an overnight flight from Los Angeles, ground controllers routed our Air France plane to an older terminal without jetways. Peering out the window, I shook my head in frustration.

"Here we go again," I said to Trish. "The ground crew's bringing out a couple of mobile stairways. You know what that means."

Trish rolled her eyes, then pressed the call button above her seat.

"I can't go down those stairs," she told the flight attendant. "Normally, they bring my scooter to the aircraft door, so I just need to use my walker to get to it."

"I'm very sorry about this," the young woman in the blue airline outfit replied. "Our regular gate at the main terminal was occupied, so they sent us over here. This has happened before."

"Is there a lift that can take me down? The last time this happened, they used one of those hydraulic lifts that brings supplies up to the galley."

"We don't have that here either. Only at the main terminal. They will move the plane over there before the next flight. But don't worry. We will get you down the stairs as soon as your scooter arrives."

Twenty minutes later, after all the other passengers had disembarked, the ground crew rolled the scooter up to the base of the nearer stairway. Two burly men in overalls brought up an aisle chair and placed it next to Trish. I reached under her arms, lifted her from the seat, and maneuvered her onto the aisle chair.

Once we had Trish stabilized, the crew members wheeled her back to the airplane door. With one in front and one behind, they lifted the chair and carried her down the stairs. As they began, Trish glanced back at me and made a gesture of futility with outstretched arms.

"I can't believe we're doing this at one of the biggest airports in the world," she said with a nervous laugh.

As I helped Trish onto her scooter, I noticed our friendly flight attendant waving to us and scrambling down the stairway. She held up Trish's turquoise shoulder purse, which we had forgotten aboard in all the tumult.

By the time we reached the baggage claim area, our black Travelpro suitcases, marked with bright red wrapping on the handles for easy identification, had been removed from the carousel. This happens to us often enough that we knew to retrieve them at the nearby baggage office.

The travel agent had arranged for a wheelchair-accessible van to transport us from the airport to our hotel. That turned out to be more uncomfortable than convenient, as Trish had to ride up a ramp into the rear and then remain on the scooter for the entire trip. We resolved to use regular taxis or public transportation from then on.

Our hotel, the Villa Madame, also presented challenges. Its one accessible room opened to a lovely, plant-filled courtyard, but the room's entry ramp consisted of a ridiculously short, steep incline. I had to push the scooter hard each time Trish entered. The room itself was spacious enough for Trish to move about, and the bath was equipped with grab bars and a roll-in shower. The sitting area, however, was in a loft atop a dozen stairs. No matter, since we planned to spend little time in the room. The hotel's location was ideal for our purposes, within walking distance of nearly every place we planned to visit, and the managers were gracious and helpful.

With the rest of the day available for exploration, we set off up the Boulevard St. Michel, onto the Île de la Cité in the middle of the Seine, site of the original settlement by the Celtic Parisii tribe and now home to Notre Dame Cathedral. I saw the cathedral at a distance on a prior visit and, of course, recognized it from a thousand pictures, but still found myself awed by its multi-fenestrated towers, stained-glass rosette windows, flying buttresses, and scores of stone gargoyles.

As I stood in the plaza staring up at the world-renowned Gothic architecture, Trish interrupted my thoughts, saying, "You've been standing there, not moving or saying a word, for about fifteen minutes. Are you o.k.?"

"I'm fine. I just get entranced looking at iconic sights like this." I recalled having the same experience at the gargantuan General Sherman tree in Sequoia National Park and at iconic Half Dome in Yosemite. That made it all the more tragic when we watched televised reports of the cathedral being consumed by fire a decade later.

While on the Île de la Cité, we hoped to see the French Deportation Memorial honoring the 200,000 Parisians, nearly half of them Jewish, deported and killed by the Nazis. We followed signs to a walled mini-park behind the cathedral. But the subterranean memorial itself turned out to be located at the base of a steep stairway and thus quite inaccessible.

By late afternoon, we looked forward to our first Parisian meal. After walking back to the Left Bank, we came upon a corner bistro with a row of outdoor tables covered in checkered cloths. Trish spoke to the waiter in French, but he responded in fluent English, presumably after hearing us talk. Quite a change from my last visit, I thought. A carafe of house red wine relaxed us, as we leisurely consumed a meal of onion soup, duck breast salad, poached salmon, and assorted cheeses. An Edith Piaf recording playing in the background rounded out a perfect beginning to our visit.

On waking the next morning, Trish declared, "What I've been most looking forward to is having a freshly baked croissant and cappuccino."

The desk clerk suggested a café a few blocks away at the Place St. Sulpice. That became the daily starting point for our explorations of Paris. We made our way on narrow sidewalks and precarious street crossings as morning traffic whizzed by us.

At the Café de la Mairie, we sat outside at a round wood table, enjoying morning sunshine and looking across at the twin towers and double levels of marble columns of the Church of St. Sulpice. Trish got her wish of a croissant and cappuccino while I opted for a double espresso. Tourists thronged the plaza in front of the church and posed for photographs around the fountain with its statues of bishops pointing in the four compass directions.

As we left the café, we hesitated at the crosswalk to the plaza. The unofficial driving rule in Paris apparently is that cars may pass through a crosswalk while pedestrians are in it, so long as the vehicles maintain a minimum distance from walkers. We were astonished cars kept coming even as we ventured out into the street, so unlike what we were accustomed to in California. We tried repeatedly, each time retreating from traffic that sped within a few feet of us.

"This is scary," Trish said. "I would never cross a street like this back home."

Seeing our dilemma, a middle-aged French woman, dressed and coiffed as if she had stepped from a page in *Vogue*, took my arm and led us out into traffic, saying in English, "I know we are French, but we will not run you over."

She was right. The cars kept coming, but they maintained a discreet distance. Upon reaching the other side, she bid us a pleasant stay, waved goodbye, and disappeared into the plaza crowd.

Eager to continue exploring, we followed Rue de Rennes, which became Rue de Bonaparte, which then crossed the Seine on the Pont des Arts, terminating near the Musée du Louvre. We observed that most major Paris streets change names at random intervals, thereby able to honor more historical figures and events. Four- and five-story masonry buildings lined most streets, dating from the vast redevelopment of Paris overseen by Baron Haussmann and Emperor Napoleon III in the mid-1800s. As urban planning professionals, we appreciated the way major streets connected all the key public buildings, monuments, railway stations, museums, and parks. We also understood, however, the massive displacement of people, homes, and businesses caused by that redevelopment, just as so often happens today.

The Louvre provided our first surprise. As we entered the sprawling courtyard of the u-shaped, 16th-century palace and approached the contemporary glass pyramid in the center, we spied a long line of waiting visitors. Just then, a museum guard ushered us to one side and led us to the entryway through the pyramid. Disabled visitors, he informed us, were admitted free of charge and not required to wait in line.

This impressed Trish. "I don't remember any accommodation like that for disabled people when I was here in France before," she told me. "In fact, I don't remember much of anything being done for them."

"What do you suppose changed that?"

"Probably the same as at home. It takes years, but eventually enough people demand that conditions change, so it happens. Sometimes, it just takes someone in a high enough position of power to understand the need for it, maybe on account of their own experience or the experience of someone close to them."

We could have spent a week touring the Louvre, but limited ourselves that day to seeing the most famous items among the 35,000 on display. More surprises soon came.

Leonardo da Vinci's portrait of Mona Lisa draws immense crowds, restrained behind a concentric series of railings. Noticing that Trish couldn't see over or past those rows of visitors, a museum staffer led us to the area in front of the barriers, where we had an unobstructed, close-up view of the lady's mysterious smile.

Other visitors treated us just as graciously. At the statue of Venus de Milo, two young men parted the crowd to allow Trish to circle Aphrodite and see all of her white-marble, partially draped form on a pedestal in the middle of the room. We enjoyed similar experiences viewing the marble Winged Victory of Samothrace atop a ship's prow, the bronze of Hercules fighting three-headed Cerberus, and many more. Now I was impressed too, and not just with the artwork. The French had developed a genuine sense of hospitality since my last visit. And they had become sensitized to the needs of disabled people, whether tourists or locals, more than any other place we had visited.

We strolled westward from the Louvre through lush floral landscaping and expansive lawns of the Tuileries Gardens. Then, crossing back across the Seine, we came to the Musée d'

Orsay, housed in a onetime Beaux-Arts-era railway station and known for its extraordinary collection of Impressionist paintings. Again we were admitted without charge and without a wait. I recalled admiring the Monet works lining the rotunda of the Boston Museum of Fine Arts, but the eighty-five of his paintings here put the Orsay in a distinct class.

"That's enough art for one day," Trish announced. "I want to do something spectacular. Let's go to the Eiffel Tower."

With slight trepidation, we caught a bus for the first time in Paris. Other riders apparently knew to wait while the driver extended a ramp from the open door, allowing Trish to ride her scooter aboard. The bus route followed Quai d' Orsay along the left bank of the Seine all the way to our destination. Trish had been here before, but I had seen the Eiffel Tower previously only at a distance as I drove through Paris. Up close, its soaring web of steel upstaged its surroundings, much as the Statue of Liberty does in New York harbor.

We found a line of visitors that snaked at least a quarter mile around the plaza beside the tower, all waiting their turn to ascend. With dusk approaching, I feared we wouldn't make it up there that day. Just as we prepared to purchase tickets, a uniformed young woman greeted us and asked us to follow her. As at the museums, they gave special consideration to disabled visitors. We bypassed the line, going straight to an elevator that took us up to the first observation deck. Trish could go no higher, but she enjoyed the view from there while I clambered up a flight of stairs to the next level for a few photographs. By the time we returned to ground level, evening had come on and lights bathed the tower in a coppery glow.

As we returned to the hotel, we noticed for the first time a bronze plaque mounted on the wall by the entrance to an adjacent school. I shuddered as Trish translated the wording for me. It memorialized the Jewish students of that school who were deported and murdered by the Nazis. Just school children, taken along with their families. More than three hundred such plaques have been installed at current and former school sites throughout Paris.

All had gone so well up to this point that I could scarcely believe the disaster that befell us that night. As usual, we plugged in the charger through a transformer and connected it to the scooter, but we discovered in the morning that the charger had failed and the scooter had no power. Hotel staff could find no phone number for a business selling scooters or accessories. We made a frantic phone call to our scooter dealer back in San Diego and arranged for him to ship a replacement charger to our hotel in Avignon, where we would be in a few days.

"We'll deal with this," Trish said. "We always do. But what about in the meantime, until the new charger gets here?"

"We can't just shut down our exploration of Paris," I replied. "You've got to ride the scooter. If it has no power of its own, I'll have to push you."

"I don't want you to have to do that. You'll hurt yourself."

"I've been training for years. I just ran a marathon a few months ago, remember? I'll be fine."

No other option presented itself. For the next two days, I would push Trish and the scooter around Paris, drawing a mix of stares and smiles.

The next morning, the few blocks to our morning café went easily, as did the short distance north to the broad, tree-lined Boulevard St. Germain. We would catch a bus from there to the Place de la Bastille, former site of the infamous prison.

That turned into a new obstacle. Unlike the bus we rode the previous day to the Eiffel Tower, the wheelchair ramp on this one would not deploy. As the driver tried repeatedly to actuate it and Trish gave me a pained look, four men attired in some kind of city uniforms, maybe transit employees, saved the day. Stepping out to the sidewalk, they picked up the scooter, with

Trish aboard, and lifted it onto the bus. We thanked them profusely as other passengers applauded.

The same quartet lifted Trish and the scooter off the bus at our destination. I then pushed her up the street to the Brasserie Bofinger, a 150-year-old establishment believed to be the first brasserie in Paris. Known for its seafood, it also featured traditional Alsatian dishes consisting of sausages, poultry, or fish combined with copious amounts of boiled potatoes and sauerkraut. Glowing reports in travel guides about that portion of the menu drew us there. Seated at a centrally located table, we admired the Belle Époque interior, with its mirrors, murals, and stained-glass domes. And we marveled even more at our lunch—a massive, aromatic platter of sausages, bacon, and cabbage, which we complemented with Alsatian blond beer.

Trish again tried speaking French with the restaurant staff, but they insisted on demonstrating their English.

"Have you dined with us previously?" inquired our waiter, clad in the restaurant's traditional white shirt, apron, and dark vest.

"No," Trish replied. "When I was in Paris before, I was a poor student and couldn't afford it."

"Ah, yes, I had that experience too," he said with a smile, before hurrying off into the crowd to fetch us more beer.

Satisfied with our lunch, we wandered through the nearby Marais district, the aristocratic part of the city prior to the revolution and later a heavily Jewish neighborhood. Grand 17th-century mansions mixed with kosher restaurants and delis, as well as trendy contemporary shops. Narrow cobblestone ways filled with pedestrians provided the most vivid street scene we encountered in Paris. Despite being full from lunch, we couldn't resist stopping for pastry at the Murciano Patisserie, with its bright blue façade and a massive brass menorah in the front window. We laughed as we passed the Panzer deli, with its sign proclaiming itself the "King of Pastrami," but the savory aroma wafting out the doorway suggested the sign might be accurate.

"They might be the king over here," I joked to Trish, "But I'd like to see how they compare to Langer's Deli in LA. We should come back here when we're hungry again and find out."

Our final destination in the Marais was the Museum of Jewish Art and History, housed in a rose-colored stone mansion and chronicling centuries of Jewish contributions to the culture of France. Strict security confronted us at the entrance, with metal detectors, searches of purses, and a requirement to leave behind bags and any objects that could serve as weapons, such as my Swiss Army knife. Their caution turned out to be justified four years later, when Paris became targeted by a series of Islamist terrorist attacks, including one at a Jewish grocery in a nearby neighborhood.

We worked our way up through the several museum levels, viewing exhibits ranging from Chagall paintings to medieval gravestones, with me pushing the scooter throughout. When the staff announced closing time, we headed to the single visitor elevator, only to encounter another obstacle. The lift that had brought us to the top level now refused to operate. We explained that to the security guard who found us stranded alone up there. He called for instructions. This had not occurred before, so they had no protocol in place to deal with it.

A tall fellow with closely cropped hair and a military bearing soon appeared and identified himself as head of security. He escorted us into a back area of the museum, off-limits to visitors. From there, a separate elevator took us back to ground level. Under his close watch, we returned to the entrance, where I retrieved my pocket knife. He opened the now-locked front door, begged our pardon for the inconvenience, and sent us on our way.

I resumed pushing the scooter, this time to the nearby Boulevard Sebastopol, where we found a bus that took us back over the Île de la Cité and dropped us by the Luxembourg Gardens, close to our hotel. We strolled among flowers, trees, and statues through the center of this sixty-acre park dating from the 17th century. Thankfully, the dirt pathways were level and smooth, making my task of pushing the scooter easier. And the changing floral aromas made the walk even more pleasant.

Our last full day in Paris turned out to be the most arduous for me. A bus on Boulevard St. Germain took us in the opposite direction from the previous day, this time dropping us across the Seine from the Place de la Concorde with its twin fountains and towering Egyptian obelisk. This largest of Paris' public squares hosted the guillotine used to execute royals during the revolution 200 years earlier, but then was renamed as a gesture to national reconciliation. It anchors the eastern end of the Avenue de Champs-Élysées, with the Arc de Triomphe at the other end.

On an unseasonably warm day, pushing the scooter up the Champs- Élysées became a challenge. After a few blocks, we paused for a light lunch of crêpes served from a cart in a park adjoining the boulevard. As we prepared to resume our trek, Trish took pity on me.

"I feel so bad you're having to push me like this."

"I know, but it's the only way we're able to see this city. Besides, this is letting me work off the big meals we've been eating. But let's hope the new charger shows up soon."

The rest of the way, while I pushed, Trish steered through crowds of Parisians in this busy shopping district. We chuckled at seeing a McDonald's hamburger joint, albeit one fancier than those at home, amid the high-priced boutiques and upscale restaurants. By the time we reached the Place Charles de Gaulle at the westerly end, we both felt ready for a pause.

The Arc de Triomphe, another Paris icon, towered 165 feet over the plaza, beckoning us to view up close its inscriptions and decorations. But a new difficulty presented itself. Twelve major streets converged there in a traffic circle six lanes wide. That produced a whirlwind of cars, motor scooters, and bicycles. I marveled at how the traffic flowed unimpeded, with only an occasional auto horn sounding. A pedestrian tunnel providing a safe route across to the monument could only be reached by a flight of stairs.

"Remember what the lady told us crossing the street the other day at St. Sulpice?" Trish asked me. "She said they may keep driving, but they won't run over us. Let's look for a break in traffic and make a dash for it."

That struck me as too optimistic, but I also wanted to get over to the monument. After positioning the scooter off the curb at the edge of the circle, I watched for an opening.

"When I say 'go,'" I warned Trish, "I'm going to push as hard as I can, so be ready."

A moment later, I saw a break and began pushing. Sure enough, somewhat to my surprise, oncoming cars slowed or veered around us, though I paused a few times to keep more distance from them. Thirty seconds later, we emerged from this obstacle course onto the circular island holding the arch. A memorial to soldiers who died in the French Revolution and the Napoleonic wars, its interior walls bear lists of military victories and famed leaders. Beneath it rests France's Tomb of the Unknown Soldier from World War I. After much staring and photography, partly to delay dealing with crossing the traffic circle again, we made another mad dash, this time a little less hair-raising than the first time.

Having survived that, we set off for what would be our final visitor experience in Paris, a boat ride on the Seine. At a dock near the Eiffel Tower, we boarded one of the motorized, barge-like boats known as *bateaux mouches* that ply the river. Riding upriver, we passed beneath bridges we had crossed and looked up at monuments and buildings we had visited. Walkways filled with pedestrians followed the river on both sides, accessible by stairways down from street level. By the time the boat passed Notre Dame Cathedral and began its return, we had a newfound appreciation of how much the Seine serves as the central artery of Paris.

"This feeling is unforgettable," Trish said with a sigh of contentment. "I understand what Ingrid Bergman meant in *Casablanca* when she told Bogart, 'We'll always have Paris.'"

The following morning, we rode by taxi to the Gare de Lyon, the railway station where we would board a high-speed TGV train south to Provence. It would be our first train ride in Europe with the scooter, a ride arranged for us by a travel agent in San Diego. We foresaw potential problems with finding and boarding the train, so we hoped for the best.

Inside the station, arriving and departing passengers bustled around us, while trains rolled in and out on dozens of tracks. A helpful station guide directed us to an office handling special-needs travelers. To our relief, they expected us. After a brief wait, an agent accompanied us to the train, ensured we boarded the correct car, and wished us a *bon voyage*.

I helped Trish into an upholstered seat and stowed the scooter in a luggage area nearby. As soon as the train began moving, I unpacked our lunch of sandwiches and fruit we had purchased at a grocery by the hotel.

Once out of the city, open countryside dotted with farms and small villages zipped by, interrupted only by a brief stop in Lyon. In less than three hours, we would arrive in Arles to begin the second phase of our trip.

"I'm excited," I said to Trish. "For years, I've wanted to ride one of these high-speed trains. And I'm looking forward to Provence, after all the great things I've read and heard."

"There's something else I bet you're looking forward to," Trish replied with a sly smile. "You're looking forward to the new scooter charger arriving."

# Chapter 11
# A WEEK IN PROVENCE

Trish in Chateauneuf-du-Pape

*Provence, May 2011*
After a week in Paris, Trish and I felt excited and energized, but also ready for some quieter touring. On a sunny spring day, we rode the high-speed TGV train south to Provence, where we would spend the next week before continuing east into Switzerland and Austria.

With memories of the Louvre, the Eiffel Tower, boating on the Seine, and lunching at Bofinger Brasserie still vivid, we stared languorously out the tinted train window at the passing golden fields, moss-green forests, and quaint villages. I marveled at the smooth, quiet ride and thought about how much a train like this would improve travel between urban centers in California.

Four hours and 400 miles later, we made a brief stop in Avignon, our eventual destination. First, though, we rode the train another thirty miles south to Arles. The station platform there was level with the train floor, allowing Trish an easy exit on her scooter. At the Hertz office across the street, we picked up the silver-gray Renault hatchback that would transport us for the rest of our time in Europe.

We made a point of visiting Arles to see the well-preserved Roman ruins and more recent artifacts relating to famed artists. But reaching them presented the first obstacle on this leg of our journey. The original walled city, some of it dating back two thousand years, sits on a hill overlooking the Rhône River. Narrow streets lead up to it, but prominent signs declared vehicle access to be limited to residents and instructed visitors to park in lots at the base of the hill.

Trish's scooter still had no power, due to the charger burning out in Paris. I would have to keep pushing her until a new charger arrived from San Diego.

"I don't see how you can push my scooter all the way up there and then around the town," Trish declared.

"You're right. I'll have to take a chance and go as far as we can in the car."

Metal cylinders two feet in diameter, rising from the pavement, blocked our way at the top of the slope. We needed a gate card to lower the cylinders and open the way. Before I could turn around, another car pulled up behind us. In the rearview mirror, I saw a large fellow get out of the car and start in our direction.

"We're stuck," I cried out in frustration. "Now the guy behind us is probably going to get angry at us for blocking his way."

"Let me talk to him in French. If I explain the situation, maybe he'll help us."

To my surprise and relief, the other driver walked up, gave us a smile, inserted his card into the control mechanism, and allowed us both to pass.

After following signs to the Roman arena, we saw no available public parking at first, but then found a vacant handicapped space nearby. I hung our California parking placard from the rearview mirror, confident that no one would challenge it.

From a circular pedestrian promenade bordered by shops, we looked through archways at the interior of the arena. Its white limestone walls and columns appeared so well maintained that I half-expected gladiators to march in at any moment.

Lanes and alleys too narrow for cars to pass led to a Roman amphitheater and temple; a decayed stone building in which Vincent Van Gogh resided during part of his stay in Arles; and a 17th-century city hall three stories high and decorated with columns and statuary at every level, evoking the onetime commercial importance of the town. Eventually, I grew weary of pushing and Trish grew weary of bouncing on cobblestones. At that point, we returned to the car and continued on our way.

An expressway parallel to the Rhône carried us back north to Avignon. We found the Grand Hotel Avignon just outside the walls of the old city, close by one of the twenty-five-foot-high stone archways piercing the ramparts. The hotel turned out to be a favorite with tour bus operators, with a constant bustle of groups arriving and departing, but was the only hotel in town our travel agent could find that had accessible accommodations.

We set out at once to explore. The old city lay on terrain that sloped gradually northward—not too challenging for me to push Trish and the scooter, though I kept hoping the new charger we had ordered would arrive soon.

A few blocks up the Rue de Republique, the main street of the old city, we found a casual seafood restaurant. After a dinner of rockfish soup, Provencal-style steamed mussels, and local rosé, we continued our exploration. As evening came on, the limestone of the main cathedral, the city walls, and the other public buildings glowed in a bath of white and gold lighting.

We returned to the hotel to make plans for the rest of our stay. With Avignon as our base, we would take day trips into the different regions of the surrounding countryside. As we pored over the maps and tour books we had used in preparing for this trip, Trish had a concern.

"All these picturesque hill towns and wineries we've been talking about visiting? I bet none of them are very accessible. Once we get there, how are we going to get around?"

"Yeah. I've been concerned about that too. In the pictures, some have smooth streets and look pretty easy to navigate. Others, not so much. I'm sure we'll get stopped from exploring certain places. We just have to take it one at a time. We always manage pretty well."

"I guess. I'm also concerned about you having to push me around those places. This won't be like rolling down a boulevard in Paris."

"I know. But we came for the towns and the scenery, so I'll have to do it. I also want to see more Roman ruins. They're all over this region, but I expect most of them will be marginally accessible too. Let's spend tomorrow here in town and start exploring the countryside the next day. I'm hoping the new charger will get here by then."

Following that plan, we took one more day to explore Avignon's old city. The aromas of bread baking and coffee brewing drew us into a café just within the walls for a light breakfast to fuel us for our explorations.

Most impressive was the fortress-like Palace of the Popes, a ten-story edifice dating to the 1300s, when a series of popes made their home here rather than in Rome. In those times, even popes apparently needed heavy stone walls and high parapets to protect them from marauders. As impressed as we were by the archways, walls, and towers, we couldn't ascend the long stairway to the public entrance. That didn't bother us much, though, as we both had seen more than our share of European cathedrals and palaces. Instead, we wandered down shaded medieval alleyways, along the riverfront esplanade, and onto the remains of the 12th-century St. Benezet Bridge, once the only pathway across the Rhône.

Along the way, we paused at the synagogue in what once was the Jewish ghetto. Avignon has had a significant Jewish presence since the 13th century, when many congregants moved there from Portugal. This building, however, dated only to the mid-1800s, replacing an earlier temple destroyed by fire. Steps leading to the doorway blocked Trish from entering, But I found the door unlocked and took a quick look at the two-story colonnaded, domed interior. Its dark wood ark and pews, as well as the elevated pulpit, reminded me of the much older synagogue we had visited on the Caribbean island of Curacao, also founded by Iberian refugees.

On returning to the hotel, we found a courier package waiting for us. To our glee, it contained the much-needed scooter charger. We rushed to our room, plugged it in, and awaited its effect as eagerly as kids on Christmas morning.

Early the following day, with a fully charged scooter, we set out to tour the nearby Côte du Rhône region and its world-famous vineyards. Starting northward, we made our first stop, after just seven miles, in the village of Châteauneuf-du-Pape, another home of popes in the Middle Ages and namesake of some of the best red wine in France. We parked in the central square, unloaded the scooter, and headed for a nearby bistro.

Seated at an outdoor table, surrounded by flowering red oleander bushes, we ordered, of course, two glasses of deep garnet-colored Châteauneuf-du-Pape. On a hilltop overlooking the village sat ruins of a castle built in the 14th century for one of the early Avignon-based popes.

"The wine is great, but we can't do this in every town," I told Trish. "By midday, I won't be able to drive the car and you won't be able to steer the scooter."

"Everything in moderation," she agreed with a laugh. "Let's take a walk before going on."

Centuries-old stone walls lined the winding back streets. We wandered about briefly but kept running into steps too high for the scooter to overcome. That soon sent us back to the car and back on the road.

We had read about a new winery north of there, Domaine de Mourchon, that was drawing much attention for combining high-tech equipment with traditional winemaking craft. But we lacked directions. Then, making our way along a rural byway outside the town of Seguret, a hand-drawn sign sitting on the ground by the side of the road pointed up the hill on our right toward the winery we sought. At the top of the hill, amid views across the Rhône Valley, we found a cluster of twenty-something men milling about outside a tan stone building with red-painted wooden doors. A sign indicated the winery was closed that day, but the apparent leader of the group informed us he had been in touch with the owners, who promised to open for a tasting. Soon enough, a middle-aged, white-haired fellow dressed in a polo shirt and khaki slacks — not my image of a French winemaker — drove up and welcomed us. The entry was level enough for Trish's scooter, but she could barely see over the top of the tasting counter.

As our host began pouring samples of his wines, he told his story. After a career as a petroleum engineer, mainly working on oil rigs in the North Sea, he had retired back to Scotland. His wife and daughter, tired of the climate there, insisted on moving to the south of France. In need of a new project, he purchased sixty acres of old-growth vineyards, studied the chemistry of winemaking, and built a winery. He pointed to the ten-foot-high stainless-steel vats behind him. Locals at first were scandalized at his high-tech approach, but quickly found his wines to be as good as theirs, if not better. By now, he was winning awards and distributing his wines throughout Europe and parts of North America. Trish impressed him with her knowledge of wines and the two of them chatted until we excused ourselves to continue our explorations.

On our way back to Avignon, we detoured to see the splendid Roman theater at Orange. Built against a rock escarpment in the middle of town, it provided seating on stone benches for 10,000 visitors, who entered through twenty-foot archways. It purportedly is the best-preserved Roman structure of its kind. The Romans hadn't thought to include wheelchair ramps, and subsequent generations hadn't added any. That limited us to viewing the interior from the entry level, but the otherwise perfect design and construction impressed us nonetheless.

Once back in Avignon, we headed into the old city again for a novel dining experience. Just inside the ramparts, a mansion built in the early 1800s for the anisette-making Pernod family had been converted into a restaurant. On a balmy early summer evening, we asked to be seated at one of the circular wrought-iron tables outside in the courtyard, looking up at the ivy-covered walls of the mansion. Trish's scooter wheels momentarily sank into the gravel of the courtyard, but a push from me got her moving again.

Determined to practice her once-fluent French, Trish began speaking to the server as soon as he approached but, like his earlier counterparts in Paris, he responded in fluent English. He presented that day's specials, and we followed his suggestions of roast quail, salad of cold roasted vegetables, and a bottle of local Viognier. After that, we both wobbled a bit on the way back to the hotel.

The relatively easy experience of our first day of exploration lulled us into a false sense of confidence. Our visit the next day to the fortress town of Les Baux disabused us of that. Built in the Middle Ages on a hilltop among rugged mountains twenty miles south of Avignon, its views dominate the surrounding countryside as its rulers once did militarily.

From a distance, the peak capped by Les Baux looked like a rock pile assembled by a mythological giant. The road up from the valley sliced through granite rock outcroppings as large as office buildings. Bunches of orange and yellow flowers, popping up in crevasses where rainwater collected, provided a stark contrast to the dark, imposing stone surroundings.

Winding our way up, getting glimpses of the castle ruins amid green forest and gray stone, Trish began to worry. "They must have carved this town right into the rock. I bet this is going to be hard for me."

"At least the scooter is fully charged. But I'll push you if I need to."

Our fears were justified. The town had indeed been chiseled into the stone. I pictured building a walled town atop some place like Half Dome in Yosemite National Park, but even more rugged.

The so-called "Dead City" — ruins of the original fortress — was largely inaccessible, with steep walkways and numerous steps too high for the scooter. Whenever the scooter slowed on an upward-sloping street, I stepped in to push, at least until we hit an obstacle we couldn't overcome. And the rough cobblestone paving had Trish asking for frequent pauses to let her back and neck recover.

The relatively newer parts of Les Baux proved more hospitable. Narrow streets, many constructed right against sheer rock walls, were less steep and less bouncy. Homes and shops lining the streets were built from rock cut right from their surroundings—like living in a quarry, but more picturesque. The engineering and sheer determination that enabled construction of this place centuries ago astounded us.

Trish pointed at a street winding up to a higher level of town. "Let's try going up there," she urged. "The view should be great."

Soon, however, the incline became too steep for the scooter. I pushed from behind, on and on, like Sisyphus with his boulder. Would we make it to the top, I wondered? No. Coming around a bend, the street metamorphosed into a series of long steps, too high and too steep for the scooter. Though we missed that view, a different route we took coming back down opened at frequent intervals to long-distance views of jagged stone ridgelines that looked like dragon spines bursting out of the surrounding farmland.

After surviving Les Baux, we were ready for any further challenges Provence might throw at us. And I felt relieved at only needing to unload and reload the scooter once in each town we visited, unlike other vacation trips where that was necessary multiple times a day, stressing my already-compromised back and wrists.

The Luberon area east of Avignon presented the richest trove of medieval hilltop towns, each providing unique experiences. In Bonnieux, we followed savory aromas to a café with a view up at the thirty-foot-high stone walls of the original fortified town. Even in this rural village, the vivacious proprietor insisted on speaking English with us. She apologized for her centuries-old building not being more accessible. After lunch, she led Trish on a circuitous route to a restroom on a lower level, deep in the foundations of the building. Then, as in Les Baux, we managed to explore a few sloping cobblestone ways but eventually encountered inclines or steps the scooter couldn't overcome.

On the way to our next destination, we encountered a triple-arched stone bridge crossing the Calavon River. Another wondrous bit of Roman engineering, the Pont Julien has survived two thousand years of continual use to become the last remaining bridge on the onetime main road from Italy into Provence. Nearby, at the edge of a roadside vineyard, we unexpectedly saw a Yucca plant covered in clusters of creamy white flowers, like something transplanted from the California desert.

Roussillon turned out to be the highlight of this segment of our exploration. We approached along a road passing through the deep-red ochre cliffs that give the place its name and apparently the reason for the town's founding in Roman times. The iron oxide ochre has been used throughout human history for body decoration and artistry, but the Romans and other Mediterranean cultures also employed it widely as coloring for walls of buildings.

We weren't prepared for the crowds here. After circling for a while, we spotted a just-vacated handicapped parking space near the town center. As in the other hilltop towns, some areas were inaccessible for the scooter. But we found plenty to see on more level ground — homes, shops, and churches, all in varying shades of ochre, stone walls topped with geraniums, and a picture-book square where we paused for coffee. Knowing of the area's famous lavender fields, we sampled lavender-flavored ice cream from a vendor near the square — the best ice cream ever in our experience. Then we drove a winding, one-way road out to the Abbey Notre-Dame de Sénanque, where lavender fields cultivated by monks for centuries stretched the length of the valley, giving off their instantly recognizable scent.

Halfway back to Avignon, we paused at dusk in Isle-sur-la-Sorgue, just to see the last remaining wooden waterwheels by which the Sorgue River once powered the town's textile industry. After finding a parking place by the river, we enjoyed an easy stroll on flat sidewalks, taking in several of the waterwheels, as well as the river itself moving through town in multiple stone-lined channels.

With my penchant for Roman antiquities, I didn't want to leave Provence without seeing the Pont du Gard, a two-thousand-year-old aqueduct spanning the Gardon River gorge fifteen miles west of Avignon. From the visitor center, we set out along a well-maintained paved pathway. As a light rain fell, the aqueduct came into sight—main arches eighty feet high, with dozens of smaller arches above them supporting a thousand-foot-long channel that once carried water to the city of Nimes. As much as all the medieval hilltop towns we visited impressed me, this outdid them all. As we stood on the river bank and stared up at the colossal structure, I exhaled deeply in appreciation of this breathtaking piece of history. After a long pause, we continued onto a stone pathway across the river at the base of the aqueduct. From there, we marveled at the thousands of three-foot-long, unmortared stone blocks with which the Romans built this masterpiece of engineering.

We celebrated our final evening in Provence by dining at a longtime restaurant in the old city recommended by the hotel concierge. But we hadn't anticipated the large step down from street level at the entrance. The restaurant waitstaff sprang into action, carrying Trish's scooter down while I helped her in. Then, to avoid further steps, the proprietor seated us at a table at the entrance level, normally reserved for larger parties. As a welcoming gesture, he brought us glasses of the locally produced *pastis* apéritif. The garlic soup, tapenade, duckling, and grilled fish all were outstanding, as was the service overseen by the owner, who returned regularly to ensure we were enjoying dinner and to chat in French with Trish.

We drove away from Provence the next morning, determined to return and explore even more. Once again, we had overcome difficult accessibility issues and hadn't allowed them to diminish our experiences. For now, we were off to a winding, breathtaking drive over the Furka Pass through the Alps and on to Zermatt, Switzerland to see the Matterhorn.

# Chapter 12
## WATER, WATER EVERYWHERE

Trish and Cary at Castle Comfort Lodge, Dominica

*Dominica, March 2014*
Trish and I have traveled to many islands. Until we visited Dominica, however, none quite met her expectations of a tropical paradise.

"I want jungle, waterfalls, blazing sunsets," she declared as I presented options for our next vacation. "Like the pictures in *National Geographic*."

Among the islands we had visited, Bonaire and Grand Turk had nice sunsets but were desert-like, with more cacti than palm trees; Grand Cayman, apart from the splendid botanical garden, had pretty sparse vegetation; on Hawaii and Maui, volcanoes were more impressive than the foliage. And so on. They all had great scuba diving, which was terrific for me but not so satisfying for Trish.

In my mind, I ran through Caribbean islands I hadn't visited and that we could reach by air with relative ease.

"How about Dominica?" I offered.

"You mean the Dominican Republic?"

"No. Just Dominica. It's further south and east. They call it the nature island or the water island, on account of its dense jungle and its huge variety of animals and plants, plus its hundred rivers and dozens of waterfalls."

"Never heard of it, but it sounds wonderful. I assume the diving is good or you probably wouldn't bring it up."

"The diving gets great reviews. We just need to research how to get there and where to stay."

"OK. What about hurricanes?"

"It's in the Caribbean hurricane belt, but we should be fine if we wait until spring."

I had read in diving magazines about Castle Comfort Lodge, a twelve-room establishment situated on the island's west coast, a mile south of the main town of Roseau. Articles described it as a "dive lodge" with a dive shop on-site and dive boats operating from the hotel's pier.

The hotel website offered an accessible guest room and described the entire property as being wheelchair-friendly. The principal hostelry in Roseau, on the other hand, sat on a hillside, with stairways connecting its multiple levels and no accessible rooms.

After seeing photos on-line, Trish remarked, "It's nothing fancy, but it looks comfortable. Let's call them."

Over the phone, Trish booked the accessible room, on the ground floor and facing the ocean, for a week. We found an American Airlines flight non-stop from San Diego to Miami, with a connection from there to Dominica.

On the advice of the hotel staff, we deviated from our usual practice of renting a car to get around the island. Narrow, winding roads, many in poor condition, coupled with driving on the left side, would be a challenge even for someone experienced in Caribbean-island driving. We would find taxis available and inexpensive, they assured us, including ones that could accommodate Trish's scooter.

Our travel karma held until we reached Miami International Airport, where the authorities and the airlines seem to go out of their way to complicate our plans. Flights get delayed. Connections require hiking miles of terminal corridors. The air stays muggy. Food vendors, except for one stand serving authentic pressed Cuban sandwiches, offer bland fare. And I'll never forget the security agent there who recoiled in fear and horror upon pulling the scuba regulator from my carry-on bag and screamed for backup, apparently thinking she had intercepted a terrorist carrying this unrecognizable (to her) tangle of hoses and valves. After a few tense moments, her supervisor intervened and calmed her down. Unfortunately for us, flying from the West Coast, most Caribbean destinations require connecting here.

This trip proved no exception. No sooner had we disembarked from our redeye flight and retrieved Trish's scooter than an announcement in the terminal informed us that our flight on to Dominica was cancelled due to mechanical problems. At a customer service counter, we learned the next available seats would be on a Seaborne Airlines flight in two days.

Advice from a travel magazine I read on the plane proved immediately useful. I called Seaborne on my cell phone and found that two seats were available on a flight departing early that afternoon. Still connected by phone to Seaborne, I asked the American agent to book us on that flight, only to be told her computer showed no such seats. In a throwback to the pre-computer era, I coaxed her into talking to the Seaborne agent on my cellphone and transferring our reservations to those two seats. Travelers around us, many of whom had been venting at the airline staff, looked spellbound by this drama. An elderly gentleman in a straw hat and a shirt printed with island motifs gave me a big smile and applauded.

Now, with tickets in hand and assurances our luggage would be transferred to our new flight, we had some time to kill.

"I've got to find a restroom," Trish informed me. "Right now!"

A hundred yards down the terminal corridor, we found one. Unfortunately, not a unisex one where I could enter and help her off and back on the scooter. After fifteen minutes, Trish called me on my cell phone to tell me she was having difficulty getting up and out. Entering the ladies' room myself seemed inadvisable, risking making a scene or even getting arrested. Instead, I asked an airport worker pushing an empty wheelchair to go in and assist Trish, but the woman declined, saying she was prohibited from physically assisting disabled people other than transporting them. I asked her to call security. She said she would as she scuttled away with the wheelchair, but I doubted it. At that, a thirtyish woman in jeans, t-shirt, and athletic shoes, who had watched this scene unfold, offered to assist. In a wonderful example of how the kindness of strangers has helped us through so many travel obstacles, she located Trish, crept under the door of the stall, helped Trish onto her scooter, and escorted her out.

"This is the one nice memory I'll have of this airport," I told Trish.

"I know what you mean" the other woman said with a laugh. "I hate flying through here, too. Enjoy the rest of your trip."

Without further obstacles, we jetted over the Bahamas and down the Leeward Islands chain, arriving at Dominica's Melville Hall Airport in mid-afternoon. On our final approach, Trish grew excited at the view out the airplane window.

"You weren't kidding about the jungle," she exclaimed. "I've never seen so much greenery packed together."

The island's rugged topography, sloping steeply in all directions from a central ridgeline, left little room for airport runways. A small airfield north of Roseau accommodated only inter-island flights. Larger aircraft like ours were routed to the main airport, near the far northeast corner of the island.

Outside the terminal, sunshine and a light breeze welcomed us to the tropics. A blue-and-white, twenty-seat shuttle bus waited to transport us and two other couples on a maze of winding roads over the mountains to the other coast. The shuttle's built-in lift raised Trish and her scooter up to the floor level, where I helped her transfer to a seat.

One of the other couples spoke Spanish and sat forward near the driver. The other couple, about forty years of age, from Ohio, turned out to be avid divers and underwater photographers also headed for Castle Comfort Lodge.

The drive across the island provided breathtaking ocean and mountain views. Bridges undergoing reconstruction creaked under the weight of the bus. Homes painted in bright shades of blue, yellow, and pink stood out against the deep green of the surrounding palm jungle. A tattered billboard advertising Colgate toothpaste bore pictures of smiling children calling out "Save the world from cavities."

"I can hardly believe the number of rivers and waterfalls," Trish said after we passed the first half dozen. "There's one flowing down every hillside. It's like water, water, everywhere."

As we swung around a tight turn and the ocean came into sight, glittering like a field of sapphires, Trish turned to me and exclaimed, "This is the best ride we've taken since the Dalton Highway in Alaska!"

By the time the bus wound its way down the grade on the island's west side and reached Roseau, we felt fatigued but excited. A rainbow marking the passing of an earlier shower arched over the town and up the mountainside. As we passed through Roseau, occasional pedestrians waved to us from covered sidewalks and shop doorways. It looked quiet but quaint, someplace to explore another day.

Minutes later, the bus pulled off the highway, into the lodge's driveway. The driver unloaded us and our luggage outside a lime-green, two-story building with indigo shutters. A circular seal by the entrance bore the hotel's name and a reef scene of fish and corals.

A hotel worker in shorts and a flowered shirt emerged to welcome us. After a quick check-in, she led us to our room in a building across the driveway. Red geranium-like flowers burst from shrubs along a three-foot-high wall surrounding the patio outside our door. A pair of chairs, a table, and a drying rack for bathing suits and dive gear left just enough room on the patio for the two of us and the scooter. She offered us an electrical transformer for the 220-volt wall outlets, but we had brought our own.

Even before unpacking, Trish set off to explore the accessibility of the property. I tagged alongside her. After circling the gardens in front of our room, we followed a smooth concrete walkway past bushes dotted with bunches of curly, white flower petals that gave off a sweet but pleasant smell, like being in an arboretum. That brought us to the lodge's outdoor dining area. A dozen four-person tables sat under a blue gazebo appointed with gauzy white curtains and covered with the usual corrugated metal roof to protect against rain and intense sun.

Steel drum music and cooking aromas wafted from a hut at the near end containing a bar and kitchen.

"There's where I'll be hanging out while you're diving," Trish said, pointing to a swimming pool surrounded by lounge chairs at the other end, next to the dive shop.

Then, surveying a menu board, she announced to the women behind the bar, "I'm ready to start partying. Two reggae rum punches, please." The smiling bartender nodded and motioned for us to take a seat.

As we settled in at the rail, looking out at sailboats bobbing at their moorings, clouds streaked the western sky and gathered at the horizon. It all turned first a deep yellow and then burnt orange before the blue-grey night sky overcame the last rays of the setting sun. In that changing scene, an inter-island cruise ship slipped across the waves and melted into the horizon, only its lights visible at the end.

"This is my idea of a tropical sunset, just what I was hoping for," Trish said, as she turned and gave me a big smile.

The Caribbean contains dozens of major islands, with almost as many different cultures, reflecting their history. We rarely go to any island more than once, and we always look forward to experiencing new ones. Just like on other islands, we loved the first evening here, as we began to immerse ourselves in the surroundings, the food, and the music.

By now, low ground lights had come on around the property, with subtle overhead lighting in the dining area. After a second round of rum punch, we dined on conch fritters, grilled lionfish, and ripe plantains, all washed down with Carib beer.

"I've never seen lionfish on a menu before," Trish said as we ate. "It's pretty tasty."

"Good thing. It's an invasive super-predator that's been spreading throughout the Caribbean. Divers have been killing them for years, trying to keep them under control. Someone discovered they make good eating, so now there's an extra incentive to remove them."

With our bellies full and our heads filled with expectations of the days to come, we returned to our room and drifted off to sleep.

I had arranged to dive each morning, and then spend afternoons exploring with Trish. The first morning, Trish joined me for a light breakfast of fruit salad, toast, and coffee at the seaside restaurant.

Midway through breakfast, she sighed and said, "I wish I could get in the water too. The dives I did in Roatan and Grand Cayman were so great. Of course, those were years ago. Now I just can't do that anymore."

"I know. But we'll make up for it with other adventures."

With that, I collected my bag of dive gear and walked down the sloping ramp to the boat. Trish waved from the breakfast table and blew me a kiss.

On the boat, I found Bob and Meredith, the Ohio couple, setting up their photographic equipment. I joined them and eight other divers on benches along the sides at the rear of the boat, each of us sitting in front of our air tank and gear. After a brief ride along the southwest coast to a site called L' Abyss, we stepped off the stern and drifted down forty feet to a coral-covered plateau. There, we swam among neon blue parrot fish munching on bits of coral; schools of black-banded sergeant majors, yellow-striped French grunts, and big-eyed red squirrelfish; pairs of graceful angelfish; and single long-snouted trumpetfish. Then, dropping over the edge of a steep wall that plunged too far to see, we descended to nearly a hundred feet, gliding past green and purple sponges, coral plates and outcroppings of every color, and waving brown gorgonians. A green moray poked its head from the reef, flashing its dagger-like teeth at me. Further out from the reef, stingrays and sea turtles soared past us.

Each day's dive sites, with fanciful names like Witch's Point and Shark's Mouth, provided new thrills and visual feasts: five-foot-tall, blue barrel sponges; pinnacles covered in green, red, and yellow corals; currents that carried us along undersea cliff faces; and more eels, turtles, and rays, along with an endless assortment of colorful fish. On one of our last dives, we swam across the floor of a dormant volcanic crater where gas bubbles streamed up from still-warm fumaroles, giving the site its name of Champagne.

But there was just as much to explore on land. Never ones to just hang out at the pool or the bar, we asked the office that first afternoon to call an SUV taxi to take us to town. Carrying a shoulder bag filled with exploring essentials—camera, guidebook, bottles of water, sunblock—we rode into Roseau. The taxi driver, a six-foot, husky, twenty-something man named Albert, would become our frequent companion during the rest of this stay. We struck a deal to call him exclusively, in return for which he agreed to a discounted rate for shuttling us in and out of town or taking us exploring around the island in his maroon Chevy Tahoe. The SUV could carry Trish's scooter in the cargo compartment, and together he and I could lift it in and out without either of us straining our backs.

On the short ride, Trish chatted up the driver, asking, "How accessible is the town for me and my scooter?"

"No worry," he assured her. "The streets and sidewalks are in good condition. The public buildings have ramps for wheelchairs. Some stores have a step at the entrance, but the more interesting shopping is from stands along the street. And no place is very crowded. You'll be fine."

Turning to me, she gave a slight headshake I knew to be a sign of at least mild skepticism. Yet, when Albert dropped us along the waterfront in downtown Roseau, we found he was right. As the national capital, Roseau is home to a fifth of the population, but that translates into just 14,000 people, so it's essentially a small town, far smaller than our neighborhood in San Diego.

Roseau maintained a casual charm in a way that was typically Caribbean. While occasional cruise ships pulled into the deep-water port to disgorge hordes of tourists, local fishermen still drew their open boats up onto a rocky beach nearby to unload their day's catch. And the town was nearly devoid of tourist-oriented souvenir shops.

Each day, we lunched at a different place in town. We are fairly adventurous eaters and were never disappointed, but we still blanched at dishes made with animal parts I wouldn't think of as food, like cow hoofs and pig tails. That first day, Albert suggested we try Pearl's Cuisine, known for authentic local dishes. The menu changed daily, so he had no specific recommendations, other than to tell us to try something new. After being welcomed into the wood-paneled stone restaurant by the enthusiastic Pearl, we fortified ourselves with an excellent lunch of pumpkin soup followed by smoked pork and chicken with callaloo—a green, leafy vegetable common in Caribbean cooking—with a side of red beans.

With vehicle traffic light, we stayed mostly in the streets to avoid dealing with occasional steps and obstructions in the sidewalks. We passed clapboard homes painted in pastel shades of yellow, green, blue, and pink, most with covered front porches. Some featured second-story balconies extending over the sidewalk in front, in the same style as buildings we had seen in New Orleans' French Quarter. Crimson spikes of flowering ginger, strands of yellow-and-red heliconia, delicate violet orchids, and gladiolus in multiple colors filled their yards.

Wherever this treasury of tropical blooms hung over a front fence, Trish paused to enjoy their distinctive aromas. At one home, a brown lizard resembling a miniature crocodile dropped from a flowering bush onto the console of her scooter, startling her and nearly causing her to topple sideways before it leapt to the ground and skittered away.

Stores crammed with everything from clothing to canned goods, from hardware to toys, spilled out their doorways onto the sidewalks and even into the streets. Shade umbrellas invited passersby to pause and look over the merchandise. Trish maneuvered her scooter past coolers filled with beer and soft drinks at the entrance of one store to get a closer look at dresses hanging from the rafters, imprinted with colorful African patterns.

Near the center of town, we came upon a local branch of the Eastern Caribbean Supreme Court housed in an unimposing two-story building of grey stone and tan stucco, with blue wood trim in need of repainting.

"Sure looks different from courthouses back home," Trish said with a chuckle.

"I like it better," I replied." It's less formal, less intimidating, like a place where regular people would feel comfortable."

A few blocks later, Trish paused her scooter.

"I'm tired," she said with a slight sigh. "Let's go back to the hotel."

I called Albert. He was on a run with another customer, but promised to pick us up soon. Sure enough, within ten minutes he appeared, ready to chauffeur us back.

We resumed our exploration of Roseau the following afternoon. Albert dropped us at the Botanical Gardens, where we wandered smooth dirt pathways, ogling the variety of native flowers, trees, and shrubs. Then, walking through town, we again feasted our eyes on the chromatic display of homes and gardens, interspersed with the occasional more austere stone church or government building.

"This is so much easier to get around than a lot of other places we've visited," Trish remarked. "The pavement is smooth and the hills aren't steep here in town. My scooter and I are both happy."

If she's happy, I thought, then I'm happy.

We came upon the New Market, where scores of produce stands featured tropical fruits like mamey and soursop not seen in markets at home, as well as local vegetables, flowers, and miscellaneous housewares. The mélange of scents was almost overwhelming, much more enjoyable than any supermarket.

Nearby, we stopped at the Juice Man's stand to try freshly squeezed juices of some of the unusual tropical fruit. I coaxed Trish into trying guanabana, a green-skinned fruit with a creamy white interior, which she declared to be delicious enough that we should try growing it.

As we rounded a corner, Trish spied a woman selling souvenirs from a jumble of tables tucked into the mouth of an alleyway.

"We need to take some things home from here," she said. "That stand looks interesting. Let's check it out."

The vendor, who was chatting with a couple of other middle-aged women, saw us approach and turned her attention to making a soft sales pitch. No need, as she already had a motivated buyer. Still, as we perused her assortment of handicrafts, shirts, and hot sauces, she sweetened the pot.

"You buy four things, I give you one free," she offered.

"Done," said Trish, who had already picked out the items she wanted. I paid the vendor and stuffed our newly acquired goodies into the scooter backpack.

Our smiles faded when we next encountered what is referred to as the Old Market Plaza, a craft market with reggae and soca music blaring in the background. The open-air structure, encircled by square plaster columns connected with wrought iron bars, began as the island's slave market in the 1700s. The pedestal on which slaves were displayed for sale remains, though used now to display local artisans' wares.

The market's interior was too crowded with vendors' stands and piles of merchandise for Trish to negotiate on her scooter. As we stood at the edge, somberly contemplating what this place had been, a young man wearing a knit cap in reggae colors of red, green, and yellow called out to me, urging me to come see the collection of music compact discs he had spread out on a nearby table. He played one after another, until he saw one catch Trish's attention, then mine. Like the woman at the souvenir stand, he quickly offered us a purported bargain and closed a sale of a CD by a local artist.

As a welcome counterpoint to the former slave market, we came upon a monument nearby commemorating the end of slavery in Dominica. The larger-than-life bronze statue, standing in the middle of a street roundabout, depicted a man blowing an upraised conch shell while broken shackles dangled from his wrists and waist.

Albert was free when we called and immediately picked us up. Before returning to the hotel, though, he drove up the steep Morne Bruce to a view point overlooking the town and the bay. An accessible path led us to the view point, from where we could see all the way to the Scotts Head promontory at the south tip of the island.

On the boat the next morning, the divemaster suggested visiting Titou Gorge, where one can swim through a narrow ravine to the base of a waterfall.

"We should do that," I told Bob from Ohio. He agreed. As soon as we returned from diving, I arranged for Albert to take us there that afternoon. Trish would not be able to experience that attraction, so she planned to read and nap by the pool. Meredith offered to hang out with her.

En route to the gorge, Albert stopped at Trafalgar Falls to give us a view of a pair of waterfalls, the taller of which drops 250 feet down a rugged stone face. Then, on to the gorge. After stripping to our swimming trunks and carrying just our underwater cameras, we entered the refreshingly cool Mome Trois Pitons River and swam upstream into the gorge. Dozens of other visitors watched, but none joined us in the water. Tree branches formed a canopy above the thirty-foot-high walls of the gorge, itself just fifteen feet across and growing narrower the farther we went. We emerged at the far end of the gorge after a ten-minute swim and regained our footing in shallower water just long enough to take a few photos of a short but powerful waterfall. Then a sudden surge from the waterfall knocked us over and sent us swimming back down the gorge again. We later learned that this stream through the gorge eventually formed the smaller of the two Trafalgar Falls.

"It's time to explore more of the island," I told Trish on returning from the waterfall adventure. "Let's have Albert take us up to the north end tomorrow." She agreed.

The twenty-mile drive took us through settlements much like those we passed on our way in from the airport—clusters of colorful homes with occasional roadside stores and restaurants. We had mesmerizing views of the powder-blue ocean and white sand beaches on one side and equally impressive views up the olive-green mountains on the other. Near the northwest corner of the island, we came upon Fort Shirley, a well-maintained stone garrison built by the British to control entry into Prince Rupert Bay. Dozens of cannons still stood guard on the parapets high above the sea. Whether from the original construction or modern renovations, most of the fort was accessible. Trish glided easily around the grassy interior, up ramps to the parapets, and along stone walkways.

"This is so cool," she exclaimed. "So different from the old forts on other islands, where all I could do was look at them from a distance."

Again, I thought to myself what a good choice we had made in coming here.

As we prepared to ride back to Roseau, Albert asked, "Would you like to take a boat ride?"

"Where?" Trish asked, sounding intrigued.

"The Indian River. We crossed it earlier just south of here. It's very scenic. Boats leave from a dock right off the road there."

"How would I get into a boat?"

"No worry. The guide will help you. And I'll take care of the scooter while you're gone."

"Well, I'd love to do it. Let's check it out."

With that settled, Albert drove the couple of miles to the river, crossed over, and parked at the side of a single-story cinderblock building with a sign advertising boat trips. The proprietor assured us his staff would get Trish safely in and out of the boat, and the ride up the river would be unforgettable. But, when he led us out and around the building to the dock on the river, Trish's jaw dropped at what she saw. The river, and therefore the boat, were nearly four feet below the level of the concrete dock, reachable only by a flight of stairs. No ramp.

"How am I supposed to get down there?" she said, more as a statement than a question, pointing at the turquoise green motorboat.

"Don't worry, he will lift you down," replied the proprietor, gesturing toward a stocky fellow tall enough to get an NBA tryout. Trish rolled her eyes and looked to me.

"It's up to you," I told her. "Only do this if you're comfortable."

"Well, we've come this far, and Albert says the ride will be great, so let's try it."

I walked down the stairs to a wooden landing and got in the boat to steady Trish once the tall fellow deposited her there. As she stood up from the scooter, Albert held her until the friendly giant reached up, lifted under her arms and around her legs, and effortlessly brought her down to a seat in the boat. I grabbed her shoulders, but she smiled and seemed alright with what had just occurred. By now, half a dozen curious onlookers had gathered on the dock, all smiling and clapping.

One of the dock workers leapt into the seat behind us, turned on the outboard motor, and guided the boat away from the dock. In moments, we were motoring upriver, out of sight of the group on the dock. Palms, flowering bushes, and other jungle plants crowded the river banks. White herons and emerald green parrots nestled in the trees, while blue West Indian ducks and golden frogs scampered along the shoreline. Sunbeams streamed down through the green canopy and played on the slow-moving river.

After a mile or so, the river narrowed, and the banks gave way to brown-green mangroves extending their roots into the water like so many tentacles, while the dank smell of decaying vegetation jolted my nostrils. The scenery took on the look of the river I remembered near the end of the film *Apocalypse Now*. I half expected warriors to emerge from the jungle and aim spears and arrows at us.

With the river becoming too narrow and shallow to navigate further, our guide turned the boat around. A half hour later, back at the dock, the giant reemerged from the office to lift Trish up to her scooter.

"Did you enjoy it?" Albert asked, with an uncertain smile.

"Yes, it was great," Trish replied, as I nodded and gave him a thumbs-up sign.

"And many thanks for your help," she added, pointing to the tall fellow. I thanked him too and slipped him some cash in appreciation of his heroic performance.

Our last evening in Dominica, we wanted to try a long-time local favorite recommended by the hotel manager. Albert drove us there, but it was closed that night, so we returned to the hotel, only mildly disappointed. Instead, we tried a few more of the hotel bar's specialties and enjoyed a meal of grilled grouper with my favorite fried sweet plantains.

"So, what do you think of this island, compared to the others we've visited down here?" I asked Trish as we lingered over a dessert of passion fruit cheesecake and gazed out at the moon's reflection on the ocean.

"It's beautiful," she replied. "The people, the food, the scenery, it's all been great. And, looking back on it, I wouldn't have missed that boat ride for anything. Plus, I finally got to see a Caribbean island that left me feeling like I'm truly in the tropics!"

Trish and Cary on Danube Cruise, Budapest

Trish and Cary at Bay Islands Resort, Roatan

Trish and Cary at Badwater, Death Valley

Trish and Cary at Hurricane Point, Big Sur

Trish and Mona Lisa, Louvre, Paris

Trish eating Lavender Ice Cream, Roussillon

Trish at Little Colorado River, Navajo Reservation

Trish with Chestnut Vendor, Ljubljana

Trish at Waimea Canyon Overlook, Kauai

Trish on Mount Hood, Oregon

Trish at Brazen Head Pub, Dublin

Trish at Medieval Walls, Altstadt, Nuremberg

# Chapter 13
## TWENTY-SIX MILES

Trish and Cary at Waterfront, Avalon

*Catalina, June 2014*

Trish loves going away around her birthday, even if just for a couple of days. We have lots of easy-to-reach getaways from San Diego, so I'm always curious where she'll pick. When I brought up the subject shortly before her sixtieth birthday, she didn't hesitate,

"I've been thinking about it," she announced. "I want to go to Catalina. We haven't been in a while."

She got an easy concurrence from me. The largest of eight Channel Islands off the coast, Catalina became a favored destination after my first time there. But, like far too many Southern Californians, it hadn't occurred to me for years to visit.

I knew it was out there. On a clear day, I could even see it from the coast. "Twenty-six miles across the sea, Santa Catalina is a-waitin' for me," sang the Four Preps. After I had lived in Los Angeles nearly a decade, I heard that the old *SS Catalina* ferry was going out of business. Never one to miss a historic event, I boarded the steamship for one of its last two-and-a-half-hours runs across the channel, to explore what the song called "the island of romance." Then, when I took up scuba diving a few years later, I found Catalina offered the best variety of dive sites within a short boat ride, with giant kelp underwater forests, abundant fish life, and playful sea lions.

Trish had visited Catalina a couple of times with her family many years earlier. We went there together for the first time in 2002 for a day-long excursion with a group of my law firm colleagues. Trish was still ambulatory then. After hanging out with the group at a beach club for a while, we rode horses in Avalon Canyon, explored the back streets of the port, and strolled about the waterfront. We returned to the island together a couple more times after that, though by then she was reliant on her scooter.

"I want to stay at the Hotel Metropole this time," she exclaimed. "We've walked past it every time, and we keep saying we should check it out."

Again, fine with me. With that, Trish called the hotel, reserved an accessible room with a king bed and fireplace. Her only disappointment was that the room faced the courtyard rather than the ocean.

In our experience, that was par for accessible rooms. Far too often, they are in the least desirable locations, even if their rates are the same as for more desirable rooms, as if hotel managers view them as a nuisance, to be given to lower-priority guests. As a result, we sometimes sacrifice accessibility in favor of better room locations, especially to gain a view. On the other hand, we have benefitted several times from being able to score an accessible room during holiday season at other locations when it was the only remaining available room in the hotel.

Early on the Sunday after her birthday, we drove sixty-five miles north on Interstate 5 to Dana Point, the nearest port from which to catch a Catalina ferry. We found the Catalina Express landing already bustling and parking difficult. With all handicapped parking spaced filled, I unloaded Trish and her scooter at the curb and went in search of a regular space. Fortunately, we had purchased tickets in advance on-line, as both that ferry and the afternoon boat had sold out. In later years, the ferry company addressed the parking problem by issuing a dashboard permit to cars with handicapped placards, allowing them to park in short-term spaces close to the landing.

A hundred passengers already had lined up on the ramp to the landing, most smiling and chattering about the good time they anticipated. Parents struggling to hold on to their children, couples with their arms wrapped around one another, guys carrying mountain bikes. As with airline boardings, crew members led disabled passengers, parents pushing strollers, and others with special needs to a waiting area at the front of the line. Soon, a white-hulled catamaran slid into its berth at the pier. Like an anthill emptying, returning passengers poured out of the boat and up the ramp past the waiting crowd.

When our turn came, I followed Trish across a ramp onto the boat, into the main passenger cabin, and then forward to seats near windows at the bow. In short order, passengers filled the indoor cabin and an upper outdoor deck. Engines sprang to life, and we surged toward Catalina, arriving ninety minutes later.

Avalon has a harbor so picturesque, so photogenic, that I compare it to the famous harbor at Portofino, Italy, a painting of which hangs above our living room fireplace mantle. Situated near the southeast corner of the island, the harbor faces the mainland. Pleasure craft of all types and sizes bob at their moorings, while gulls and occasional pelicans float above them. Visitors sprawl on the bayfront beach and wander along the adjacent walkway. Hotels and shops cluster around the harbor, with homes inching up the chaparral-covered hillsides of the island's central spine. From its perch atop Mt. Ada, the white, green-roofed mansion built by chewing gum family scion William Wrigley, now a luxurious inn, surveys the entire scene.

Thanks to the Wrigley family's conservationist bent, Catalina remains largely undeveloped. After gaining control of the Catalina Island Company a hundred years ago, they turned most of the island into a nature preserve.

"I always like arriving here," I said. "It's close to home, but it feels like entering another country."

"I know what you mean. Remember what we read, about how some visitors think it is another country? They ask what language is spoken here and whether they can spend US dollars."

We waited while the crowd cleared, then made our way up the long metal ramp to claim our luggage. Trish's scooter strained at the steepness of the ramp until I gave it a shove. Then, pulling our wheeled overnight bags, I walked alongside her through summer crowds, following the promenade around the curving harbor into the heart of Avalon. After making our way through the shops of the Metropole Marketplace, we rode an elevator up to the lobby. Our room was spacious enough to accommodate the scooter and had the usual accessible bathroom features. By noon, we were ready to get out and reacquaint ourselves with the town.

"Before we start exploring, I need lunch," Trish informed me. "Do you think we could get a table at the Wrigley Mansion restaurant?"

"No, it's not accessible. Remember when we looked into staying there and found all the guest rooms are up a flight of stairs? There are stairs to the restaurant too."

"Too bad. Any other ideas?"

"Bluewater Grill, right on the waterfront. But don't overdo it. Save your appetite for birthday dinner tonight."

Knowing even moderate heat can worsen her MS symptoms, Trish threw on a broad white sunhat and oversized tortoise shell sunglasses for protection from the sun, now directly overhead. I settled for a baseball cap and the aviator-frame sunglasses I had been wearing since my Navy days.

The restaurant proved a good choice. Despite a crowd, the staff seated us at an outdoor table within minutes. After a quick glance at the menu, Trish ordered a platter of fried calamari accompanied by a margarita. I opted for a bowl of New England clam chowder and a tall glass of Modelo Especial, a golden Pilsner I first encountered in Yucatan a dozen years earlier and that was now available in California. As we ate, hopeful seagulls perched on nearby railings, waiting for handouts from restaurant patrons.

"There's something special about eating at a waterfront," I said. "The salt air, the smells from fishing boats, the harbor sounds. It's just different from anyplace else."

"Yeah, especially a scenic waterfront like this," she replied with a wave of her hand.

After lunch, we headed toward the Casino, a six-story, circular structure whose white stucco walls and red tile roof anchor the westerly end of the harbor. Notwithstanding the name, it was never an actual gambling establishment. Wrigley built this venue, with its dance hall and restaurant, to attract tourists from the mainland during the between-wars years. Along the way, we passed the Tuna Club, the century-old private club that has hosted presidents, tycoons, and celebrities, and is considered the birthplace of big game sportfishing. Trish rolled up to the white clapboard building extending out on a pier and posed for a photo before the club's signature bronze statue of a four-foot-long tuna leaping high to snatch a lure.

We followed a turquoise-painted wood railing along a smooth, paved walkway to the far side of the Casino. Gentle waves lapped against a wall of granite boulders that hinted at stormy weather occasionally striking the island. Overhead, a colonnade of forty-foot royal palms provided shade from the midday sun. A stucco wall bearing mosaic panels depicting island scenes ran along the inland side of the walkway. Nearing the building, we saw scuba divers emerging from the Casino Point underwater park.

The path led us to the Descanso Beach Club, where we had hung out with my colleagues twelve years earlier. It provided a restaurant and bar on the beach, along with lounge chairs and umbrellas.

"That brings back memories," Trish said with a sigh. "Our first time here together."

I have a photo of us enjoying ourselves there on that visit. Now, dependent on her scooter, she could no longer venture out onto the sand to lie on a beach chair and have a drink.

"Oh, well," she said, breaking the brief silence. "We have lots more to do."

With that, she turned the scooter around and started back into town on Casino Way.

Catalina is casual, but we dressed up a bit for dinner at the Avalon Grille. I wore a blue blazer and slacks while Trish put on a black wool skirt and a multi-colored beaded top. We have found that being even a little overdressed at restaurants often gets us a better table and better service.

Once seated in the white-wood-paneled restaurant, we started with their fabled Wrigley martinis—strong, oversized martinis that Phillip Wrigley, William's father, originally served at the bar in his Chicago office building. Trish grew excited at hearing from the bubbly, twenty-something server that the restaurant offered pan-fried sand dabs as a special that evening. These small, sweet members of the flounder family had virtually disappeared from restaurant menus.

"I love sand dabs. I haven't had them in years," Trish gushed. "That's what I want. And a glass of Prosecco."

Knowing I would have a chance to taste Trish's entrée, I opted for sauteed, locally caught scallops.

"Happy birthday," I said, raising my martini glass and draining the last of it. "It's been a good year. Here's to another one."

"Agreed," Trish replied, clinking her sparkling wine against my still-upraised glass.

Back out on the street, laughter and music poured out of waterfront bars. The evening had cooled during dinner, so I took off my jacket and draped it over Trish's shoulders. From the railing overlooking the harbor, we saw the faint glow of Los Angeles coming over the horizon across the inky ocean. I wrapped my arm around Trish and gave her a long hug.

"Happy birthday, again," I said, bending down and kissing her.

"That's all I get to celebrate my birthday?" she said with a note of sarcasm.

"Wait 'til we get back to the hotel."

On waking the next morning, Trish announced, "I want to do something more for my birthday than just hang out. Let's take one of those island tours."

After a quick continental breakfast at the hotel, we made our way to the Discovery Tours office across from the waterfront and bought tickets for their afternoon inland motor tour. While waiting at nearby Island Plaza to board the open-air tour tram, I photographed Trish in front of an octagonal fountain covered in multi-colored tiles. I assumed those came from the famous, now-defunct Catalina Tile Company whose products decorate many Southern California homes from the 1920s and 30s.

I helped Trish board the tram and stowed her scooter at the tour office. We took along a collapsible walker for her use if we exited the vehicle.

The tour began with a winding ten-mile drive westward on a good paved road into the island's central mountains until we reached Catalina's unique Airport in the Sky. With a short runway constructed across two flattened mountaintops and a filled ravine, approaches and takeoffs both occur over deep canyons, leaving no room for mistakes coming or going. The airport's wind sock blew horizontally in the brisk ocean breeze. I reminisced to Trish about having flown in there twice, both times experiences that left me breathless and doubting I would do that again.

"I'm glad you're not flying anymore," she said with a grin and a shake of her head. "Every time I hear about a small plane crashing, they say it was pilot error. I know you well enough to know you're not incapable of making an error." I rolled my eyes and laughed, but I knew she was right.

After a brief stop at the Catalina Nature Center by the airport, we followed a smooth but unpaved road downhill into the valley that holds El Rancho Escondido, the former Wrigley family ranch. Manzanita bushes, oak trees, sage scrub, and prickly pear cactus — all foliage suited to the island interior's dry climate — covered hillsides along the road.

The tram driver provided a running commentary on the island's natural and historical features. We might see wildlife, he suggested, including some of the island's wild bison, descendants of a group left behind after a film shoot in the 1920s and now part of a herd of 150 or so. He described how the ranch had been established to raise Arabian thoroughbreds. Today it features equestrian gear, awards won by its champion equines, horse barns, and ranch houses in the neo-Spanish style popular in its early days. With the aid of her walker, Trish saw enough of the property to satisfy her curiosity.

The tram continued to a viewpoint on the west side of the island. From there, we looked out at the wilder, surf-battered side, and up the coast toward the isthmus that almost divides the island. Looping back eastward, the dirt road ran through hills and valleys even drier than those we passed on the way in. Then, as teased earlier by the driver, we saw a half dozen brown, shaggy bison. They stood on a rise perhaps two hundred yards away, looking out of place here.

By the time our two-and-a-half-hour tour ended back at the plaza, we felt famished. A staffer at the tour office recommended The Lobster Trap, a casual seafood restaurant just up the street on Catalina Avenue. An exterior painted with palm trees against a sunset gave way to a crowded, stucco-walled room decorated with fishing photos and memorabilia. We ordered crab cakes and Mexican shrimp cocktail to start, then moved on to sharing an ample bowl of cioppino. Dehydrated from the tour, we washed all that down with a pitcher of Lost Coast Brewery ale.

After changing into fresh clothes at the hotel, we ventured out again. Lights came on around the harbor and twinkled on sailboat masts as we strolled the turquoise-painted dock commonly known as the Green Pier. Turquoise-green seemed to be the most popular color in the Catalina Island Company's palette.

Back on Crescent Avenue along the waterfront, we came across Luau Larry's, a *faux* Polynesian bar. We heard the crowd inside singing along with a Jimmy Buffett imitator. Many wore straw hats made to look like woven palm fronds.

"Everyone in there looks happy," Trish said. "Let's check it out."

In we went. The atmosphere proved infectious. We ordered a round of mai tais, then another. We even joined in the singing from time to time. After a while, seeking a quieter finish to the evening, we staggered to the nearby Marlin Club, an old-time dive bar as popular with locals as with visitors. I remembered from a previous visit the boat-shaped bar with a white hull and dark, polished wood top, and the bartenders in the middle. Also, the walls painted with an Art Deco underwater seascape of big fish, little fish, giant kelp, and Neptune-like figures. A vague aroma of cigarette smoke still permeated the room, left over from past times. The crowd here also was in a happy, celebratory mood. Trish struggled a little to get her scooter through the narrow aisles, but we made it to a booth alongside the mural, where I helped her transfer to a padded bench. Another round of mai tais finished off the evening.

On our last morning in Avalon, we lay about until I coaxed Trish to get up for some late coffee and pastry downstairs. The ferry back to Dana Point wouldn't leave until late afternoon, so the hotel held our luggage after we checked out. Meanwhile, we had time to browse like tourists. I stepped into a dive shop on the pier and bought a tee-shirt with a scuba graphic. As if determined to be even more of a tourist, Trish bought a caramel apple on a stick from a nearby confectionary.

"I really liked The Lobster Trap, where we ate yesterday," I told Trish. "Let's have lunch there as our last meal here before going home."

We wound up with the same server as the day before, a thin, middle-aged, sunburned brunette who remembered us and welcomed us back.

"What's the best sandwich?" Trish asked.

"Go with any of the tuna sandwiches," she recommended.

Heeding her advice, Trish ordered seared ahi, and I picked smoked albacore, both on French rolls. This time, we limited ourselves to a single glass of beer each.

Too soon, we needed to retrieve our luggage, make our way to the dock, and check in for the ferry. As we waited in line, Trish mused at how easy it is to visit Catalina.

"This place is really scooter-friendly. We should find another opportunity to come back here soon," she said.

"I agree. Maybe come for New Year's Eve. And maybe bring along friends. Like people who've lived in San Diego their whole lives but have never come over here."

# Chapter 14
# TAKING IT EASY

Trish in Front of Trading Post, Cameron

*Arizona, October 2016*
Imagine a journey that combines the most stunning scenery in the country with a major dose of Native American culture, a stay in two architectural gems, and a slice of rock music history. That's the trip Trish and I took in late 2016.

Earlier that year, Trish had received an invitation from her onetime neighbors, Joe and Janelle Atkinson, to join in the hundred-year anniversary celebration of the Cameron Trading

Post, which their family operates on the Navajo Reservation in Arizona. Trish and I had long been interested in Native American culture, and both of us had done professional work with tribes in California.

"I'd really like to go," Trish said. "The whole thing sounds fascinating. And Cameron is right by the Grand Canyon. We always enjoy visiting there."

I agreed. We accepted the invitation and set about planning our itinerary.

"As long as we're driving over 500 miles each direction, we should think about any places we want to stop along the way," I suggested.

As she pored over an Arizona road map, Trish grew excited, exclaiming, "Look at this! Winslow! Is that the same one that's in *Take It Easy*, that Jackson Brown song the Eagles turned into a big it? You know, 'Standing on a corner in Winslow, Arizona.'"

A little research disclosed that, not only did Winslow occupy a legendary spot in music folklore, but it is home to La Posada, the last of the classic railroad hotels designed by architect Mary Colter for the Fred Harvey Company and the Santa Fe Railway in the early 20th century. A perfect place to stop for the night on the way to Cameron. And we could couple that with a stay, after the festivities, at the El Tovar Hotel, perched on the south rim of the Grand Canyon.

Early on a cool, bright October morning, we departed San Diego in our Explorer with Trish's scooter loaded in the rear. Interstate 8 wound over the crest of the Tecate Divide and through the bare, broken rock of the Jacumba Mountains before dropping into the lower Colorado Desert. By mid-morning, we crossed the Colorado River at Yuma and entered the Grand Canyon State. After another hundred miles of barren desert interrupted by occasional solar energy farms, we stopped in Gila Bend for gas and takeout food. The service station had an air-conditioned, accessible restroom, spacious enough to accommodate the scooter.

Once we got past Phoenix, the drive grew more interesting. US Highway 87 wound through the Tonto National Forest, where towering rock formations stood behind thousands of forty-foot Saguaro cacti with their multiple upraised arms. The road rose to the heavily forested Mogollon Mesa, then led straight into our initial destination of Winslow.

On entering town, signs directed us to the street corner supposedly immortalized in the song *Take It Easy*. We found a park, a wall with a sign identifying the location, and a statue resembling Jackson Browne. Trish circled the corner on her scooter.

"Less impressive than I expected," she commented. "But it's still cool to see the place I've been hearing about in that song for years. And I guess it's a memorable place for tourists to have their picture taken and connect with pop culture in real life."

La Posada fronts on a remnant of historic Route 66, dubbed the Mother Road by John Steinbeck, that carried generations of migrants and tourists out to California. The hotel's neo-Spanish exterior, with tan stucco walls rising two stories to a red, barrel-tile roof, stands within a desert garden. Winslow once boomed as the Arizona headquarters of the Santa Fe Railway, and as a stop on Route 66 before I-40 bypassed it. Today, though, the neighborhood looks tired, in contrast with the restored hotel.

A young woman led us from the check-in desk to our accessible room, furnished with handmade wood furniture and Mexican woven rugs in every primary color. We noted rooms named after celebrities who had occupied them—President Franklin Roosevelt, Albert Einstein, Amelia Earhart, John Wayne, and a score of others.

Once in our room, Trish commented, "The walkways, gardens, halls, entries, it's all level and accessible. An architect ahead of her time."

Ten hours on the road had us looking forward to a relaxing evening, beginning with a dinner of grilled elk and red wine. We then took our server's suggestion and made our way to the rear patio, facing several sets of railroad tracks. Seated beneath soft lights, we sipped wine and joined other guests in watching teams of locomotives pull endless freight trains in and out of the station, their horns blaring and their wheels clicking on the rails. We enjoyed this entertainment for an hour, then returned to our room for a good night's sleep before completing our drive to Cameron.

---

In the morning, after a casual breakfast of omelets, corn muffins, and coffee, we drove west to Flagstaff and then straight north to the community of Cameron, at the western edge of the 27,000-square-mile Navajo Nation. A few minutes before reaching Cameron, we passed the eastern turnoff to Grand Canyon National Park that we would follow two days later.

The trading post sprawls across several acres. What began a century earlier as an outpost at which Navajos could trade handicrafts and livestock for store goods now encompasses a motel, restaurants, shops, gardens, a truck stop, and a gallery of spectacular Navajo crafts work. The vast shop in the main building sells contemporary handicrafts. Nothing comparable, though, to the century-old chiefs' blankets, fine silver jewelry, and other treasures in the stone gallery building, which is open only by invitation. For many years, the trading post hosted an annual auction at which Native weavers, potters, and silversmiths offered their best craft work. Trish bought several fine woven blankets at auction, some of which hang in our home today.

We pulled up to an accessible parking space near the motel office. Trish's friends had arranged for us to have an accessible room in the original motel structure built into a hillside above the Little Colorado River, a tributary of the main Colorado. Newer buildings holding scores of hotel rooms stood nearby. A single-story building at the head of the entry off the highway contained shops and restaurants. The entire compound bustled with the 200 guests invited for the anniversary celebration, as well as the usual tourists.

Once we had settled into our room, we went in search of the Atkinsons, finding them ensconced on a patio behind the main restaurant, welcoming arriving guests. Joe rose from his seat to greet me and embrace Trish, then handed us each a commemorative black t-shirt with a graphic of a Navajo ceremonial dancer on the back.

"I'm going to need one of these pretty soon," he told Trish with a laugh, pointing at her scooter.

"Good thing you've made this place so accessible," she replied. "I can get around here more easily than a lot of places in the city."

Since we had some free time that afternoon, Trish and I drove to a nearby park on the reservation. It overlooked a gorge on the Little Colorado River, where azure water rushed between auburn stone cliffs. Though the dirt road into the park was well-graded, Trish's scooter had to contend with bumpy terrain in the parking area and on trails. While modest compared to the nearby Grand Canyon, the views still made the effort worthwhile.

The festivities began that evening with a welcome dinner in the main restaurant, serving contemporary versions of traditional Navajo cuisine of lamb and corn. From then on, activity swirled about us for the next two days. Tribal medicine men blessed the proceedings. Men in stitched western shirts, blue jeans, and cowboy hats danced with women in long traditional dresses, moccasins, and turquoise jewelry.

Musicians, artists, and craftspeople presented exhibitions. Culinary feasts punctuated the rest of the events.

The second evening, traditional Navajo, Hopi, and Apache dancers took turns performing within a ring of guests on the main patio. As Trish sat on her scooter at the edge of the crowd, two Apache dancers, heavily painted and swooping about like great eagles, swirled around her for the longest time. Nearby guests pointed at this curious display.

Once the performance ended, I said to Trish, "That was a real highlight of the evening, having those dancers moving around so close to you."

"Yes! It reminded me of how I felt when the stingrays hovered around me in Grand Cayman. Remember how the divemaster there said he had seen that before with disabled divers? I wonder if that's what prompted those ceremonial dancers."

Trish commented on it to Joe Atkinson over breakfast the next morning. He shook his head and said he hadn't seen them do anything like that before, but he agreed that it must have had something to do with their perception of her disability, since she was the only one they reacted to that way.

We stayed and chatted with our hosts a little longer and thanked them for including us in this unique experience. Then it was time to move on to our final destination, the natural wonder a few miles away that we never tired of visiting and viewing.

---

I love watching visitors getting their first glimpse of the Grand Canyon. It takes me back to my own first visit, in the 1960s. The magnitude of the canyon, with one unique formation after another, in layer upon layer of different colors, is so striking, it exceeds the senses' ability to absorb it all at once. Most people just stand and stare, as if hypnotized, just as I did. A few let out shouts of amazement. Many immediately raise their cameras, as if afraid they may lose the image if they don't capture it at that very moment.

Trish is an admirer of Mary Colter's architectural work, so we made our first stop at the Desert View overlook, where Colter's fifty-foot, cylindrical stone tower provides unobstructed, multi-level views down to the Colorado River and across the broad gorge at the eastern end of the canyon. The scooter managed the quarter-mile paved pathway from the parking area, but Trish had to content herself with looking out over the canyon from a platform at ground level while I made a quick climb up the tower.

"I wish I could get up there too," she lamented, "but it's a pretty great view even from here. And I can appreciate the design and construction of the tower. Colter had an amazing sense of fitting her designs into their surroundings."

Our arrival at El Tovar, in Grand Canyon Village, upped our level of excitement. We had spent a memorable New Year's Eve here a few years earlier, culminating in a snowfall at the stroke of midnight. This time, bright sunshine greeted us as we found an accessible parking space in a lot across the way from the hotel's entrance.

Trish surveyed the broad steps leading up to the front porch and grumbled, "I forgot. No ramp." Instead, we entered through a side door and followed the hallway to an atrium lined with dark-brown-stained logs and decorated with mounted, ten-point deer heads. We planned just an overnight stay on this visit, as an accessible room was available for only one night. Besides, we had been there recently and, doubtless, would be back again. Our room turned out to be spacious, similar to the one we had occupied on our last visit. Far larger than the tiny one we had to settle for on our first time here together, when we came over the holidays and got the last available room in the hotel.

From the canyon rim, we surveyed what over the years has become our favorite landscape. The paved pathways following a low stone wall provided Trish with a smooth ride. Far off, on the north rim, we could just make out the other lodge we had stayed at two years earlier. And filling the foreground was the channel that the Colorado River had carved through countless rock layers over hundreds of millions of years — over a mile deep and nearly twenty miles across in some places, interrupted by a multitude of high formations left standing by the relentless river. No wonder explorers and cartographers over the years gave those formations mythological names like Vishnu Temple, Walhalla Plateau, and King Arthur Castle.

We stopped half a dozen times along the winding pathway, The view changed from each angle, revealing different formations in this diverse landscape. The gnarled trunks and needle-covered branches of pinyon pines jutted out just below the rim.

As she looked down from the Bright Angel trailhead, the popular trail leading from Grand Canyon Village down to the river, Trish gasped, "Look at those dots down there, by that green area. They must be hikers."

"Yes. That's the trail I hiked the last time we were here. It passes through the Indian Gardens oasis that you see down there. The trail between there and the rim isn't too difficult, so some people hike down that far to experience more of the canyon. You'll recognize people up here who hiked even part way into the canyon by their big smiles."

Two years earlier, I had experienced a special view of the canyon when I hiked with a friend from the distant North Rim to Phantom Ranch at the bottom, across the Colorado River, and up the steep trail to the South Rim. This time, there was no hiking. We contented ourselves with visiting the viewpoints that Trish's scooter could reach.

With evening approaching, we relaxed and drank margaritas on the veranda outside the hotel lounge. Shadows draped the ridgelines, mesas, and towers within the canyon, followed by a reddish-orange glow that painted the undersides of scattered clouds. As the canyon settled into evening darkness, we left to prepare for dinner.

The elegance of the hotel called for us to dress up for dinner, more than the informal ambience of Cameron. I had brought a blue blazer, white shirt, and repp-stripe tie for the occasion, while Trish wore a white silk blouse and silver necklace over black slacks that wouldn't get caught in the scooter wheels. Supper in the main dining room, with its historic murals surrounded by stone and wood walls, brought back more memories of previous visits. The maître d' gave us a table wide enough for Trish to pull up to sideways on the scooter. And our meals of steelhead trout straight out of the Colorado River and roast duck with local, sweet prickly pear sauce fit the location.

Morning came all too soon. With a long drive home ahead of us, we devoured a quick breakfast, loaded the car, and bade the Grand Canyon farewell. There would be no overnight stop on this drive, only 550 miles of steady driving. Sixty miles on Arizona Highway 64 connected us to Interstate 40. From there, it would be freeways almost all the way home. skirting Flagstaff and Phoenix, and stopping once to refuel.

Just west of Gila Bend, our stop on the way out five days earlier, a billboard caught my eye.

"Look!" I yelled. "Date shakes at the next exit. I haven't had one in years." With that, I made a dash across traffic lanes to get off the freeway.

Date milkshakes are a Southwest delicacy or peculiarity, depending on your tastes. I love them, Trish, a little less so. Alongside the freeway, baking in the afternoon sun, stood the little food stand advertised on the huge billboard, selling date shakes, as well as the usual highway fast food of burgers and fries. I ran in and got a couple of each to fortify us for the rest of the drive. We gulped down the food, but savored the shakes for the next twenty miles.

An orange sunset filled the western sky as we crossed the Colorado River again, back into California. Midway across the highway bridge, Trish commented, "Just a few hours ago, we were looking at the Grand Canyon. It's hard to believe this tame little river here is the same one that carved that incredible canyon."

"Yes. Between being blocked by a couple of huge dams and having most of the water pumped out of it after that, there isn't much left by the time the river gets here."

Less than three hours later, we arrived home, back in the bustling urban core of San Diego. After all we had seen and experienced, we both were quietly reflective during the last part of the drive. As we relaxed in our living room, with Trish having transferred from the scooter to her favorite reclining chair, we became more animated again.

Trish summed up the trip, saying, "I love the Grand Canyon. I can't wait to go back again. But you know, the festivities at Cameron were something unique I'll never forget. And the stop in Winslow, well, that's going to make me remember this whole trip every time I hear *Take It Easy*. Put on the Eagles' CD and let's listen to it right now."

# Chapter 15
# DESERT MAGIC

Trish at Borrego Air Ranch House

*Borrego Springs, California, March 2017*
In warm months following a rainy winter, the desert community of Borrego Springs draws a wave of visitors to see an unrivaled wildflower display. Magenta sand verbena line roads north of town. Golden California poppies, white rock daisies, blue lupine, and dozens of others hover over yellow cups and desert five-spots in sandy washes. Scarlet Indian paintbrush and bright yellow brittlebush decorate rocky canyons running up the

foothills. And thorny stands of ocotillos produce their own show of red floral streamers soon after, followed by blooms on thousands of barrel, cholla, and beavertail cacti.

During a "super bloom," the occasional phenomenon when the springtime flowers reach a visual crescendo, visitors outnumber the town's year-round residents four to one. Something like what New England villagers experience when autumn leaf-peepers descend on them. One has to ignore the crowds and enjoy the visual experience.

In 2017, Borrego Springs experienced such a spring. It had been twenty years since conditions were that good, and Trish and I wouldn't miss the opportunity. Since the town's handful of hotels could only accommodate a small fraction of visitors, each day saw a new onslaught of arrivals. We planned on a three-day stay at our Borrego Air Ranch house and brought with us another couple who were regular desert-goers.

On a bright but cool Friday morning, we loaded my Explorer with Trish's scooter and provisions for our stay, and set out on the ninety-mile drive from San Diego to Borrego Springs. Forty miles east of San Diego, soon after passing the Viejas Indian Reservation, we exited Interstate 8 and followed a winding rural road northward into the Cuyamaca Mountains. That took us through mature evergreen forests, some still showing signs of past wildfires, and swung around Lake Cuyamaca, fuller than usual due to recent rains. From the former mining camp of Julian, now a tourist magnet famous for its historic downtown and its apple pies, another rural road led down the even-more-winding Banner Grade into the desert. I slowed in the curves to keep the scooter from sliding around.

"It's hard to believe they cut roads by hand into these mountains to reach mines back in the 1800s," Trish remarked.

Ten miles after reaching the eastern base of the mountains, a side road took us over Yaqui Pass, named for a Native American tribe that historically lived in the area. Just past the crest, we got a panoramic view of Borrego Springs and surroundings.

"I'm not the biggest fan of the desert," Trish exclaimed, "but this first view of the valley always gives me a lift."

I understood. In our view descending from the pass, the steep slopes of the Santa Rosa and San Jacinto Mountain ranges framed the north and west sides of the valley. The Salton Sea, California's largest inland water body, glittered to the east. Badlands rose to the Font's Point escarpment across the northern part of the valley. And a road carved into the cliffs like a goat path wound down Montezuma Grade on the far side of the valley, ending at the main street of Borrego Springs.

Moments later, the Air Ranch came into sight two miles to the right. At the bottom of the grade, we passed La Casa del Zorro (House of the Fox, in English), a longtime resort favored by San Diegans, tucked into a grove of palm and tamarisk trees. We soon arrived at the Air Ranch and followed the palm-lined entry road that became an aircraft taxiway crossing the end of the runway and running straight past our house.

I got Trish her scooter, then gave her a push to help across the sand driveway and up a concrete ramp to the front gate. While I unloaded the car, she drove about the front yard, inspecting the desert plants around the perimeter. On her own, she cautiously rode up a second ramp and through the front door of the house.

"This place makes me feel as if I'm stepping back in time," Trish mused. "It's like something out of an early *Sunset Magazine* spread."

True enough. The mid-century-modern, one-bedroom house was built in the 1950s by Ed Fletcher, creator of the Air Ranch and a member of one of San Diego's early developer families. Floor-to-ceiling windows at the front look out at a walled yard surrounding an elliptical swimming pool, two mature native fan palms, a pair of spiny ocotillos that sprout crimson blooms, and a creosote bush that produces tiny, white flowers. Glass panels in the wall provide a view of aircraft taking off and landing on the nearby runway. The wrinkled slopes of the Vallecito Mountains fill the horizon. The interior décor of the house resembles a 1950s motel room, with orange-and-black-striped curtains, Art Deco wood chairs upholstered in avocado-colored vinyl, and garishly colored table lamps, all dating-from the years the home was used by the Travelodge company as an executive getaway place. I repainted the house and garden wall a tan earth tone to blend in with the desert, but colored all the facia and trim bright blue to evoke the Air Ranch's relationship to the sky.

The coziness of the house appealed to me when I bought it thirty years earlier, long before I knew Trish. For her, however, it now meant difficulty in maneuvering her scooter among closely placed furniture and through narrow spaces. A counter separating the living room and kitchen blocked her from the sink and pantry. Even though we widened the bathroom doorway, the tiny room still presented a challenge for her.

By the time we unpacked, our friends Mike Jenkins and Barbara Filner arrived. I had known Barbara since working together in politics forty years earlier. A slender blonde with a pixie haircut, she grew up in Pakistan, where her father was a missionary. A lean, bearded lawyer-turned-urban-planner, Mike knew Trish for several years through professional circles. He and Barbara both now worked as mediators. They often camped here in the desert. So, an easygoing couple well suited to be company for the weekend.

We sat in the shade on the patio beneath the long front overhang, drank beer, nibbled on guacamole and tortilla chips, and chatted about San Diego politics. A light breeze carried the smoky aroma of creosote bushes. By late afternoon, as the sun moved behind the San Jacintos, shadows formed on the Vallecito range, creating a mosaic that continually changed before us.

"Drink up. I made a six o'clock dinner reservation at Carlee's," I announced. The café, with its Art Deco touches, for decades has anchored the east end of Palm Canyon Drive, Borrego Springs' two-lane downtown business strip. Newer restaurants serve classier cuisine and the town also features some very good Mexican food, but Carlee's remains the best place in town for eclectic, traditional cooking. In making the reservation, I requested a particular corner booth that had room alongside it to park Trish's scooter after she slid over onto the semicircular, dark brown leatherette bench.

Along the road into town stands a scattering of rusty metal sculptures of long-extinct animals that inhabited the valley in bygone eras—giant sloths, wild horses and camels, pygmy mammoths, eagle-like birds. More of them surround the north side of town. Created by artist Ricardo Breceda, they sit on private land whose owner funded these installations. Although the sculptures received a cool reception from locals at first, they soon became a major visitor attraction and a quirky but beloved feature of the town.

"I remember being blown away by these things the first time Cary brought me out here," Trish commented as we drove past them. "I had heard about them, but they turned out to be more fanciful than I ever imagined."

Notwithstanding the early hour, we found a crowd gathered outside the restaurant. I expected that during wildflower season. We nudged our way through and found our booth waiting. After a round of drinks, we plowed through several selections from Carlee's expansive (though not expensive) menu—a Reuben sandwich, a platter of liver and onions, a cheeseburger heaped with Ortega chiles, and a bowl of penne pasta drenched in Italian sausage marinara.

"Now it's time for some stargazing," I said, as we drove back to the Air Ranch. "It's a clear night and there's almost no moon."

We clustered outside in the yard near the pool, Trish on her scooter and the rest of us on slingback chairs. The dark sky had reloaded with stars, as well as a few planets.

"I never get over this view," I said. "The only thing more spectacular is seeing meteor showers out here. Sometimes, you can barely keep up with all the streaks and flashes. That's one of the things I love most about the desert, that makes it so different from being in the city."

"I know," Mike replied. "The last time we camped here, we saw the Perseids. Amazing."

Trish moved forward to turn her scooter and look at the sky back over the house. "Careful," I warned her. "I don't want to have to fish you and the scooter out of the pool." As if to emphasize my warning, a lone coyote let loose with a long, soulful howl.

Saturday morning, after a breakfast of *huevos rancheros* and coffee, we prepared to do some serious exploring.

"Let's hold off on the flowers until tomorrow morning," I suggested. "It'll be less crowded than on a Saturday. And there are plenty of other things to see today."

With the scooter again loaded in the rear of the Explorer, we drove south, first traversing mile-wide San Felipe Wash. We left the highway on a sandy track that led us to the Cactus Garden, a conglomeration of hundreds of cacti, some as tall as an adult. Like the wildflowers, the succulents bloomed early this year. Groups of delicate golden blossoms popped out of the tops of barrel cacti, while magenta flowers erupted along the edges of beavertails. Bright sunshine magnified the colors.

Trish watched from the car at first as we photographed this display. Then, when I found a turnout of firm sand, I unloaded her scooter so she could ride close to some of the magnificent blooms. Thank goodness, I thought, for the hoist that spared my back and wrists the stress of lifting the scooter in and out of the car.

We took another jeep road down into the Borrego sink, the floor of the valley. Hillsides parched for years now burst forth with fields of yellow daisies. Windblown sand formed troughs and ridges along the roadside. Topographic maps I acquired decades earlier through the Park Visitor Center helped guide us through the valley and into the badlands. Trish's scooter bounced in the rear, as did the passengers in front of it, while we negotiated rougher and narrower paths.

"That's Font's Point," I said, gesturing toward a high spot in the escarpment rising above us. "Let me show you the view from up there."

"I won't be able to join you," Trish added with a sigh. "But you'll love it."

With a nod from my passengers, I threaded my way out of the badlands, followed a paved road back toward town, and then turned up the Font's Point wash. We knew the steep, soft slope at the end of the wash made it impossible for Trish's scooter to climb to the view spot. Fortunately, she had reached it by foot on earlier visits here, before her mobility declined.

"Enjoy it," Trish called to us as we exited the car. "Times like this are when I most miss the days when I could walk."

I led Mike and Barbara up there for a brief but stunning view in all directions, with the late afternoon sun spreading mountain shadows over the town and across the valley.

Once back at the house, Trish declared, "I am so glad to get out of the car and back on my scooter, I may have to sit on this for hours, but at least it doesn't bounce me around."

We drank margaritas and devoured snacks as the sun dropped behind the mountains. To the north, the last sunrays cast an alpenglow across the ridges of the Santa Rosas. As we watched, a songbird-sized bat appeared from the fronds of the far palm and skimmed across the pool, catching tiny insects off the surface.

I barbecued dinner on a charcoal grill. We soon gathered around the patio table, washing down chicken and corn with bottles of Pilsner Urquell. Trish related how we stopped in the town of Plzen on a visit to the Czech Republic, just to experience drinking pilsner at its place of origin.

In the morning, over a light breakfast of fruit salad, yogurt, and coffee, we set our itinerary for the day.

"First, we should drive around the best wildflower areas," I suggested. "Later, before you go home, I have a surprise for you, something I'm pretty sure you've never seen out here before."

We again piled into the SUV, this time driving past the center of town and through the remaining citrus groves and palm farms that once filled the north end of the valley. Roadside verbena glowed in the morning sun and a collage of flowers filled abandoned pastures. At the mouth of Coyote Canyon, we encountered an expected traffic jam, as mobs of visitors descended on the most vehicle-accessible area in which to see the super bloom.

I joined a caravan of cars rolling up a dirt road in the middle of the broad canyon, as scores of vehicles passed us in the other direction. White desert poppies and long-stalked desert sunflowers dominated at first, but were soon joined by a cascade of blooms — orange apricot mallow, orchid-like monkey flowers, and too many more varieties to count. I pulled over occasionally, allowing us to get out, look more closely at the blooms, and take photos, especially of ground-hugging flowers like evening primrose and yellow tack stem. Desert flowers have subtle scents, but the profusion of blooms created a noticeable perfumed aroma. Most cars turned around when the road grew rougher, leaving the small number with four-wheel drive to continue. As the elevation increased, flowers grew even more varied and profuse.

Three miles up the canyon, we encountered a forest of mature ocotillos in full bloom. Their ten-foot woody stalks extruded pea-sized green leaves, and strands of flaming-red flowers extended from their tips. I pulled over and parked for us to get a better view. The ground was solid, so I unloaded Trish's scooter. The four of us then wandered about, viewing the ocotillos and the variety of flowers.

After exiting the canyon, I took a circuitous route to see more of the Breceda sculptures, including a group of farmworkers, a Spanish missionary with his burro, and a weathered prospector. The biggest treat for visitors, though, is the 350-foot-long, serpent-like dragon undulating into and out of the earth, and culminating in a scaly, fire-breathing head. I pulled off the road, parked near the head end, and again got out the scooter so Trish could join us in a close-up view.

As we returned to the house, I reminded Mike and Barbara that I had a special treat in store for them. This time, I followed another soft, sandy road out the north side of the Air Ranch, back toward the Borrego sink. After two miles of bouncing on this track rutted by off-roaders, I swerved right up a steep hillside and pulled to a stop next to a stone monument inlaid with a brass plaque. It marked the site below of San Gregorio, where the de Anza expedition first camped in the future California after walking up from Mexico. Knowing from abundant surface vegetation they would find water, they dug wells, rested, and fortified themselves before continuing on to the coast.

I first came upon this site while searching for the original Borrego spring years earlier. Knowing a little about de Anza, I felt stunned at realizing he and his expeditioners had been right there, fifty feet below the ridge where I stood. That feeling drew me back to this spot repeatedly over the years and motivated me to bring Trish here on one of her first visits. Sometimes, when visiting alone, I stood there for many minutes, mesmerized, as if transported back in time. I have experienced that in other places — the Concord Bridge battle site outside Boston, a Moorish fortress in Spain, the Mauthausen concentration camp in Austria.

I turned to Trish, viewing this from her seat in the car, and said, "You know, standing here, if I close my eyes, I can almost see and hear the soldiers, settlers, and livestock milling around, like I was there with them 250 years ago."

"Maybe you were," Trish replied, as Mike and Barbara stood by and smiled. "You sometimes talk about having experienced past lives. Maybe you were here."

# Chapter 16
## TICKETS BUT NO RESERVATIONS

Trish at Brandenberg Gate, Berlin

*Berlin to Vienna, October 2017*
In our first three days in Berlin, Trish and I covered the highlights of this capital that had been heavily damaged during the Second World War, then was divided for decades between occupiers from the Soviet Union and the other Allied nations, eventually was reunified, and in recent years was rebuilt again

into one of the great cities of Europe. We strolled down Unter den Linden boulevard to the iconic, neoclassical Brandenburg Gate, with its twelve stone columns rising fifty feet to a bronze statue of the Roman goddess Victoria driving a horse-drawn chariot; walked silently among the 2700 stone blocks of the Memorial to the Murdered Jews of Europe, as well as the museum beneath it documenting the persecution and killing carried out by the Nazi regime; wandered the tree-lined pathways of the Tiergarten, the city's central park; toured the Museum of the Wall near the onetime location of Checkpoint Charlie, for years the militarized transit point between East and West Berlin; and browsed numerous other museums and historical sites.

On our last day here, we visited the Berlin Wall Memorial. After making our way along the cracked concrete remnant of the wall lining the south side of Bernauer Strasse, we viewed monuments to individuals who had died trying to escape East Berlin. We then paused for a picnic lunch in what had been the "kill zone" inside the wall, but now was a broad expanse of park filled with visitors.

I sat down on a low stone wall, the remaining foundation of a building in a cemetery that was relocated when the wall went up. Trish remained on her bright red, three-wheeled mobility scooter, her auburn hair blowing lightly in the afternoon breeze. Graffiti on the wall near us displayed a post-Cold War message to the former East German authorities: "We have never had to put a wall up to keep our people in."

Silently, overwhelmed by the gravity of our surroundings, we ate sandwiches and cake purchased that morning at a deli near our hotel. With our visit to this historic city nearing its end, I found myself thinking ahead to our travel plans for the next day.

"I'm a little uneasy about the train from here to Vienna," I told Trish. "We've got a tight itinerary for the rest of this trip, with hotel reservations in Vienna and Ljubljana, picking up the rental car in Vienna, and the flight home out of Munich. Plus, I don't want to miss the opportunity to stop off in Braunau and visit Karin." That was my childhood friend with whom we planned an overnight visit in my hometown north of Salzburg.

"The train is the one thing that's pretty much out of our control," I continued. "We're counting on them providing accessible services for you and the scooter."

Trish gave me a quizzical look. "Don't we have tickets for an accessible train car?"

"We have our tickets, and the travel agent in San Diego told the ticket office here what we need, but you know how easily these things go sideways. We're not far from the main train station. Let's go over there and confirm our arrangements. I'll feel a lot better."

Trish shrugged in agreement. The breeze grew chillier as we prepared to leave the park, so I helped her put on her black leather jacket.

At that moment, a twenty-something man, carrying a video camera, approached us. I took him to be Middle Eastern, maybe one of the recent refugees.

"I heard you speaking," he said. "Are you Americans?"

"Yes, why do you ask?"

"I am a reporter with the Algerian national television network, here to cover the German elections, but I also am making a documentary about the Berlin Wall. I am asking people of all kinds why they are visiting here, what it means to them. May I film your answer?"

I looked at Trish. When she nodded, I turned back to the reporter, who had set up his camera and was ready to begin filming.

"Alright," I began, "I'm interested in the Berlin Wall because I lived in Germany as a child, until just before construction of the wall began. I saw the early years of the Cold War, and the wall is the ultimate symbol of that. I lived in Austria previously. It also was occupied and divided after the war, but the occupation ended there without incident. Here, it was different. The Cold War had heated up and Germany stayed divided. Berlin too. We could never visit here in those days, so this is my first opportunity to see what's left of the wall and understand what it meant for people here."

Trish had spent the Cold War years in the United States, but she seconded my feelings about wanting to see this Cold War symbol up close.

The reporter thanked us and set off to find more visitors to interview. After viewing photos and artifacts at the Berlin Wall Documentation Center across the street, we found a trolley that took us to the Hauptbahnhof. Upon seeing Trish astride her scooter, the smiling but proper young woman at the information kiosk just inside the front doors shook her head.

"I cannot help you," she told us. "You must go to the ticket office on the second level."

From the glass elevator, we surveyed a train station so vast that it reminded me of an airline terminal. Two stacks of platforms, each four levels high, with multiple tracks on each level. In between, a four-story, glass-covered atrium lined with acres of shops, restaurants, fast-food stands, and services catering to travelers. A cascade of aromas flooded out at us from the food establishments we passed, and the roar of trains pulling out to destinations across Europe echoed through the open station interior.

In the ticket office, ringed by a dozen counters and filled with travelers waiting for their number to be called, we found the desk serving disabled travelers closed. A middle-aged, chubby blond woman summoned us to the adjacent counter. In passable German, I explained what we thought was a simple purpose.

"We are traveling in the morning to Vienna. We have our tickets." I pulled the 4- by-8- inch tickets from my left front pocket, unfolded them, and laid them on the Formica counter top. They showed two first-class seats from Berlin to Vienna, with a transfer in the Czech town of Breslav. "I want to find out where we will board the train and to be sure we are in a car that my wife can enter on her scooter."

The women surveyed the tickets for what seemed like far too long, then pursed her lips.

"Your passports, please," she finally said, looking up at me and raising her brow.

"I don't have the passports here. They are at our hotel. I will have them tomorrow when we travel."

"There is a problem. I must see your passports."

Why would there be a problem? I thought. We have tickets. They're aware we need accessible accommodations. But I knew there was no point in arguing.

"Alright," I conceded wearily. "I will get our passports and return."

"We close at 10," she informed me. I glanced at my watch and saw I had almost four hours, surely long enough to resolve any issues.

As we left the ticket office, Trish said, "You were right about needing to come down here, but what now? What if there really is a problem?"

"There are always problems when we travel," I countered, "but we always find a way. Whatever it is, somehow, we'll work it out."

"Yes. Somehow, we always find a way."

Outside the station, we boarded a trolley headed back to Friedrichstrasse. There we descended by elevator to a subway line going south toward our hotel. The first three trains had thresholds too high for the scooter, but the fourth had a level entry. After ten minutes and three closely spaced stops, we disembarked at the city center station, went up another elevator and walked two blocks to the Hilton.

Feeling a mix of urgency and trepidation, I retrieved our passports from the room safe. Now, speed was important, so we agreed I would return to the station by myself. I made sure Trish was comfortable, then dashed out of the hotel, descended stairs at the subway entrance across the street, and ran down a long tunnel to the station. A northbound train arrived just as I did. I dashed aboard and dropped into a seat by the door. Now I felt chilled. In my rush, I had not thought to bring a sweater or jacket from the room.

Reversing our earlier course, I rode north for three stops. Luck was with me again, as a bus to the train station arrived within a couple of minutes. There, I went back up the elevator to the ticket office. Still catching my breath, I pulled a number from the ticket machine and pressed the button for accessibility help. This time, the counter I wanted was staffed. But the elderly woman being served didn't budge for the longest time, while a steady stream of customers was called to other counters. I sat on the closest bench, eyes fixed on the overhead monitor, as travelers around me chattered in a half-dozen languages and train sounds rushed in each time the electronic office doors slid open for a new arrival.

When my number appeared on the overhead monitors, I sprang forward, as if afraid they might change their minds. At the counter stood a tall, middle-aged fellow wearing a bright red, sleeveless sweater. He looked friendlier than the woman I had dealt with on my earlier visit.

"How may I help you?" he greeted me in German, with a slight smile.

"I speak only a little German," I replied. "Can we speak English?"

He frowned, but repeated, this time in English, "How may I help you?"

I recounted my earlier experience, showed him our tickets and passports, and again asked for confirmation of our travel arrangements. He nodded, then turned to his computer monitor. His facial expression remained deadpan, other than an occasional further nod.

After a minute or so, he turned back to me and shook his head.

"You have tickets," he acknowledged in an emphatic tone, "but you have no reservations."

A few times in my life, I have had the sensation of having entered the twilight zone or fallen down the rabbit hole with Alice in Wonderland. This was one of those moments. I heard what he said, tickets but no reservations, but I could make no sense of it. "Really?" I thought. "Really?" My lips moved, but no words came out.

"I don't understand!" I finally blurted out in exasperation. "What does that mean? If I am holding tickets for a particular train on a particular day, how can there be no reservation?"

"You have first-class tickets for the train, but you need reservations for seats. Only one car on the train can accommodate wheelchair passengers, just a few, and this car is second class. There may not be seats there anymore. Also, we have a lift to help your wife board the train, but we are required to notify our colleagues in the other countries where you are traveling so they will be ready to assist you. That must be done at least two days in advance, but you are traveling tomorrow."

It was my turn to shake my head. "My travel agent spoke directly with your main ticket office by telephone three months ago. I was there. She told your people exactly what we needed when she ordered the tickets. We expected all the arrangements to have been made. Someone here should have done that. We are on a vacation trip and must be in Vienna tomorrow evening."

I looked him in the eye and said, in my sincerest tone of voice, this time in German, "I know it is not your fault, but please help us with this."

The agent nodded yet again. "I will try," he said, in a more sympathetic tone than before. "It is difficult, but I will try. Please wait."

So I waited as the agent made phone calls, typed on his computer, and jotted down notes. His voice and expression gave no hint of success or failure. I listened intently, trying to decipher whatever he said. Fifteen minutes later, he turned back to me.

"I have done all I can do," he told me, now sounding weary. "I have made the seat reservations for you. I am arranging for you to change trains in Prague rather than Breslav. That will be easier. And I have notified the railroad authorities in Prague and Vienna about the scooter, but I have not received a confirmation. So, unless you hear from us still tonight, you should come to the station in the morning for your train. Hopefully, it will be alright."

He handed me back our tickets, along with printed reservation confirmations showing our seats in the accessible car and the new routing through Prague. I no longer felt compelled to ask why we needed the separate reservations. Some things in life must be accepted. But I also knew better than to relax yet. Sure enough, just when it appeared that our problems had been solved, I stumbled over a final obstacle.

"Please give me your cell phone number," the agent said, "so we can reach you if we hear back from the other authorities and they say no."

I closed my eyes momentarily and took a deep breath. I didn't want to tell him that our cell carrier had screwed up both our phones and we had no service outside the US. So, I just said, "We have no cell phone. We are staying at the Hilton downtown. Please use that number."

The agent cocked his head and gave me a pitying look. I imagined him thinking, Who doesn't travel with a cellphone? But he accepted that.

"We are finished!" he declared. "In the morning, come to the side of the information kiosk downstairs. Someone will take you to the train and help you board. Good luck."

"Thank you, *danke*," I gushed. I grabbed my travel documents and rushed out, afraid that, if I stayed another minute, some other issue might arise.

No messages came that night from the ticket office. In the morning, we took a taxi to the railroad station and checked in at the information kiosk. The agent there, a rumpled, middle-aged woman with sharp features, looked at our documents, threw up her hands and went off in rapid-fire German. There still was a problem. Yes, we had both tickets and reservations, but there were no arrangements in the computer for a disabled passenger. In as calm a voice as I could manage, I related my experience at the ticket office the previous evening and the assurances I had received.

"Come with me!" she ordered. "Your wife waits here."

I looked over at Trish, who rolled her eyes, then motioned for me to go. So I followed the information agent back up to the ticket office. Of course, the fellow who had helped me the previous evening was not yet on duty so early in the day. Instead, she began another rapid harangue at a much younger woman seated at an information desk there, thrusting our travel documents at her. Soon, both of them were waving their arms and growing increasingly excited. Agents at various counters, along with waiting passengers, all stared at our commotion.

Then, just as the excitement seemed to reach a pitch, as the agent from downstairs began to tell me we could not board the train under these conditions, her colleague from the information kiosk rushed in and thrust a small piece of paper at her. She looked at it, then up at me.

"Lowe? You are Lowe?" she asked, reading my name from a handwritten note, presumably from the red-vested agent.

"Yes," I replied cautiously, uncertain where this was leading.

"Everything is good!" she exclaimed, with the first smile I had seen on her face that morning. "Come downstairs with me. We will take you to the train."

Three disability assistance workers led us to the elevator serving the lower platform, loaded our bags, and operated a mobile lift to get Trish and her scooter aboard. We settled into one of three sets of seats that had space for wheelchairs or scooters. They weren't the first-class seats we had paid for, but at least they were ours. Minutes later, in a smooth motion, the train departed for Prague.

Once we were actually underway, Trish asked, "So, what happened back there? First, there was a big problem, then there was no problem."

I related the events in the ticket office, shaking my head. We both laughed, but with a nervous edge. We still had two stops to go.

An hour or so out of Berlin, the conductor who earlier had punched our tickets returned to talk about the disability arrangements. A plump, twenty-something woman with long blond hair and ruddy cheeks, she spoke fluent English.

"I will get off the train at the Czech border," she told us, "and a Czech conductor will come aboard. I will make sure he knows about your train change in Prague. I already called ahead to make sure they will be prepared to help you off this train and onto your other train."

I thanked her and related our misadventures at the station in Berlin.

"Don't worry," she assured us with a laugh. "We won't abandon you!"

We never saw the replacement conductor. An hour after crossing the border, the train pulled into Prague. We had visited Prague twice in recent years, but knew we would not see anything on this stop other than the inside of the railroad station. We waited and waited for the lift and assistance that never came.

"I'm getting concerned," Trish said, as the time approached for the train to depart. "You need to find someone to help us, or we're going to wind up in Budapest rather than Vienna."

I desperately searched for help. On the platform nearby, I saw a fellow dressed in what I took to be a conductor's uniform.

"Hello," I called to him. "Do you speak English? *Sprechen Sie Deutsch?*"

"I speak a little English. Can I help you?"

"Are you the conductor for this train? We need a lift to get off. It was arranged for us."

"I know nothing of this."

I sighed in disbelief. "Did the German conductor not tell you?"

"No one has told me. Now there is little time, but I will call for help."

A lift arrived shortly, and we disembarked. But as soon as we and our bags were on the platform, the lift operator drove away and the conductor disappeared onto the train, leaving us alone without direction. With four suitcases and Trish's walker, we set off to find our other train and, hopefully, confirm arrangements for getting aboard.

An elevator from the platform took us down to a brightly lit, underground concourse of shops and restaurants. Also the ticket office, where I approached the agent at an open counter, smiled and hoped for the best.

"Do you speak English?"

"A little."

"*Deutsch?*"

"No."

"We have tickets to Vienna. We need help to get on the train." I pointed to Trish on her scooter behind me. She waved and smiled at the agent hopefully.

The agent got an alarmed look and darted off. She returned a minute later with an English-speaking colleague in tow. I repeated our request.

He shrugged and shook his head. "You must make arrangements for wheelchairs," he declared, apparently thinking this would be news to me.

"We made arrangements in Berlin. They sent the request yesterday. And the conductor on the train today confirmed it."

"We have no information."

I felt like we were back down the rabbit hole with Alice. I resorted to what had worked in Berlin.

"I don't know what happened, but please help us. We must get on the train to Vienna."

"Yes, yes, we will help you. Go back up to the waiting area. The board there will tell you which platform for your train. I will call for a lift."

Off we went again. Once we found the electronic schedule board, Trish tugged at my arm. "I feel like they just see me as a piece of baggage, something they have to deal with," she said, sounding quite annoyed.

"I know, but at least they're dealing with the situation."

As soon as our train number appeared on the board, we joined a herd of passengers racing down a long tunnel and up the ramp to our platform. There, to my relief but mild surprise, a lift stood ready. But, this time, it proved unnecessary. As we approached our car, the conductor swung open a built-in lift from inside the door.

"Wow!" Trish exclaimed. "We need a picture of this to show people at Amtrak back home." I obligingly pulled out my camera and snapped a photograph.

The conductor brought Trish onto the train, then our luggage. We again found a pair of seats with space for the scooter. Soon, we were en route to Vienna.

But we had one last challenge. The friendly conductor looked at our papers and said, "Your tickets are only good to come to Prague. You have no ticket to Vienna."

"No," I protested, "our tickets are to Vienna. Our reservations too."

He looked and looked. Finally, he brightened. The first page of the ticket was just for the Berlin-Breslav (now Prague) segment, but the second page showed us going all the way from Berlin to Vienna. So we dodged another bullet and all was well.

At the Hauptbahnhof in Vienna, the conductor again deployed the built-in lift, and we descended at our destination. I hugged Trish. We both smiled, this time broadly, without the previous nervousness.

Standing on the platform, waving goodbye to the conductor, we finally felt free to exhale.

# Chapter 17
# STAIRS ARE NOT A PROBLEM!

Trish at Dragon Bridge, Ljubljana

*Slovenia, October 2017*

When I first suggested including Slovenia in a trip to Europe, Trish reacted skeptically.

"We'll be in Austria, and Slovenia is right next door," I said. "It's beautiful that time of year, and it won't be packed with tourists."

"Yeah, but this isn't Prague or Budapest," she countered. "This country was cut off from the rest of Europe for decades. How accessible do you think it's going to be?"

"Probably less than those places," I agreed. "More like those hill towns we visited in Provence. But remember how helpful people were, and how well it all worked out?"

While growing up in Austria and Germany, I traveled around much of Europe with my family, but some places were off-limits—mainly Eastern Europe and the Balkans. Even when the Cold War subsided a bit, my father's American security clearances barred us from going. As a former Czech national, he risked being detained if he visited any of the Soviet-bloc countries. The closest we got to Slovenia was the border with Italy at Trieste. During her student days, Trish had crossed a small part of Slovenia on her way to Dubrovnik, down the Adriatic coast.

Slovenia was the northernmost part of Yugoslavia, but is now an independent, democratic republic, part of the European Union. That means Euros as currency and no restrictions on driving a rental car there. Although not a party to the open-borders Schengen Agreement, its borders are mere formalities. A friend in San Diego whose family had immigrated from Slovenia gave us lots of travel tips and assured us that English is commonly spoken. But she had never paid close attention to how well the country accommodated disabled people.

What we found on the internet reassured us at first. The Slovenian Tourist Board hosted a website extolling travel for the disabled, and other websites promoted hotels and tourist attractions purporting to be accessible. But our enthusiasm was tempered by a notice on the Tourist Board site that the country had just begun addressing accessibility and recognized it still had much work to do in that regard. Notwithstanding that caution, we decided to go for it.

Six months later, at the end of a four-day visit in Vienna, I picked up a rental car from the Hertz franchise on the Kaerntner Ring, walking distance from our hotel. I savored the morning stroll along the broad, tree-lined boulevard as my last one this trip in one of the most walkable cities. I recalled walking here in my childhood, when Vienna still showed heavy wartime damage, and on many later occasions, after the streets, parks, churches, and other buildings had been restored.

Finding a car that accommodates our needs can be a challenge in some places. This time, we secured a new, maroon Kia mini-SUV. With a hatchback, a rear deck low enough for me to lift the scooter in, and a passenger entry high enough for Trish to enter and exit easily (with my help), it met all our criteria. An hour later, we were on our way out of Vienna, southbound on a high-speed *autobahn*, bound for Slovenia.

We breezed through a hundred miles of open country, fields, and forests interrupted only by the historic city of Graz. I recalled that was the hometown of bodybuilder, actor, and politician Arnold Schwarzenegger. Just before crossing into Slovenia, we stopped at a service station to purchase a window decal allowing us to drive on the motorways there. At the border, a billboard welcomed us to Slovenia and a border guard required only a glance at our passports. Other than that, the crossing was seamless, except that highway signs now bore Slavic rather than German names.

The highway followed the emerald-blue Soca River westward through a valley of the same name, headed toward our destination of Ljubljana another sixty miles away. The rugged Kamnik Alps, rising to over 8,000 feet, filled the horizon to the north, lapping back over into Austria. In the foreground, wooded hillsides, vineyards, and castles dotted the landscape. It all seemed familiar, very much like the countryside in the Tyrolian part of Austria where my family often drove in my childhood.

Approaching Ljubljana, our GPS failed us, sending us off the expressway and onto a city street, rather than routing us around the city to an exit much closer to our hotel. This cross-town arterial took us through business districts filled with storefront shops and offices, residential neighborhoods of mid-rise apartment buildings, and occasional parks.

"It all seems clean and well-kept, but I'm disappointed at how plain it looks," Trish said to me midway through our transit of the city.

"I know. A lot of the city was destroyed when the Germans and Italians occupied it during World War II, and then local militias fought for control. But the photos we saw of the older neighborhoods that survived looked really interesting."

We had picked the Hotel Cubo out of a travel guidebook that described it as a boutique establishment located close to the city center and the historic Old Town. The manager responded quickly to Trish's email inquiry and assured her an accessible room was available. We knew from experience, though, that accessibility in European cities typically is not synonymous with ADA standards at home.

I spotted the hotel ahead on the right, turned the corner, and found a handicapped parking space near the hotel entrance. That seemed like a good omen. Once again, we displayed our parking tag from home.

English did indeed turn out to be widely spoken there. The hotel desk clerk was fluent. She explained English is taught as the second language up to high school, at which point students can opt to continue English or switch to Italian.

Our room turned out to be reasonably accessible, roomy enough for Trish to navigate her scooter from the door to the bed and the window, but her joy turned into a familiar frustration when she attempted to enter the bathroom. As promised, it was outfitted with grab bars and a roll-in shower, but she couldn't get to them.

"Who designed this?" Trish moaned. "The cabinets in there are so close to the door, I can't make the turn to get inside the bathroom."

The manager apologized, explaining this resulted from retrofitting an older building, and no other room in the hotel was more accessible. At least the bathroom fixtures were modern. Fortunately, we had brought with us a collapsible aluminum walker, which enabled Trish to reach the sink, toilet, and shower.

As evening approached, we set out to explore, beginning with the block-sized Congress Square across the street. A park full of mature trees filled the center of the square. We followed the downtown pedestrian mall, a cobblestone way lined with upscale shops. That led us to Presernov Square, the city's most popular gathering place, surrounded by 19th-century stone buildings with ornate doorways and window frames. The square swarmed with people enjoying a comfortably cool evening. Aromas of meat and sausage grilling wafted from food vendors around the perimeter. On a promontory ahead of us, the brightly lit Ljubljana Castle loomed over the Old Town, like a sentinel still protecting the settlement below.

"This is gorgeous," I said to Trish. "We'll come back tomorrow in the daytime. Right now, let's head into the Old Town."

We crossed the Ljubljanica River on the famous Triple Bridge carrying vehicles on its central span and pedestrians on two narrower side spans — one of eight bridges along the downtown area. Lights glowing from buildings on either side of the river created a festive, holiday-like atmosphere.

At the suggestion of the hotel staff, we made our way along the main thoroughfare to Julija, a restaurant specializing in traditional Slovenian cuisine of stews, soups, sausages, pastas, and rich deserts. Lots of Austrian and Italian culinary influences, The restaurant entrance had too large a step for Trish's scooter to overcome, but we were happy to be seated at one of their outdoor tables, where we got a view of the passing street scene. And the brisk air of the autumn evening felt perfect for drinking lots of local red wine.

Full from a dinner of vegetable soup, carpaccio, roast lamb, and grilled chicken, we wandered farther down the street, now filled with evening walkers and shoppers. Every restaurant we passed sent mouth-watering smells into the street. Voices echoed off the three-story, tile-roofed, stone buildings lining the way. Although the street was paved with cobblestones, these were flatter than ones we had encountered in some other cities.

"Thank goodness," Trish declared. "What a relief not to get bounced around on these stones."

A lighted arcade took us under a commercial building and back to the river. We walked along a paved pathway until we came to a café with a nice view of lit-up buildings across the river. There, we paused for a nightcap of Slovenian nut cake and brandy.

"It's wonderful so far," I said to Trish as I finished the last crumbs of cake.

"Yes, I'm glad we came. This Old Town is really charming."

The following morning, after an oversized breakfast of cold cuts, omelets, pastries, and coffee provided by the hotel, we ventured back to Presernov Square. It looked even more impressive in daylight. We paused to look up at the 30-foot-tall monument to national poet France Preseren and to admire the shocking-pink and white cathedral on the north side of the square. Then Trish noticed a vendor nearby.

"He's selling roasted chestnuts," she exclaimed. "I haven't had those since my student days in Bordeaux."

We bought a bagful, fresh off the roaster, after which the vendor posed for a photo with Trish. Then we were off across the Triple Bridge again, into the heart of the Old Town. As we walked, I alternated between eating the still-warm chestnuts myself and popping them into Trish's mouth.

"Just like what I remember from France," she reminisced.

"Just like I remember from my childhood," I joined in.

We walked in the opposite direction from the previous evening, toward the base of the hill below the castle. We passed an eclectic collection of buildings, from simple, yellow, stucco-clad structures with small windows to ornate granite edifices with arched windows and sculptured doorways.

Standing alongside a moss-covered stone wall, waiting in line to ride the funicular up to the castle, we noticed people staring and pointing at Trish's scooter.

"I hate them staring like that," Trish said, sounding annoyed. "It's like they've never seen a scooter before."

"I know," I replied. "But think about it. We've seen a couple of people in wheelchairs, but not another scooter, so I guess it's a curiosity." Trish shrugged as the line moved forward and peoples' attention shifted.

The ride up gave us our first panoramic view of the city, a sea of three-and-four-story buildings with red-tile roofs, interrupted occasionally by taller, modern office buildings. We also spotted the thirteen-story building known as the Skyscraper, once the tallest residential building in Europe.

Most of the castle as it stands today was built in the 15th century, but the foundations and the original construction go back another 300 years. A Roman fort is believed to have occupied the site a thousand years earlier. Until modern times, the stronghold served as the home of rulers of Carniola, a historical region encompassing much of present-day Slovenia. All the way back to my childhood, I loved clambering around old castles, like those along the Rhine River, imagining the people who occupied them, the military battles to take and defend them, and the gruesome events that occurred in their dungeons.

Of course, structures that old turned out to be only partially accessible. Long flights of stone stairs led from the central plaza up to the parapets and tower or down to interior rooms. I made a few quick scrambles up or down to take pictures, then wandered with Trish around the plaza to view historical exhibits.

After descending on the funicular, we crossed the river again, this time on the Dragon Bridge. Five-foot-tall bronze statues of winged dragons, dull green from oxidation, occupied pedestals on either side at both ends of the bridge, evoking a medieval feel to the crossing. The Ljubljanica flowed peacefully beneath the bridge, in sharp contrast to the ferocious-looking dragons. Trish posed at the base of one of the statues, the dragon towering over her as if warning her not to cross.

Clouds and wind gusts dampened our plans to spend more time walking about town. Wanting to explore more of the country, we decided to take a day trip, beginning with a visit to the famous caverns at Postojna, thirty miles to the south. We expected to find a crowd waiting to see the magnificent stalagmites and stalactites in the world-renowned caves. Still, after an hour of driving through lush countryside, the hundreds of visitors gathered at the cavern entrance astonished us. Thankfully, we found a handicapped parking space close to the entrance. The crowd meant a wait, but it gave us time for a quick lunch of sausage and beer at one of the nearby food stalls.

Viewing the caves required first riding deep into a mountain on an open, narrow-gauge train, then disembarking and walking through various rooms and passageways. We managed the first part, leaving Trish's scooter behind at the platform. The train whisked us through a two-mile-long tunnel carved by the Pivka River. Along the way, lights shone on columns, curtains, and icicles of stone created over eons by mineral-laden water emerging from the surrounding rock.

When the train halted and passengers exited to walk through the rest of the cavern, we faced a familiar dilemma. The walking route was too rough for a scooter, and we had left it behind, anyway.

"I know you wanted to walk through the cave," Trish said, "but obviously I can't do it, and I don't really feel safe alone here." She sounded frustrated, even a little upset.

"I agree," I replied, though she probably detected disappointment in my voice. "Maybe we'll see more on the way out," I said, trying to sound upbeat.

With us as the only passengers, the train then proceeded to the reloading point. As we waited for the others, I saw an opportunity. The loading platform opened to the last large room of the cavern. Now that we were in a well-lit area, with many people nearby, I felt secure leaving Trish for a short time.

"I'll be right back," I promised, as I pulled out my camera and made a dash across the platform. Beneath the cavern room's twenty-foot ceiling, I found a dazzling display of formations a hundred times more impressive than the ones we saw in the tunnel—groups of stalactites hanging from the ceiling, stalagmite columns thick as barrels rising up to meet them, and patterned walls, all in colors of white, green, and gold. As the rest of the group filtered back to the train, I snapped pictures to share with Trish later. It wouldn't be the same for her as seeing the cave features in person, and I knew that bothered her, but we had long ago agreed that this would have to suffice as a best alternative at places she couldn't reach.

By the time we emerged from the cavern, the clouds had scattered and the wind died down. This looked like an excellent time to continue on to our second hoped-for destination of the day, the postcard coastal town of Piran at the end of a peninsula extending into the Adriatic Sea.

Along the way, we made a slight detour to see the Predjama Castle, a white, stone redoubt built into the mouth of a massive cavern in an even more massive cliff. We knew in advance we would not be able to enter the castle, as the long, rocky pathway to it was inaccessible for a scooter. Instead, we drove to the nearest parking spot and viewed the castle from a distance, marveling at how 13th-century builders constructed such an imposing structure in such a remote place.

As we wound our way from there to Piran, on another thirty miles of local roads, the sun shone brighter, as if blessing our decision. Piran turned out to be as picturesque as advertised. Finding no available spaces in the town itself, we left our car at a parking structure back up the narrow entry road. On our walk down the hill from there, we got a splendid panoramic view of the harbor, red-roofed buildings clustered around a central square, a fortress-like church along the water, and a cathedral on an opposing hillside. The sunshine and salt air couldn't have been more different from conditions in the cavern just two hours earlier.

"Beautiful," I commented. "It's a classic Mediterranean fishing village.

"Yes, it reminds me of small towns around Dubrovnik," Trish replied wistfully. "That was one of my favorite stops in my travels back in my student days."

The smooth road along the waterfront took us past scores of sailboats and fishing boats, all bobbing gently in the quiet waters. Across the street stood blue and yellow apartment buildings, hotels with lush frontage landscaping, and a plethora of tourist businesses.

Soon, we came to the square we had seen from the hillside, dominated by a bronze statue of a man in 18th-century attire holding a violin—unidentified, but presumably a noted local musician. Signs harkened back to when Slovenia was for decades part of Yugoslavia, with the plaza itself named 1st of May Square and a nearby street named Via Lenin.

The red-brick cathedral tower, a virtual twin for the one at St. Mark's Cathedral in Venice just up the coast, loomed in the background. Austere government buildings and festive-looking outdoor restaurants surrounded the square. We settled into a cafe' with a view toward the water and stuffed ourselves with a platter of fried calamari accompanied by local dry white wine.

As the sun set off a brilliant crimson show behind the harbor lighthouse, we started the trek back to Ljubljana. En route, the weather changed again, turning to a heavy drizzle that followed us all the way to the hotel.

Our last evening in Ljubljana, we went in search of Restoracija Ronin, which we heard described as the best seafood restaurant in the city. We found it, beneath a miniscule sign in an older stucco building at the end of the Old Town close by the castle funicular. As we so often discovered with older European buildings, entry involved climbing a few steps. At home, we keep a portable metal ramp in the car for moments like this, but it's too heavy to take traveling.

"So much for that," Trish said with a sigh.

At that moment, seeing us outside, a waiter emerged to welcome us.

"We would like to come in," I said, "but we can't get up the stairs."

"Stairs are not a problem!" he declared, disappearing back inside. In a moment, he returned with two more waiters and the restaurant manager. Together, they lifted the scooter, with Trish aboard, ready to carry her up the stairs and into the establishment.

"Are you sure about this?" she asked, looking back at me and grimacing. I also felt anxious but didn't want to show it, as the men seemed to have everything under control. I guessed they had done this before. On being put back down, Trish breathed a sigh of relief and let out a loud laugh. That made me feel better too.

Inside, the restaurant was quiet on this midweek evening. Conversation from a few tables blended with recorded zither music. Whenever the kitchen door opened, aromas of fried and grilled seafood flooded the room.

Seated beneath the arched ceiling of the whitewashed interior, we lingered over a dinner of fried squid, Greek salad, seafood risotto, and grilled sea bass, accompanied by a bottle of local white wine, all as delicious as anything we had on this trip. Afterward, the restaurant staff carried Trish and the scooter back down the stairs and waved us off into the night.

Our path out of Slovenia took us north toward Salzburg and my hometown of Braunau, where we would visit my childhood friend Karin Zinecker. Shortly before reentering Austria, we exited the motorway for a brief visit to the lakeside resort town of Bled. Hotels, restaurants, and parks lined the walkway skirting the lake. We parked the car and took a long walk, with only an occasional tree root or pavement crack causing Trish any problem on her scooter. On this overcast day, the lake didn't show its famous emerald color, but the historic church on an island in the lake and the castle on a promontory overlooking the scene still made for memorable views. As we walked, little brown ducks and swans the size of dogs followed us, hoping for handouts.

After passing through a three-mile-long tunnel beneath the Julian Alps and then another brief border stop, we continued through mountain passes well into Austria. Snowy peaks and glaciers towered over lush meadows, mountain villages, and onion-domed churches. Along the way, Trish and I talked non-stop about all we had seen and done during our first visit to Slovenia. Meanwhile, I noticed road signs bearing more and more names of places I remembered from my childhood. Finally, getting my first glimpse of the white Salzburg castle on its ridge overlooking the city, I smiled and nodded in recognition. I felt back at home, but I looked forward to returning to Slovenia someday.

# Chapter 18
# NOT SO EASY IN THE BIG EASY

Trish Eating Beignets at Café du Monde, New Orleans

*New Orleans, April 2018*

Trish and I love visiting older, historic cities in the United States, but those places often present accessibility issues. We received a fresh reminder of that when we traveled to New Orleans for the national conference of the American Planning Association, where we were to make a joint presentation.

I had visited many times before, including twice for Mardi Gras. Trish had been there once on business many years earlier and another time with me on vacation. However, her visits to the town known as the Big Easy took place before MS made her reliant on a mobility scooter.

A warm, muggy evening greeted us on arrival at Louis Armstrong Airport. Summer comes early to the South, with far higher temperatures and humidity than we had left behind in San Diego.

The middle-aged woman staffing the airport shuttle desk looked warily at Trish's scooter.

"Honey, can you get off that and step up into a shuttle bus?" she asked, in a tone that suggested she already knew the answer.

"No, I can't do stairs. I need an accessible shuttle," Trish replied.

The woman nodded. With thousands of conventioneers arriving, besides the usual tourist traffic, I assumed she already had a hard day.

"OK," she said with a weary smile. "Some lifts aren't working, but we'll fix you up. It'll be just a short wait.

The wait turned out to be pretty long, close to an hour, before a shuttle with a lift arrived where we waited outside the terminal. The driver held off the twenty other passengers from boarding while he directed Trish onto the flatbed lift, raised her into the rear of the vehicle, and secured the scooter with cargo tie-downs. I helped her off the scooter and onto the nearest bench seat.

Thirty minutes later, we arrived at the Hilton New Orleans Riverside, at the foot of Poydras Street, midway between the Morial Convention Center and the French Quarter. By the time we checked in and unpacked, we were too fatigued to go out anymore that evening.

To our relief, the restaurant in the lobby still was serving. Seated in plush, brown leather chairs beneath the nine-story atrium, we filled up on barbequed gulf shrimp and seafood gumbo, bookended with glasses of Abita amber. Not the best food in town, but just fine under the circumstances.

Our room itself was as accessible as the hotel reservation clerk had promised. "If only hotels that aren't part of a big chain could be this accessible," Trish lamented. "I guess that's the tradeoff, convenience versus charm."

From our sixth-floor window, we saw the broad Mississippi River glowing in the moonlight, backed by the lights of Gretna. I marveled at this artery of American exploration and commerce that ended its 1,500-mile journey just beyond our view. We fell asleep to the sounds of boat horns from the river and occasional passing streetcars.

Our first morning there, we followed a crowd from the hotel to the convention center, four blocks or one trolley stop away. The wide, smooth sidewalk along Convention Center Boulevard had no obstructions, but reaching it required negotiating a brief labyrinth out the front of the hotel—steering along a narrow walkway around the side of the building, across a couple of cracked parking lot entrances, and through a puddle of water from a recent rain.

Once inside the cavernous lobby at the north end of the convention center, we claimed our credentials from a mobbed counter and headed off to our morning conference programs. The two-level convention center sprawled for eight blocks along the river. As we scanned our conference program and map, we realized we would be wandering back and forth, up and down, through that building for three days.

"Don't let me forget to charge my scooter every night," Trish implored, recalling past incidents where her scooter battery died, and I wound up pushing her back to our hotel. "And I better carry the charger with me the rest of the time we're here."

"Yes, and keep your cell phone on you. We won't always be at the same programs. It's going to be challenging finding each other in this crowd, especially with you sitting so low."

Eight hours later, exhausted but excited from a day of listening to and talking with colleagues from around the country, we headed out for an evening on the town. After passing the gaudy, neo-Vegas Harrah's Casino across the street, we went two long blocks north on Canal Street before turning right into the French Quarter. Decatur Street took us to Jackson Square, the iconic central meeting place of the Quarter. The triple spires of St. Louis Cathedral on the far side of the square stood dark against the evening sky, while floodlights illuminated the rest of the building in a golden glow. In the foreground, silhouetted against the cathedral, stood a bronze memorial to Andrew Jackson. He was still honored for defeating the British in the Battle of New Orleans 200 years earlier, though his reputation for exterminating Native Americans was catching up to him, maybe leading eventually to removal of that statue.

By now, we noticed scents of beignets frying at Café du Monde, pralines baking at Aunt Sally's across the street, and gumbo being ladled out in nearby restaurants. Our first destination, however, was Pat O'Brien's, the bar that originated the rum drink known as a hurricane, served in a glass shaped like a bulbous hurricane lamp.

Moving about the French Quarter, with its narrow sidewalks and bumpy streets, was hard enough for someone walking but downright difficult for a wheelchair or scooter rider. On some blocks, utility poles or trash cans obstructed the sidewalks, and some corners lacked ramps. Fortunately, we encountered little vehicle traffic at that time of evening, so we stayed mostly in the streets.

Pat O'Brien's is always packed. We found the main bar, with its ceiling of hanging beer steins, too crowded for Trish to maneuver on her scooter. Hoping outside would be a better bet, we exited the side door and followed the carriageway to a brick-lined patio bar landscaped with potted plants surrounding a fountain. Just as we arrived, a couple got up from one of the low wrought-iron tables and motioned to us to take their places. While I got us a couple of hurricanes, Trish started a conversation with another couple still at that table. They turned out to be attending the same convention, as were drinkers at two other nearby tables. By the time I returned, drinks in hand, they had a small party going within the patio crowd.

Between sips, we talked about the convention and about our urban planning work. We found a thirtyish couple from a small Midwest city especially amusing, as they related how little planning and land use regulation existed there compared with comparable cities in California.

"I served on the City of San Diego Planning Commission for six years," Trish told them. "We probably dealt with more regulations in every meeting than it sounds like you do in a year." They laughed but had to agree.

Another round of hurricanes later, I checked the time.

"We need to go!" I announced to a startled Trish. "We've got a dinner reservation at Tujague's in fifteen minutes."

Tujague's, which locals pronounce "two-jacks," fronts on Decatur Street near Jackson Square. Although close to tourist venues, its Creole cuisine draws more of a local crowd. Backtracking on our earlier route, we arrived at the restaurant just in time. Inside, the white linen tablecloths, picture-lined walls, and courtly servers remind patrons of the restaurant's 150-year history. Diners already occupied all the tables in the front room and the adjoining room was a step down. To reach our table, we followed the maitre'd around the front room, through the pantry, and then into the second dining room.

We ordered Sazerac cocktails, a locally favored combination of rye whiskey, absinthe, sugar, and bitters. By the time we finished our appetizers of seafood gumbo and crawfish tails with tangy remoulade sauce, we felt at home. Meanwhile, the aromas from the kitchen sent our senses into overdrive.

"I like this place much better than some of those stuffier French restaurants here," Trish opined. "And the food is better. Remember how disappointed we were the last time we ate at Antoine's?"

"It's hard to get a bad meal in New Orleans, but I agree with you."

I went for a main dish of poached pompano with asparagus. Trish picked the duck breast with Lyonnaise potatoes. We traded off and both finished happy.

We welcomed the walk back to the Hilton. The brisk evening air felt refreshing after two hours in the warmth of Tujague's packed dining room. As we reached the high-end Canal Place mall, a few blocks short of the hotel, I got what I thought was a bright idea.

"We can save some distance by going around the back of the shopping center," I suggested. Trish didn't argue. I soon had second thoughts, though, as Iberville Street took on the dark appearance of a back alley behind the monolithic rear wall of the mall, empty of other walkers. An ideal spot for a mugging, I thought. Trish had the same thought.

"Let's get out of here, now!" she declared, speeding up her scooter.

"Yes. I wish I hadn't suggested this. But it's closer to keep going than to turn back."

I scanned the shadows ahead of us and repeatedly looked back over my shoulder for what seemed like an eternity. I didn't know if seeing another person would be comforting or scary. Every sound from within the mall made me flinch. Fear of this kind of situation had led me to take a *krav maga* martial arts course the previous year, but I hoped never to have to use it. And, even if I could fight off a single unarmed mugger, what would I do if there was more of a threat than that? Could I protect Trish in that situation?

Then, within minutes, we were back out on crowded Convention Center Boulevard. The well-lit hotel lobby looked especially inviting after our brief adventure.

"Lesson learned," I said with a nervous laugh. "No more back-street shortcuts."

Our conference presentation, entitled "Going Out on Your Own," was scheduled for the next morning. The ninety-minute program aimed to acquaint planners and lawyers thinking of leaving their jobs at private firms or public agencies with the business, legal, and ethical issues involved in setting up their own businesses, as Trish and I both had done. Wanting to appear professional, I dressed in a lawyerly grey, pinstriped suit and patterned maroon tie, while Trish wore her most business-like Navy-blue suit with a white blouse and a gold lapel pin.

By our start time of 9:00 am, 300 or so people crowded into the hall, many carrying cups of coffee and slouching in their seats, still recovering from late-night partying. Trish and I sat at a raised dais, with a ten-foot-high PowerPoint projector screen to our left. As promised, conference staff had fitted the dais with a wheelchair ramp for Trish. She and I carried on a lively conversation for over an hour, interspersing legal rules with anecdotes from our respective experiences. We then opened up to questions and comments from the audience, who lined up at microphones in both aisles to query us. At the end, we received an appreciative applause, allowing us to feel the effort to make this presentation was worthwhile.

With no other morning program that interested us, I suggested an early lunch.

"Let's go to the Central Grocery," I urged. "I've been wanting a *muffuletta* since we got here." The Italian sandwich, a round loaf of sesame bread stuffed with salami, provolone, and highly seasoned olive salad, originated a century earlier as a staple food for dockworkers on the nearby river. Located between Jackson Square and Tujague's, the grocery's aromas wafted outward in all directions. Well before noon, a line already had formed inside between shelves of olive oil, pastas, cheeses, and assorted Italian delicacies.

Although the grocery sells its famous sandwiches by the quarter, we bought a whole one, ten inches across, and carried it over to the river for an *alfresco* lunch on the lawn atop the levee.

"You haven't said a word since we stopped here," Trish remarked, as I devoured half the sandwich.

"This is so good, I can't think about anything else," I replied, swallowing the last bite and wiping olive oil from my face with a wad of napkins. Meanwhile, Trish had eaten just half of a quarter sandwich. I wrapped up the rest and tucked it into the backpack of her scooter, to take with us for a mid-afternoon snack.

"Now what?" she asked. "We've got over an hour before the afternoon programs."

"That sandwich needs a dessert. We can't leave New Orleans without eating beignets at least once, and Café du Monde is right there."

We made our way through the mid-day crowds. Street musicians at Jackson Square blended with hundreds of tourist voices into a cacophony. Horse-drawn carriages ambled by carrying visitors on French Quarter tours, the horses' metal shoes clicking on the street pavement.

The café, famous for its French pillow-like doughnuts covered in powdered sugar, was crowded as always, but we got lucky again. I spied a couple getting up from a table at the edge of the covered outdoor patio at the front and made a dash for it. Trish followed close behind, threading her scooter among the closely spaced tables. Within minutes, a blond teenage waitress clad in the café's trademark white blouse, apron, and white paper cap appeared to clear the table and take our order. Like most of the other diners, we asked for two orders of beignets with chicory café au lait. Every bite of beignet exploded with flavor in my mouth, the sugar complementing the fried taste of the dough. The coffee cleansed my mouth of both, leaving a light chocolaty aftertaste.

When the afternoon conference programs ended, it was time for more food and some New Orleans-style entertainment. We intended our first stop to be a reception hosted by a lawyer group within the APA. Conveniently, the location was close to our later dinner destination. We made our way up Canal Street again and headed back into the French Quarter. Passing the Acme Oyster House, site of many memorable lunches, I wanted in the worst way to stop in for a half dozen Mississippi River oysters, but a line snaked out the door and down the block.

The address we sought was right next door, though with a catch. A flight of at least twenty stairs led up to the reception room. A smiling young woman wearing a conference tag stood at the base of the stairs to screen those entering.

"How do we get up there to the reception?" I asked her. "Where's the elevator?"

That drew a blank stare and a long silence.

"There's no elevator in this building," she finally responded. "Can you go up the stairs?" she asked Trish.

Trish gave me a quizzical look, then turned back to the conference woman and said, "No, I can't," loudly enough to draw looks from passersby. "I can't believe someone would schedule an event in a place that is totally inaccessible!"

"I'm sorry," the young woman told her. "I'm just here to greet people. I had nothing to do with setting up the party."

True, but irrelevant. Trish shook her head in frustration, then turned back to me.

"Planners," she fumed. "They think about access issues all the time in their work, but when it comes to something like this, they totally forget how to plan."

Seeing no solution to this obstacle, I shrugged. "Galatoire's is just around the corner. Let's see if they'll take us early."

As we turned down Bourbon Street, we encountered a six-piece brass band leading an impromptu parade. Anywhere else, this would have seemed an anomaly, but it's an everyday occurrence in the French Quarter. With horns, saxophones, and a tuba blaring and a bass drum pounding, the band paused in front of our destination, providing us with a brief concert before we entered.

Galatoire's exuded an airy elegance, with its expansive dining room, high ceiling, and widely spaced, linen-covered tables. I started with oysters Rockefeller, baked in their half-shells and covered with herbed spinach. The dish originated at Antoine's, but has since become a New Orleans staple. Trish, not a fan of oysters, opted for turtle soup with sherry. But what makes Galatoire's famous, and what we came for, were the crab dishes. From past visits, I knew I wanted basic crabmeat au gratin, lump blue crab meat baked with a topping of bechamel sauce and bread crumbs. Trish went with the more exotic but equally luscious crabmeat Yvonne, featuring artichoke hearts and mushrooms in a meuniere sauce.

As we shared a dessert of pecan pie with whiskey sauce and whipped cream, I announced, "We're in New Orleans. It's time to hear some jazz."

A few years earlier, I would have suggested Preservation Hall, but most of the original band members there had died or retired. Besides, I wanted something livelier. A few blocks down Bourbon Street sat Fritzel's European Jazz Pub. I had walked past it many times but never gone in, perhaps put off by its odd name. This time, I had learned more about it and was eager to experience a house band known for some of the best and hottest jazz in the French Quarter.

Music blared from the narrow entryway, wanting to draw us in, but I saw a problem—a step at the front door much too high for Trish's scooter. The doorman saw it too and proposed a solution. The adjoining alley led to a courtyard and then to a rear door, all level. He summoned another pub employee to help him move trash cans that crowded the alley, after which he led us to the rear and inside.

The pub's interior presented another challenge. While a young woman pointed us toward two seats right in front of the corner stage, we couldn't see a wide enough path for the scooter through the densely packed rows of tables and benches.

Turning to me, Trish said, "I can't get through there. I'd be banging into people and running over their feet."

At that moment, the band took a break. With some good-natured cajoling, the waitress got enough guests to turn in their seats and move their legs to allow us to pass. They waited patiently while I helped Trish into a chair and then rode her scooter back out, parking it just inside the rear door.

Once seated, with a couple of Crescent City pilsners ordered, we took in the room. On one side of the center aisle, patrons sat in chairs at rectangular tables facing a twelve-by-twelve-foot stage. On the other side, people sat on long wooden benches at equally long tables, all facing the side of the stage. Bookshelves, concert posters, and framed photographs of musicians covered the walls. Overhead fans circulated air well enough to keep the room comfortable.

The musicians soon returned. A middle-aged, crewcut man in a white shirt sat at the piano to our left. Two younger, bearded players, on drums and bass, occupied the rear of the stage. In front, a young trombonist and a middle-aged clarinetist filled out the group. They launched into the first of a series of upbeat jazz tunes that shook the small room and had the audience clapping and nodding. Two sets and two more rounds of beer later, we were ready to call it a night. I retrieved Trish's scooter and helped her exit, again with the cooperation of intervening patrons.

"I don't want to walk back to the hotel," I said. "Let's head down toward the river and catch a streetcar."

Trish nodded in agreement. New Orleans' streetcars, like the one immortalized in Tennessee Williams' *A Streetcar Named Desire*, form an integral part of the visitor experience. We followed Bourbon Street and then Ann Street back toward Jackson Square, passing beneath blocks of black wrought-iron balconies hung with baskets of geraniums.

Soon after we arrived at the outdoor Dumaine Street station, a forest-green streetcar approached. We saw, however, that it was filled to overflowing with partiers coming from the cluster of clubs in the nearby Marigny neighborhood. The trolley driver leaned out, pointed at the full train, and assured us another one would be along shortly. I wondered, but he was right. Within a few minutes, a second trolley pulled up, only half full, with vacant wheelchair spaces. Four stops later, we exited at our hotel.

The conference wrapped up the following morning, leaving us the rest of that day to explore. I had reserved a Toyota RAV4, a crossover SUV with a hatchback for loading Trish's scooter. Hertz had the new, electric-blue vehicle waiting for us at their office across from the Convention Center.

We followed busy Canal Street, lined with hotels and retail businesses, north to City Park, the Central Park of New Orleans. On smooth walkways, we strolled the Botanic Garden among centuries-old oaks draped with Spanish moss, crossed bridges over lazily drifting bayous, and paused to admire modernist sculptures set in the landscaping. Aromas of blossoming spring flowers filled the air. The only sounds were of laughing children running about the lawns and gardens.

Back in the car, we drove Interstate 10 toward the river. Having lived for many years in Los Angeles, where the western terminus of I-10 slices across the city, and also having lived at its eastern end in Jacksonville, Florida, I always feel a special connection when I drive or cross that transcontinental highway in faraway locales.

We trailed a streetcar down St. Charles Avenue into the historic Garden District with its block after block of splendid 19$^{th}$-century homes—antebellum mansions fronted by thirty-foot-high columns, villas adorned with wrought-iron trim, and gingerbread-decorated shotgun cottages. And the neighborhood housed the restaurant that would be our final treat on this visit.

We knew we wouldn't be able to eat at all the great New Orleans restaurants. I would have loved to have a platter of Mississippi River oysters at the Acme Oyster House and a brunch of trout Nancy with bananas Foster at Brennan's. Not to mention other old favorites like the Cajun home cooking at Mother's or the namesake dishes at the Gumbo House. But I had made a dinner reservation for that day at Commander's Palace, the century-old Creole restaurant, set in a turquoise, turreted Garden District mansion, that had launched legendary chefs like Paul Prudhomme and Emeril Lagasse.

"I haven't eaten there since my first visit to New Orleans, almost forty years ago," I told Trish. "And as long as we're here, I want to walk through the old cemetery across the street."

I parked under towering sycamores outside the stained, whitewashed walls of Lafayette Cemetery No. 1. After making our way along a sidewalk disrupted at intervals by ancient tree roots, we wandered through the wrought-iron gates and started down the central aisle, flanked by rows of family crypts. The cemetery filled an entire block and contained over a thousand of those stone structures, like tiny houses, built to hold graves above ground on account of the high water table. French names from the early 1800s gave way to later English and Italian ones.

As guards prepared to close the cemetery for the day, we crossed the street to the restaurant. I liked it even better this time. The staff and the atmosphere seemed more relaxed, a reflection of changes in New Orleans as a whole. We treated ourselves to gulf seafood gumbo, shrimp with ham and pickled okra, pecan crusted redfish, and pecan pie a la mode. It made a perfect finale to our stay.

The next morning, we started on a 350-mile drive to Shreveport, in the northwest corner of the state, to visit my cousin, Steve Cahn, and his wife, Gail. At Breaux Bridge, amid the bayous of Cajun country, we stopped for a boiled crawfish lunch at a café with a ten-foot, metal crawfish sculpture out front. Two days later, we drove south through the piney woods of east Texas to visit my daughter, Coralea, in Galveston, Texas. The port city's imposing 19th-century architectural treasures, its beaches, and its fresh-off-the-boat seafood had made for many enjoyable visits over the years.

As we rode the ferry from Bolivar across the bay to Galveston Island, we thought back on the past week. After sharing recollections of favorite places and meals, Trish summed up her experience, saying, "I loved it all, but sometimes it felt really frustrating getting around. They may call New Orleans the Big Easy, but it wasn't always so easy for me."

# Chapter 19
# THE LOOK OF LOVE

Trish at Beach in Kapa'a, Kauai

*Kauai, December 2018*
By our third day on Kauai, known as Hawaii's Garden Island, I felt the familiar ache in my wrists and thumbs from lifting Trish's ninety-pound, three-wheeled mobility scooter in and out of the back of the rental SUV and helping Trish herself stand up from various seats. I took in a deep breath, then sighed a slow exhale, knowing this could get worse over the rest of the week.

At home in San Diego, Trish can drive her larger scooter up a ramp into her specially outfitted Toyota van, and my Explorer has a lift built into the rear. We furnished our home with chairs and toilets tall enough to allow her to stand up on her own, except on days when her MS symptoms weaken her more than usual. But on vacation, we find hotel rooms rarely as accessible as advertised, toilets and restaurant seats awkwardly low, and rental cars with ramps or lifts nonexistent. Thankfully, the bright red travel scooter is lighter than the monster at home—just light enough that, for now anyway, I can lift it up and forward to load it.

My cellphone alarm woke me a little before six a.m. in our condo near the center of Kapa'a, midway up Kauai's east coast. I wanted to stay close to California time, and I needed to be up early anyway on alternate days to drive myself down to Koloa to catch a dive boat. On the other days, we would explore the island together. This day, we planned to drive around the north coast.

I did my daily morning stretching to loosen my arms, legs, and back. After drawing back the blackout curtains in the living room, I gazed through the sheers at the bright green lawn dotted with pink ginger flowers and yellow hibiscus blooms. Ocean waves murmured from a hundred yards away. Thin clouds covered the morning sky, with sunshine already peeking through. It would be a pretty day, a little cloudy, warm but not oppressive—perfect for driving and exploring.

I soon had a pot of coffee brewing. Maui coffee with a smooth, subtle flavor, hard to find at home. Trish called from the bedroom, needing help to get up. She had to sleep on the opposite side of the bed from her normal routine at home, as her scooter wouldn't fit around the usual side. That meant she had to rely on her weaker left arm to prop herself up and reach for the scooter.

"Ahhh, this is so hard," she said with a tone of resignation. "Please help me stand up."

Placing my hands under her arms, bending my knees, and then straightening, I lifted her up and toward me. A little shot of pain went through my left hand below the thumb. I winced for a just a moment. Once she was standing and stable, and able to grasp the steering yoke of the scooter, I released her. She pivoted to her right, lowered herself into the scooter seat, and headed off to the bathroom. I returned to the kitchen to cut up a strawberry papaya and warm a couple of croissants.

Five minutes later, Trish called again. I knew what she needed.

"Why do they make such low toilets?" she asked in exasperation as I entered the bathroom.

I stepped between her and the scooter. This would be more difficult than in the bedroom, with less room to maneuver. I leaned forward, slipped my hands under her arms again, counted aloud to three, then lifted up and back. Once she found her balance, she grasped the scooter as I turned her toward it and onto the seat. I gave her a hug before stepping awkwardly out of the way, tripping over the scooter's platform and banging my elbow against the wall to my right.

"Ow, dammit," I muttered.

"I'm sorry. Are you OK?"

"Yeah, I think the wall got the worse of that."

I didn't want her to feel bad about it. I see the back and wrist pains, the occasional bumps and bruises, as little potholes in an otherwise smooth road. I just hope the pain doesn't worsen and I don't lose strength to a point where I can't do this anymore. That would make it impossible to keep traveling independently or even to continue without live-in help at home.

Trish rode to the dining table, where I had removed a chair to allow her to pull the scooter up. I poured her a cup of coffee, adding enough milk to make it mocha-colored, the way she likes it. After bringing that out to her, I returned for the croissants and fruit.

We eat at different speeds, I much faster, partly because she has difficulty grasping cups and silverware. We've gotten used to that. As soon as I finished breakfast, I reached for the island map and spread it on the table between us.

I love travel planning, especially using maps Traveling has been an important feature of our relationship from the start. We have introduced each other to our respective favorite places and discovered many new ones together. It's become more difficult, of course, as Trish's condition has worsened, but I work with her in designing trips that give her lots to see and do.

We find ways to make most places accessible. The joys of experiencing travel together keep giving me reasons to make an extra effort, like giving her a needed boost up steep streets in Provence hilltop towns or lifting her scooter in and out of the baggage compartment of the bus to the Arctic Ocean in Alaska.

"Here's where we are now," I began, placing my right index finger at a mark on the map. "This is the highway up and around the north shore."

I pointed out a botanical garden, a lighthouse, various beaches, the town of Hanalei, and the end of the road at the island's northwest corner, where a trail begins down the rugged Napali Coast. I would have loved to hike that trail across knife-edge ridges and lush valleys, as I did thirty years earlier, but I didn't want to leave Trish alone for another morning. It turned out the trail was closed anyway, still being repaired from storm damage.

"What do you think?" I asked, leaning back from the table.

"I love the tropics and I love exploring. It looks great. I just don't want you to have to load and unload the scooter too often."

"We'll see a lot from the car. A few stops will be OK."

Once we finished breakfast, it took Trish nearly another hour to wash up, dress, and gather what she wanted to bring along for the rest of the day. She just needed me to pull up the tight compression socks that help the circulation in her feet. I packed a shoulder bag with her sundries, along with the map, caps, sun block, an umbrella, and snack food.

Trish headed for the door, making a sharp left turn out of the condo's narrow interior hallway. The building maintenance crew had been kind enough to fabricate a small wooden ramp to help her get past the too-high doorway threshold, but it was still a tricky maneuver making a sharp turn entering and exiting, requiring me to hold the scooter seat from the rear with both hands to keep it from tipping.

"Go ahead," I told her, "I've got you."

"Don't strain yourself, I can take it slowly."

I had parked the rental car in one of the handicapped spaces near the building entrance, providing Trish with ample room in the adjoining striped area to pull up to the passenger side. Walking ahead of her, I opened the passenger door, placed our bag behind her seat, and swung up the rear hatch. I removed a red-handled brace from the door pocket and inserted it into the lock latch, so Trish would have something to hold on to getting into the car. Once she had positioned the scooter close to the car and stood up, I stepped between her and the open door, held her at the waist, and helped her turn to fall into the seat. The high lip at the base of the door opening made it difficult for Trish to lift her legs into the car, so I knelt in front of her and raised each foot up and in while she straightened in the seat.

I remembered an old friend commenting that I had become a man of infinite patience. He was right. I sometimes even surprised myself with that.

Then came the hardest part of going anywhere in a rental car—loading the scooter without the aid of a lift or ramp. After driving the scooter to the rear of the SUV, I lowered and locked the steering tiller, disengaged the transmission, and lifted the seat off its cylindrical base. My left hand grabbed the tiller at its base while my right hand locked onto a handle above the motor, behind the seat post and battery pack. My arms could just reach across that distance and still have enough leverage to lift the vehicle.

Awkwardly, like a weightlifter raising a bar that has much more weight on one end than the other, I sucked in a breath, tensed my abs, and jerked the scooter off the ground up to the level of the SUV's deck. In a much-practiced move, I swung the heavy rear end into the back of the car, rolled it in as far as it would go, turned the front end in, and dropped it into position. Next, I reengaged the transmission to keep the scooter from rolling around. Finally, I lifted the seat from the ground, placed it against the scooter, and closed the hatch. After that, I could exhale and forget about how many more times I might need to perform that maneuver over the course of our stay.

Traffic along two-lane, coastal Kuhio Highway was light, lighter than I expected, once we cleared downtown Kapa'a. After twenty minutes of driving through lush tropical shrubbery and crossing half a dozen streams, we reached the turnoff toward Kilauea Point lighthouse. The road ended two miles up at a cul-de-sac with a view of the ocean. From the car, looking over a corrugated metal barrier, we saw the lighthouse. Its white structure balanced on a point extending from the shore, like a bite of bread at the end of a knife blade. Other visitors clustered at the barrier to get a better view.

"That's great," Trish said. "I can see it well enough from here. You don't need to get the scooter out." I closed my eyes momentarily, feeling relief and appreciation. I stepped out of the car and strolled over to the barrier to snap a few photos of the lighthouse and the coast.

Back in the car, I wanted to find Kauapea Beach, known to locals as Secret Beach. Following my usually good directional instincts, I made the first right turn on the way back to the highway. That took us past a row of lushly landscaped estates and down to the shore. But we gave up the search and turned around when the road narrowed and became heavily potholed.

On the way back, as we approached the Kilauea Point wildlife refuge, Trish suddenly gestured to her right and yelled, "Nene!"

Alongside the road strode several Hawaiian geese, or nene, their distinctive black-and-white striped feathers ruffling in the coastal breeze. Escapees from the refuge, I guessed.

"Remember when we saw them on the Big Island!" Trish exclaimed. She grabbed our camera from the console and snapped several shots as the geese stopped and seemed to pose.

We continued another five miles on Kuhio Highway, passing among towering plane trees and prehistoric-looking ferns in Kahiliwai Valley. The smell of damp vegetation filled the air in the shaded gullies. We soon arrived at the Hanalei Valley lookout. I pulled into a dirt parking area from where we could survey taro fields, ponds, and small farm houses in one of the last of the old agricultural areas on the island, the way much of it looked before the era of industrial-scale pineapple cultivation and tourist-serving development.

"Beautiful," Trish sighed. "What a great view! I don't need to get out." I felt relieved, but wondered if she just said that for my sake. In any case, the day was going well.

Back on the road, after several hairpin turns, Hanalei Bay came into sight, framed by sharp ridgelines that had allowed it to stand in for mythical Bali Hai in the film *South Pacific*. In the foreground stood the town of Hanalei, featuring art galleries, restaurants, one of Hawaii's most picturesque beaches, and a few hundred residents. A sign warned us of a road closure ahead.

"Keep going," Trish told me. "Let's see how far we can go."

Three miles past Hanalei, soon after getting our turn to cross the single-lane bridge over the Wainiha River, we encountered a long line of cars waiting to be convoyed through the last stretch of road. Sensing this could take a long time, we turned back to town.

"Let's go down to the bay," Trish said. "I want to see some big waves."

Happy to oblige, I turned off the highway at the edge of town and drove a few blocks north to Wai'oli Beach Park, fronting on the bay. Our parking karma was good enough to get us a scarce space in the dirt lot, but one with barely enough room for Trish to get out and mount her scooter. Now, I had to undertake the scooter lifting exercise in reverse. After disengaging the transmission, I raised the rear of the scooter enough to slide it toward me and roll it back. I lifted it again by the tiller and the rear handle, pulled it off the deck, and lowered it precariously, letting it drop the last few inches to the ground. Removing the scooter from the car is always more difficult than putting it in, as gravity seems to fight me twice as hard. My left hip and SI joint let me know they were unhappy with that movement. I would be seeing my chiropractor soon after returning home. And to keep doing this I would have to maintain my routine of ab exercise in the gym.

I rode the scooter up to the passenger door, again inserted the red handle into the lock latch, and swung Trish's legs out of the car. We were parked on a slight slope that dropped off to the right, so I had to squat more than usual to place my hands under her arms and get enough leverage for my legs to lift her up and out of the car. Earlier rain had left the ground slippery, and I struggled to keep my balance as I lifted and then turned her onto the scooter seat.

We went off to explore the beach. I walked beside Trish, with my arm draped over her shoulders. A grassy lawn led past picnic tables and restrooms down to the sand. Breakers rolled in from a storm to the north, creating a salty mist. At the east end of the bay, surfers took advantage of the winter conditions, though the waves weren't approaching the twenty-footers predicted on the previous night's weather report. Just as I took a photo of Trish with the bay behind her, the rain returned with a vengeance. We dashed under the spreading cover of a fifty-foot ironwood pine tree and chatted with some locals until the downpour abated.

Trish wanted lunch, so we drove a few blocks into the center of Hanalei and found a parking space alongside the Tahiti Nui restaurant and bar. My back and shoulders tensed more than usual, having had too short a rest since last loading the scooter and now needing it unload it again.

We made our way into the crowded restaurant. A friendly bartender found us a table that Trish could reach with her scooter. Looking around at the Polynesian décor of banana bark matting and bamboo furniture, I remembered attending a luau here thirty years earlier.

As we got back into the car after lunch, Trish gave a sigh of fatigue and said, "I've had enough adventure for one day." I didn't object, so we started a leisurely drive back to Kapa'a.

On arriving at the condo, I looked forward to sitting on the patio and enjoying a mai tai or two. We had dinner reservations that evening at Merriman's Fish House in Koloa. I looked forward to that too, as I recalled an exceptional dinner at their restaurant on the Big Island two years earlier. Right now, though, I needed to help Trish out of the car and unload the scooter. By the time I finished that, the carpal tunnel pain in my wrists felt like the stabbing of an ice pick. I would have to be very careful the rest of the day and take some Ibuprofen.

The drinks and medication helped a lot. By the time we rested a while and then dressed for the evening, my aches and pains had subsided.

"How do I look?" Trish asked. She wore a black silk dress with a pattern of red and white hibiscus flowers, purchased on a previous Hawaii trip. A necklace of pink coral beads stood out from the dark background of her dress.

"You look great," I said, scanning her up and down appreciatively. "As pretty as on our first date."

I dressed more conservatively, in a Hawaiian silk shirt of black Polynesian block print patterns on a white background and my usual grey slacks. Focused on the evening ahead, I winced only slightly in loading the scooter into the SUV again.

Rush hour traffic had subsided, and we enjoyed a smooth drive south along the coast to sprawling Lihu'e.

"We'll be coming this way again tomorrow," I told Trish. "If you liked what we saw today on the north shore, wait 'til you see where we're going next."

We planned to drive around the south side of the island the next day, first to see the twin Wailua waterfalls near Lihu'e and then on to Waimea Canyon, a half-mile-deep, twenty-mile-long crack known as the Grand Canyon of the Pacific. I had visited there many years earlier and had two vivid recollections—Waipo'o Falls dropping eight hundred feet down a reddish volcanic cliff face on the opposite canyon wall, and the coastal view north across the jagged, green ridgelines of the Napali Coast.

From Lihu'e, we drove inland for a few miles, and finally south on a local road into Koloa. Merriman's sat atop a row of shops in Koloa's upscale Kukui'ula Village shopping center. Our parking karma held again, as we found a blue space at the start of the walkway leading to the restaurant.

We had to forego the restaurant's wide entry stairway in favor of an elevator. The restaurant interior evoked an old Hawaiian plantation house, with white woodwork, a steeply pitched roof, and openings at window level all around the sides. We asked for a table by a window, to enjoy the indoor/outdoor ambience of the place.

As usual in restaurants, Trish preferred to transfer from her scooter to a chair with armrests. She needed my help in standing up and then dropping into the chair. I smoothed the back of her hair, then sat down opposite her.

We ordered a round of mai tais made with fresh fruit juices and Hawaiian rums, and scrutinized the menu of local seafood and produce. We shared a plate of local fish ceviche, then sampled each other's wok-charred ahi and macadamia nut-crusted kampachi. Between bites, we talked about the day, our plans for the rest of the week, and how lucky we were to be able to enjoy a trip like this. At one point, I reached for Trish's hands, lifted them and kissed them. That drew a huge smile. I hardly paid attention to the surrounding diners, except to notice a couple smiling and hugging in a booth behind Trish.

We took our time finishing our dinner as the restaurant emptied. After clearing our dishes, the waiter approached us with a curious grin.

"I have a surprise for you," he told us. "Another table would like to buy you dessert."

With that, he placed a handwritten note on the table between me and Trish. Below a row of hand-drawn hearts, it read:

*To the lovely couple by the windows:*
*As newlyweds it's so nice to see another couple show us what true love is!*
*God bless.*
*XOXO*
*The couple in the booth.*
*M&M*

Trish and I looked at each other and both smiled, then leaned forward and kissed. Turning back to the waiter, I asked who had sent it. He pointed to the booth behind Trish, but the previous occupants, the romantic couple I noticed earlier, were gone. The waiter disappeared briefly, returning with a tray of tropical ice creams.

As we enjoyed our dessert, I thought about how, in the flow of routine daily events, good and bad, distracted by needing to overcome myriad obstacles, I too often forget about the love that underlies the extra efforts I make for Trish, even if I'm actually showing it. Especially when traveling, the back pains, the difficulties in handling the scooter, the need to help Trish stand and sit, all conspire to distract me from what I feel underneath. Sometimes, it takes an outside observer to notice and to remind me.

# Chapter 20
# A TRAIN, A PLANE, AND AN AUTOMOBILE

Trish and Cary at Multnomah Falls, Colombia River Gorge, Oregon

*Oregon, May 2019*
If Trish and I had let our initial concerns get in the way, we might never have taken our memorable train trip to Portland. We both had fond memories of traveling by train. For several years, before I moved from Los Angeles to join her in San Diego, we had what we called an Amtrak relationship, with one or the

other of us riding the Pacific Surfliner up and down the coast. We enjoyed two longer train rides together — 350 miles in Alaska from Anchorage to Fairbanks and a similar distance in Europe from Berlin to Vienna.

But, when we talked in early 2019 about taking another trip like that, maybe longer, Trish had one serious concern. "You know I love riding trains, but remember all the trouble we had getting on and off them in Europe?"

I remembered only too well. Station platforms were far below the rail car doors, requiring passengers to climb several steps up or down. We needed to make special arrangements in advance for a lift to bring Trish and her scooter up to door level, and even then, we had to scramble repeatedly because the pre-arrangements didn't reach the responsible people on time or at all.

"I thought about that. It hasn't been an issue so far on the trains we've ridden here. Amtrak says most of their trains have level entries, or they have ramps or lifts available. Yet, they still tell you to include that in a reservation. I know, it didn't work so well in Europe, so I guess there's still some risk."

We decided to take the risk and go. But to where?

"I'd like to ride a train all the way up the Pacific Coast," I offered. "I've driven it, but I haven't gone north by rail past Santa Barbara."

"We liked Seattle and Vancouver. Do you want to go back there?"

"No, I was thinking of going as far as Portland. I visited there for a conference thirty years ago and it seemed kind of dull then. But now I hear great things about it, in terms of food, culture, architecture, everything we like in a city. Plus, there's beautiful scenery outside the city. We could rent a car there, drive along the coast and into the mountains."

We brought up the Amtrak website on Trish's computer so we could see the route of the Coast Starlight train. Then I spread out a map of Oregon showing the attractions in and around Portland.

"It sounds good, with one caveat," Trish cautioned after surveying the timetable. "It's almost a thousand miles from here to Portland. That'll take a day and a half. I'm not riding the whole way sitting up, not even in a business-class car. I want to see what kind of sleeping accommodations they have."

Among the options Amtrak offered on that route, the accessible bedroom caught her eye. Within a space measuring about seven by nine feet, it contained two seats that converted to a bed, a drop-down bunk bed, and a sink and toilet behind a screening curtain. It cost nearly three times the fare for a pair of business class seats, but it included meals and provided a level of comfort and privacy that made it worthwhile. A private compartment less than half the size cost nearly as much as the accessible room.

"That's the one I want," Trish declared. "You get the upper bunk. The whole setup is a little cozy, but it'll do for one night."

Cozier than we realized from the inviting picture on the website. Despite our experience with less desirable features in older Surfliner rail cars, it didn't occur to us that the same might hold true on long-distance trains, that we could pick a class of service but not the particular type or age of car.

Searching on-line, Trish found a boutique hotel, the Monaco, in downtown Portland within walking distance of a lot of attractions that interested us. She called them, satisfied herself as to the features of their accessible rooms, and made a reservation. Their rates were so reasonable that she booked a mini-suite, just to have more space to move around on her scooter.

Two months later, as dawn broke across San Diego Bay, we boarded the Surfliner to Los Angeles at the neo-Spanish Santa Fe Depot downtown. As with the airlines, Amtrak allows disabled and elderly passengers to board early. While I rolled our two suitcases, Trish bounced across two sets of tracks and up to the business class car, where we grabbed a pair of seats on the lower level, facing one another across a table. We've found the small extra cost of business class on this route to be well worth it for the roomier seating, quieter ambience, and complimentary refreshments.

After helping Trish into her seat, I stowed our bags and parked the scooter in the wide space between our seats and the door. As the train pulled out of the station on time at 6 a.m., we felt both nervous and excited. We needed to connect with the Coast Starlight in Los Angeles, but then it should be smooth sailing, or rolling, all the way to Portland.

I got us coffee, pastries, and the morning newspaper from a counter at the front of the car. As many times as we had ridden that route, we still stared silently at the ocean as the train hugged the coast from Del Mar through Encinitas, Oceanside, and the rest of the beach cities, and on into Orange County. Early rising surfers rode perfect curls that reflected the morning sun, while flocks of brown pelicans glided above them. Halfway to LA, Trish needed to use the restroom. I retrieved the scooter for her, then held open the wide, sliding door as she rolled into the spacious interior.

After three hours and ten stops, the train arrived at Los Angeles' historic, high-ceilinged Union Station. We spent the one-hour layover in an upstairs lounge supplied with snacks and reading material. Shortly before our departure time, Amtrak personnel escorted us down to the train and into the sleeping car where we would find our accessible bedroom. At first glance, Trish looked shocked.

"Are you sure this is the right room?" she asked the sleeping car attendant. "It seems so much smaller than what we saw on the Amtrak website."

"It's your room alright," the smiling young woman assured her. "This is an older car. They're a little bigger on the newer trains."

With that, we moved in and settled down for the journey ahead. The attendant handed us dining car menus and offered to bring us our meals.

I wasn't comfortable leaving our suitcases on the luggage rack in the hallway twenty feet from our door, where anyone could have access to them. Instead, we sacrificed some of our valuable space, placing the bags against the rear wall of the room. Along with the scooter, that left little floor space to move around.

We sat in facing seats, with a fold-down table in between, much like the arrangement on the Surfliner. The window by our seats conveniently faced west, where we would have better views most of the way.

The car jolted as the train pulled out of Union Station. Now we could relax, read, sleep, and take in scenery until the following afternoon. The hum of the locomotive soon faded into the background, like audial wallpaper.

The early part of the ride, through sprawling older suburbs of Los Angeles' San Fernando Valley and sprawling newer suburbs of Ventura County, was familiar territory, a route I had traveled dozens of times on business. North of Ventura, the tracks returned to the coast. Waves crashed against stone rip-rap on one side, while steep bluffs rose a hundred feet on the other. During a pause in Santa Barbara, we noticed how similar the station looked to the ones in San Diego and Los Angeles, with its high ceiling beams, tile work, and archways, from the era of the early 1900s when long-distance train travel was regarded as stylish adventure.

I took a walk through the lounge and dining cars to check out their offerings and their accessibility. Narrow hallways, jostling cars, and lack of an elevator made it obvious we would need to take our meals in the room.

Five hours out of LA, just before reaching San Luis Obispo, the tracks turned inland to get around the Santa Lucia Range and the rugged Big Sur coast. Vast vineyards of the Paso Robles area soon filled our view. Then, on to the tomato, lettuce, and celery fields of the Salinas Valley—John Steinbeck country, often called America's Salad Bowl.

By this time, we felt a bit cramped for space in our temporary home. As long as we remained seated at the window, we were comfortable, but getting anything out of the suitcases or moving about the room required some gymnastics. Especially for Trish, who needed to get onto her scooter, roll six feet, then dismount, just to use the toilet.

A knock at the door announced the return of the car attendant, checking on our dinner plans. We told her we would need meals brought to us and gave her our order. To our pleasant surprise, she returned within a half hour with our entrees, salads, desserts, and drinks packed in separate containers, all at the right temperatures.

As we began to eat, Trish gave a complimentary nod and said, "This roast chicken is way better than I expected. It's actually quite good."

"So is my steak. And the vegetables are cooked perfectly. Remember when my friend, John Kelly, worked on the long Amtrak routes years ago? He always remarked on how good the food was. I guess it still is."

Mid-evening brought us into the San Francisco Bay area. The bright lights and tall buildings overwhelmed us after riding in rural countryside most of the day. Soon after, the attendant returned to help us make up our room for the night. The seats we had occupied since leaving LA folded together to form a single bed for Trish. A bunk slid down tracks from the wall above, and a ladder attached to the side wall allowed me to climb up there.

"Too bad about the bunk beds," Trish sighed. "It would be so much more romantic to curl up together here."

We soon fell asleep, lulled by the gentle swaying of the rail car and the clicking of wheels. When I awoke at 7 a.m. and pushed aside the upper-bunk curtains, I saw dense evergreen forests. I could almost smell the pines through the window.

As I climbed down, I called out, "Wake up, Trish. I think we're in Oregon." A stop soon after at Klamath Falls confirmed that.

By the time we dressed and returned the beds to their original configurations, the attendant came by to take our breakfast order. The omelet and French toast tasted as good as the previous evening's dinner. We sipped cappuccinos and watched the scenery turn more and more mountainous. Between there and the college town of Eugene, the train climbed a 6,000-foot pass through the Cascades. Sunshine reflected off alpine lakes and filtered down through virgin forests. As we climbed up to the pass, a pair of deer peered at us from fifty feet away.

"This is as unspoiled as what we passed through on the train in Alaska," I said. The scenery overcame any lingering discomfort with the accommodations.

Once out of the mountains, we headed straight north. The rest of our route paralleled Interstate 5, the same highway the Surfliner briefly followed out of San Diego the previous morning. Other than a stop in the state capital of Salem, we spent the remaining hours whizzing past farms and small towns. When we tired of looking out the window, we ordered a nice lunch of Caesar salad and turkey grilled cheese sandwiches.

A half hour out of Portland, the attendant alerted us over the intercom that passengers getting off there should begin preparing, as the train would pause for just fifteen minutes before continuing on to Seattle. Once the train pulled into Union Station, we needed every minute of that for Trish to get on her scooter and make her way down the hall and out onto the platform, while I followed with our suitcases. It surprised us to see no other rail traffic in the cavernous station.

Outside, a sunny afternoon welcomed us to Portland. We found an SUV cab in short order, loaded the scooter and bags, and headed for the Hotel Monaco. The hotel turned out to be a good choice, and not just because of the spacious accessible room. Management put on lively events for guests in the lounge off the lobby, from tasting Willamette Valley wines to musical performances and sampling of baked goods from locally famous Voodoo Donuts.

A multitude of restaurant choices lay within blocks of the hotel. Our first evening, we followed the recommendation of the concierge and had a splendid dinner of northwestern seafood — clam chowder, crab cakes, and grilled salmon — at Jake's Famous Crawfish, a century-old establishment whose wood-paneled walls and white-coated servers reminded me of favorite restaurants in New Orleans and San Francisco.

The downtown area proved as walkable as we had hoped, with an efficient transit system, as well. Our first morning there, we rode a trolley from flower-filled Pioneer-Courthouse Square to the weekly market by the Willamette River. I led Trish in threading our way among local crafts merchants, fragrant food booths, and street entertainers, all of a higher quality than we typically found at street fairs or farmers' markets at home.

We followed a wide, inviting promenade along the river. From there, we meandered through the Pearl District, admiring restored previous-century buildings and unique street art, like a series of ten-foot-tall, vase-like structures, each painted in a different wild design. For an older neighborhood, sidewalks were in remarkably good condition, allowing Trish a comfortable ride.

"I love these historic districts," Trish said after a few blocks. "This one kind of reminds me of Galveston, but I'm happy the streets and sidewalks aren't as bumpy."

After eating sandwiches and sampling beers at the Deschutes Brewery, we stopped at Powell's City of Books, billed as the world's largest independent bookstore, with over four million volumes spread out over an entire city block. I surveyed shelves of books by and about immigrants, and purchased a couple that related to a writing project of my own.

By good fortune, we happened to be in Portland at the time of the annual Starlight Parade, an evening event downtown that combined the best elements of the traditional Rose Parade and the more whimsical Doo-Dah Parade in Pasadena, California. Parade viewers graciously allowed Trish to pull her scooter up to the front of the crowd. From there, she got a clear view of a pink streetcar promoting breast cancer awareness, a marching band decked out in tie-dyed shirts and strands of lights, a Native American group in fancy traditional attire, floats carrying witches and a polka band, and dozens more paraders.

We picked up a rental car the next morning. Hertz didn't have the mini-SUV we had requested, so they offered us a larger one at the same price. I accepted reluctantly. Without a lift like the one in my Explorer at home, this would require me to manually raise the scooter higher to get it in and out of the rear of the vehicle, putting a strain on my back.

We spent that last day in Portland exploring some of the city's many parks. From a viewpoint along a well-compacted dirt trail in hilly, wooded Mount Tabor Park east of downtown, we got a spectacular view of snow-capped Mount Hood, our next destination. It looked so close we could almost reach out and touch it. We drove through Forest Park, eight square miles of woods, gardens, and trails northwest of downtown, but most of its terrain looked too steep for the scooter. In adjacent Washington Park, we were fortunate to find a handicapped parking space close to the International Rose Test Garden, where accessible pathways allowed us to wander among thousands of rose bushes whose blooms flooded our senses with every imaginable floral color and scent.

The next morning, we were off to Mount Hood, the 11,000-foot volcanic peak that dominates the Cascade Range. We had reservations to spend the night at Timberline Lodge, a historic landmark built high on the mountain by the Works Progress Administration and the US Forest Service during the Great Depression. It provided the backdrop for scenes in the film *The Shining*.

We drove a scenic highway through the mile-wide Columbia River Gorge, lined with granite cliffs and evergreen-covered slopes. Wind created whitecaps in the river and whipped spray at us, while the dense forests scented the air. Twenty miles from Portland, we exited Interstate 84 and drove up a winding road to Crown Point, a state park offering a panoramic view of the gorge from a parapet outside a domed stone building seven hundred feet above the river. After returning to the interstate, we next stopped to view Multnomah Falls, a 500-foot, two-level cascade reminiscent of Yosemite Falls and the tallest of many cataracts along tributaries of the Columbia. Trish's scooter made it up the smooth, paved walkway to a viewpoint near the base of the falls, but it couldn't continue on the stepped trail to a bridge higher up and closer to the tumbling water.

At Bonneville Dam, the massive system of navigational locks and hydroelectric facilities that spans the river forty miles east of Portland, we toured the historical museum. Trish took my picture standing in front of a ten-foot-high propeller that once served the hydro generators. We then followed a paved pathway of switchbacks alongside fish ladders where salmon the size of dogs leapt upward toward their spawning grounds while younger ones headed down toward the ocean.

"I'm glad to see so many of them," Trish said with a laugh. "They're my favorite food, you know."

At the town of Hood River, we turned south into the mountains, climbing on a well-maintained highway I could imagine crowded at other times of year with winter skiers or summer tourists. Halfway up, the peak of Mount Hood came into view. Soon after we reached the snowline, a narrower Forest Service road led up to the lodge. Its steep, turreted roof and heavy stone base made for a dramatic picture against the snowy peak towering over it.

We found handicapped parking spaces near the main entrance but, with no way to negotiate the wide stone steps, had to use a side entrance leading to an elevator up to the main lobby level. The lodge was a labyrinth of hallways, stairways, lobbies, and elevators. Its landmark status limited the Forest Service in making structural modifications. As a result, we found the building overall to be less accessible than one might wish, but a little persistence helped us find accessible, if circuitous, routes.

The desk clerk gave us a spacious, wood-paneled, accessible room one level down with a fireplace and a view of the peak. Getting from there to the hotel lounge required taking an elevator back to the lobby, transiting that space, and then taking a second elevator up another level. Later, we were happy to find a ramp provided access to the dining room, where we enjoyed a dinner of wild game and locally grown vegetables while gazing out at dusk falling over the mountain scenery.

"This place so much reminds me of the Ahwahnee in Yosemite," Trish mused as we lingered over pancakes and coffee in the dining room the next morning before checking out. "I love all these old lodges. Too bad we're not staying another night."

"Yes. I had no idea it would be this spectacular. We should come back."

We drove a different route back down, following a scenic path through Mt. Hood National Forest, past the eastern suburbs of Portland, and then on toward the coast. Midway through the vineyards, farms, and dairies of the North Willamette Valley, we began to feel and smell cool coastal air.

At the ocean, we stopped overnight in Pacific City. The Inn at Cape Kawanda faced a dune-lined beach where fishermen pulled dories up at dusk. Offshore, a haystack-shaped rock at least a hundred feet high dominated the view, especially silhouetted in the sunset.

Our winding drive north up the coast the next day took us through Tillamook, famous for its cheeses. The drive also presented unusual views of more of those haystack-shaped rock formations, volcanic monoliths that dot this section of coastline. The largest one, actually named Haystack Rock, rises to a height of two hundred fifty feet offshore at Cannon Beach.

We paused there for a lunch of clam chowder and grilled fish at the Driftwood Inn. Staff there were exceptionally helpful, providing us with an easy-to-reach table and guiding Trish to their hard-to-find restroom. Another scenic highway, traversing deep-green Tillamook State Forest, took us back to Portland in time to catch a return flight to San Diego.

As we winged our way south, I looked out the plane window at the mountains, coastline, and cities — much the same terrain we had travelled on our way up the previous week. The flight would take about five hours, including a plane change in San Francisco, compared with the thirty-four hours we spent riding trains.

"What do you think?" I asked Trish. "Was the train ride worth it? Would you take another long rail trip, rather than flying or driving?"

"I loved being on the train. There's something romantic about traveling that way. I wish it had been a little roomier but, sure, I'd do it again. Maybe just a little shorter ride."

"OK. I'll start thinking about other destinations, ones a little closer to home."

I pulled out an Amtrak brochure I had picked up in LA and began perusing routes.

"How about taking the Texas Eagle to Tucson? Or the Southwest Chief to Flagstaff, to visit the Grand Canyon again?"

Trish looked up from her book, gave me a big smile, and replied, "The Grand Canyon. Now that would be worth a train ride. When do you want to go?"

# Chapter 21
## DO YOU SPEAK ENGLISH?

Trish and Cary at Newgrange, Ireland

*Dublin, September 2019*

After years of trying, I got Trish interested in traveling to Ireland. Strange that it took so long, as her ancestry is three-fourths Irish. With auburn hair, a pale complexion, and scattered freckles, she fits one stereotype of Irish appearance. Enough so that an immigration agent at Shannon Airport, seeing her American passport, once asked why a nice Irish girl like her would have moved to America.

Actually, most of her ancestors—Butlers, Farrells, and O'Donnells—emigrated from Ireland to the United States and Canada during the famines of the 1800s. As a child, she lived in a heavily Irish neighborhood in Detroit before her father's work brought the family to California. While growing up, she attended Catholic parochial schools taught mostly by Irish priests and nuns. Yet, for years, as we planned dozens of other trips, she showed little interest in visiting the Emerald Isle.

"This is your heritage," I told her. "I know you enjoyed your brief visit there during your junior year abroad. And the country has really modernized since then. I bet the accessibility is pretty good."

After two trips to the places of my family origins in Eastern Europe, Trish began to show interest in exploring her own roots, but remained evasive about returning to Ireland. What underlay this reluctance dawned on me as I observed Trish's interaction with her parents. Her mother reveled in the family's Irish heritage but spoke bitterly about the starvation and oppression that forced so many Irish to emigrate, and about the poverty families like hers endured in a new country. Trish's father, half Irish and half German by ancestry, expressed even greater pride in his Irish roots but showed no interest in the circumstances of his family's immigration to the United States. Whatever happened to either side of the family back in Ireland was virtually off-limits as a topic of exploration or discussion during Trish's years of growing up in that household, and afterward as well.

A couple of years after both her parents died, I tried again. As we discussed possible travel destinations for the fall of 2019, I challenged her.

"I would really like to see Ireland. I've seen most of the rest of Europe, but haven't been there. It's full of interesting history and culture, and I understand the food has gotten pretty good. Plus, hanging around with you and your family, I feel like I've become part Irish myself."

After considering this for a few moments, she surprised me. Smiling and nodding, she declared, "Fine, let's do it!" It was as if I had given her permission for something she secretly wanted to do all along but had kept bottled up.

As we performed research and scanned maps, Trish's enthusiasm grew. She became even more enthusiastic as we found lots of references to places being accessible. We decided to first spend several days in and around Dublin in the northeast part of the country, then drive to the west coast and visit the areas around Galway and Killarney.

"On my first visit, I spent too much time in pubs and didn't explore much," she confessed. "This time, I want to check out more of the culture and the history. I have a friend, Sinead, an Irish woman I know through work. We can get suggestions from her."

As we went on with our trip planning, it fascinated me to learn how widely people there still speak traditional Irish rather than English, especially in the more rural western counties. Also, how prominently memorials to the centuries-long struggle for independence from English rule show up, particularly in travel guides to Dublin.

Our overnight flight from San Diego to Dublin followed an unusual route, with a plane change in Chicago. On arriving in the Irish capital, we picked up our rental car, a crimson hatchback Kia Sportage, and headed into the city. My first shock came from remembering I would be driving on the left side of the road, something I had done with considerable trepidation on a couple of Caribbean islands. The second shock was the realization that we should have requested a vehicle with GPS. The route we took from the airport into the city center involved driving several miles on a heavily traveled boulevard that changed names frequently and offered little signage for orientation.

Concerned I had overshot, and knowing we needed to get on the south side of the River Liffey, I took a left turn on Church Street, which became Bridge Street, then High Street, and finally

Bridge Street again. When we passed St. Patrick's Cathedral, I knew we were close to our hotel, but one-way streets and streets that intersected at odd angles left me uncertain how to proceed. It reminded me of Prague, where our GPS quit working and we became so confused by the street layout that our hotel sent someone to guide us in.

With perseverance, we found the Brooks Hotel on narrow Drury Street. It lay within walking distance of virtually every place we planned to visit in Dublin and had a car park across the street. Passing beneath the hotel's marquee, through the eight-foot-high glass doors, and into the tan-wood-paneled lobby, we felt comfortable and relieved, at last. We had reserved a deluxe accessible room in the boutique hotel to make sure Trish would have ample space to maneuver her scooter.

We paused just long enough to unpack. Then, famished from our lengthy journey, we returned to the lobby and marched straight through the wide entry of Francesca's restaurant. Seated at a window table, we watched a steady stream of pedestrians of all ages out for the evening. We had to begin with drinks of Irish whiskey — regional brands like Dingle and Connemara that turned out to be smoother than any we tasted at home. Turning to dinner, we shared plates of Irish venison and a flatfish known as plaice that reminded me of flounder.

"I want to see the Book of Kells today," Trish announced on waking up the following morning.

From the moment she agreed to visit Dublin, Trish fixated on seeing that illuminated manuscript of the New Testament Gospels created by 9th-century monks, now considered one of Ireland's cultural treasures and kept in a temperature-controlled glass case in the Trinity College library. To prepare for our first-day excursion, we fortified ourselves with a traditional full Irish breakfast of fried eggs, bacon, pork sausages, fried tomato, mushrooms, black and white puddings, bread, and coffee.

Through a maze of narrow streets, we first made our way to St. Stephen's Green, Dublin's largest public garden. Most street corners had wheelchair ramps, but the heavy pedestrian traffic created something of an obstacle course for Trish.

I noticed that street and location signs here in the middle of town commonly bore names in both English and Irish. For instance, Harcourt Street and Sráid Fhearchair, or St. Stephen's Green and Faiche Stiabhna.

We took our time wandering shaded paths lined with flowers, lingered by a fountain spraying in a dozen directions at the center of a forty-foot-wide pool, and crossed a footbridge over a lake providing home to scores of brown ducks. All of it was scooter-friendly pavement or packed earth. Amid all this nature, several monuments and exhibits paid tribute to the Irish fighters in the celebrated 1916 rebellion known as the Easter Rising, in which armed Irish nationalists declared an independent republic and battled British troops for a week, with heavy casualties on both sides.

Across from the park's northwest corner, we noticed Butler's Chocolate Café. Trish couldn't resist. We sampled the chocolate candies and departed with two cups of intensely flavored hot cocoa.

Grafton Street, a smooth, five-block-long pedestrian mall comprising Dublin's main shopping district, took us directly to Trinity College. We found the library in one of the original buildings, dating back to the late 1500s. But reaching the Book of Kells in its dimly lit upstairs chamber appeared to require mounting stairs. Trish's initial anguish turned to smiles when a timely docent led us to an elevator behind a rope barrier. Once in the exhibit room, Trish rose from her scooter to get a good look at the book, opened to pages that showed the exquisite craftsmanship of multi-colored graphics, medieval Latin lettering, and liberal use of gold leaf. Library staff turn a page each day to reveal different contents.

I held Trish steady from behind so she could stand without needing to lean on the display case. After sitting back down on the scooter, she turned to me and said, "Amazing. I can imagine those monks toiling away in their cloisters, spending days on each page."

"You got that right," I replied. "Remember that book I got you for your birthday, *How the Irish Saved Civilization*, about monks in Irish abbeys keeping learning alive during the Dark Ages in Europe? This is the kind of thing it was talking about."

We followed a tour group into the Long Room, the original book stacks of the library, where the 200,000 oldest volumes in the collection now reside on shelves two stories high, flanked by rows of white marble busts of famous philosophers and writers, beneath an arched, dark wood ceiling. Midway down the central aisle, we paused at another Irish national treasure, a wood harp reputed to have belonged to 11$^{th}$-century King Brian Boru, the ruler credited with unifying Ireland and freeing it of Viking domination.

Though revered as Ireland's most illustrious educational institution, the college manages not to take itself too seriously. A blue banner hanging from a lamppost outside the library read "Trinity Arts & Humanities — generating dangerous ideas since 1592."

We continued on to the other destination Trish had expressed the most interest in visiting—the Irish Emigration Museum, on the opposite bank of the river. The museum admitted disabled visitors at no charge.

We made our way through a succession of rooms filled with films, photographs, dioramas, and other displays, providing a dazzling history of the famines, wars, and social upheavals that sent millions of Irish abroad. Most went to North America, but substantial numbers wound up in Australia and other parts of the world. Far from being entirely tragic, the stories on display also celebrated the cultural, athletic, political, and economic contributions these emigrants made to the lands where they settled. The museum regularly wins honors as being among the most visited tourist sites in Europe.

Trish lingered at exhibit after exhibit, as if reluctant to break away from the connection it provided to her own family's history. When she occasionally spotted a reference to someone with one of her family names, she called me over to share her glee.

As we left the museum, we spotted the replica sailing ship *Jeanie Johnston* moored at a dock nearby. Known as a famine ship, the original transported thousands of emigrants across the Atlantic to North America in the mid-1800s. During that saddest episode of Irish history known as the Great Famine, a million Irish died of starvation and disease, while a million more left the country. It made for a sobering finish to our museum visit.

A few blocks away, on broad, tree-lined O'Connell Street, we came to the General Post Office, stronghold of insurrectionists in the 1916 Easter Rising and the place where they declared a free Irish republic. Bullet marks in the Ionic columns remain as vivid reminders of the Irish independence struggle. Trish teared up at seeing this place, one of the few legendary sites she recalled hearing about in her childhood.

We planned to have dinner at the Winding Stair, a restaurant overlooking the river, recommended by a friend who had visited Dublin recently. After making our way up crowded Great George's Street and through the entertainment district known as Temple Bar, we arrived at the restaurant, only to find it situated on the second floor of a building with no elevator. Just the winding staircase from which it took its name.

"We managed to avoid roadblocks like this all day," Trish said, tightening her lips and shaking her head. "I suppose it was expecting too much for our good luck to continue the whole trip."

Thankfully, a cozy restaurant at street level just around the corner, serving excellent contemporary Irish cuisine, accommodated us. After dinner, we stood by the river and viewed the Ha'Penny Bridge, its 200-year-old, cast iron structure brightly lit and reflected in the water below. But stone steps at both ends kept us from crossing. Retracing our earlier path, we returned to the hotel and resumed sampling Irish whiskeys from the glass display case in the Jasmine Bar.

The next day, we explored in the opposite direction. The Dublin Castle, which for centuries had been the seat of English occupation government, sounded intriguing. We crossed a bridge over a dry moat and entered a central courtyard at least an acre in size. A collage of structures surrounded it, from a 13th-century castle turret to more recent construction holding offices, residences, and ceremonial spaces. We found the architecture interesting, but passed on touring the interior.

Instead, we continued on a few more blocks to the remnants of the original city walls—stacked stones that once repelled incursions by native clans from the countryside. Hungry now, we crossed the street to the Brazen Head Inn, Dublin's oldest tavern, dating from the 12th century. We entered the brick structure through a passageway into a stone-paved courtyard. Despite the establishment's age, we found the courtyard and interior wheelchair-accessible. At an ancient wooden table in a crowded room lined with historical memorability, we lunched on Irish stew, fish and chips, and pints of Guinness. The beer tasted smoother and richer than the bottled version we got at home, but then the brewery producing this draft sat just blocks away.

The route back to the hotel took us past St. Patrick's Cathedral, the grey stone structure built on the site of a well where Ireland's most important saint conducted baptisms in the mid-5th century. Though we both had toured innumerable European cathedrals, and had bypassed several other large churches on our walks here, this one demanded a visit. At first, steps at the entry blocked us, but a security guard escorted us to an unmarked gate, down a pathway past a cemetery filled with Celtic crosses, and through a side door level with the interior. We roamed about, taking in the basilica's awesome features: the multi-vaulted, hundred-foot-high ceiling supported by a series of limestone arches; highly detailed stained-glass windows rising to a series of peaks behind a stone altar in the shape of a miniature church; stone floors of ever-changing, colorful mosaics, giving way in some areas to ancient, well-worn brown tiles; and scores of crypts of Irish notables, including that of author Jonathan Swift, who once served as dean of this cathedral.

Trish paused at a table against the rear wall to light a votive candle and place a donation in a wood box. As we moved on, a twenty-something priest approached us.

"I saw you light a candle," he said in a strong Irish accent. "I assume you're Catholic. Can I answer any questions for you?"

"I'd call myself a lapsed Catholic, and my husband here isn't Catholic at all," Trish replied. "But we're interested in the history of this place."

The priest frowned for a moment, but then gave us an enthusiastic recounting of the cathedral's construction dating from the year 1220, its temporary conversion to an Anglican Church during the English Reformation of the early 1500s, and its reconstruction in the mid-1500s and 1800s. We thanked him and moved toward the exit. On the way out, we placed a donation in a box beneath a sign requesting support for continued restoration of the cathedral.

That evening, we explored the Temple Bar neighborhood, filled with pubs and restaurants. We began at a raucous establishment bearing the same name as the neighborhood. With a crimson, wood exterior, two upper stories decked out with strands of pale blue lights, and a vertical neon sign announcing its name, it stood out from its neighbors.

When Trish had difficulty getting inside on her scooter, the pub's greeter opened a wider door to give her an easier passage. Turning to me, he began to explain how we should arrange for that door to be opened again when we were ready to leave, but caught himself in mid-sentence.

"I'm sorry," he blurted out. "Do you speak English?"

"Yes, all the time."

"Oh, good. I don't speak Irish."

Trish caught my eye and covered her mouth to stifle a laugh. Once inside, she exclaimed, "I can't believe that guy thought you're Irish, and traditional Irish, no less! You don't look the least bit Irish!"

"Well, you do, and I'm with you. Plus, I'm wearing a green shirt." Still, with my solidly Eastern European Jewish ancestry, it did seem peculiar. Ireland has a small Jewish population, two of whom were even elected mayors of Dublin, but I doubt many speak Irish.

The greeter called over one of his colleagues to help us navigate the thick and rowdy crowd. He parted a way for us through the crowded bar, past a traditional Irish band in mid-performance, and into a dining area where he made space for us at a packed table. Over the music ricocheting in from the next room, we struck up conversations with our table mates, twenty-something locals. Meanwhile, a server took our orders and promptly delivered pints of Guinness and a platter of house-made charcuterie. An hour later, we bid our new friends goodbye, worked our way back through the crowd, and moved on to several other equally hospitable but quieter pubs.

Seated at the next pub, I took a long sip from my pint of Smithwick's, then said to Trish, "Those people in the Temple Bar were so welcoming. It was like we were out drinking with old friends."

"Yes, it's like that here," she explained. "People spend a lot of time socializing in pubs, and they assume everyone is a friend. It was like that in the Irish neighborhood I grew up in too, and when I was here years ago. It'll be even more that way when we get out to the western counties."

After immersing ourselves in Dublin for a few days, we decided it was time to begin exploring the countryside. I looked forward to that, but anticipated the stress my wrist and lower back soon would feel from repeatedly lifting Trish's scooter in and out of the car.

Trish missed seeing the Wicklow Mountains, south of Dublin, in her previous visit. Now within a national park, the mountains rise a short distance from the coast. Although highly visible, finding a way in proved challenging. I suspected directional signage was a low priority in Ireland, and our later experiences in more rural areas confirmed that. We also learned how locally many people stayed. After driving miles up a road that seemed likely to lead into the park but coming to a dead end, we asked directions from a woman standing in her front yard, only to be told that she was not aware of any national park in the area. That experience, too, repeated itself numerous times. We learned later that many national park designations were just lines on a map, and that local residents were not necessarily informed of them.

The challenge of finding our way here and elsewhere was compounded by roads typically just wide enough for two small cars to slip past one another, and sometimes even narrower, with stone walls often inches away and roadside vegetation growing out well into the right-of-way. Little more than wagon tracks paved to accommodate motor vehicles. Driving on the left side of the road added another layer of complexity. The side of our car soon bore so many scratches and scrapes that I shuddered at the prospect of returning it to the rental company.

Despite all that, we got a visual reward when we found the high road that traversed the park from north to south, winding up in the village of Glendalough. For twenty miles of winding road, we viewed sweeping hillsides covered in red-brown heather and littered with granite boulders, pristine lakes below jagged cliffs, mountain tops rounded down by eons of wind and rain, and bursts of red and yellow flowers amid rock outcroppings. Puffy clouds hovered overhead, and the wind carried a barrage of fragrances. To the east, farms marked by windrows covered hillsides and filled occasional valleys. At one point, where the road leveled off, I got out to walk around. The low, dense vegetation, springy beneath my feet, reminded me of Alaskan tundra.

On the outskirts of Glendalough, we came across Lynham's of Laragh, a restaurant housed in a stone-and-stucco building with bright red geraniums hanging from upper-story windows. The entry and interior were free of steps. Seated in the dark-wood-paneled dining room, we fortified ourselves with a lunch of roast beef and beer. On the way out, I noticed a grey stone plaque commemorating "the men and women who gave their lives in the insurrection of 1798," an uprising inspired by the American and French revolutions.

The next day, we drove north to the Boyne Valley, a UNESCO World Heritage Site containing numerous Neolithic tombs and monuments. In particular, we wanted to see Newgrange, a circular hilltop tomb and cultural site constructed around 3,000 B.C., earlier than Stonehenge or even the Egyptian pyramids.

After ascending the hill on a paved path and viewing the wall of the 300-fote-wide structure, I turned to Trish and said, "Look how perfectly they placed these thousands of stones. And all without metal tools."

A passageway just wide enough for a single file to enter extended into the center of the structure, below a corbelled stone roof covered by a grassy mound rising to a height of forty feet. The opening and passageway had been oriented so that the sun shines directly into the interior at the winter solstice.

Steps at the opening and the narrowness of the passageway prevented Trish from entering. She explored the engraved stones on the surrounding grounds while I made my way inside with a guide and a dozen other visitors. In the dim light and dank smell of the interior, I could imagine us as members of the agrarian community that built this structure over many years and came here to worship. As we crowded into the rear of the structure, the guide turned on a light at the entrance that simulated the effect of the winter solstice. That drew gasps from several in the group.

The return to bright sunshine jolted me back to reality. Our guide pointed out nearby hilltops that bore similar structures or other cultural sites from the same Neolithic Period.

In the nearby town of Slane, we drove up the famed Hill of Slane, which Irish mythology holds to be the site where St. Patrick lit a bonfire on Easter in 433 to call the pagan people of the region to come and convert to Christianity. While the story may be only myth, standing there on the hilltop and looking out over the still lightly developed Boyne Valley, I found it easy to imagine such an event and such a time.

We made our way back to Dublin by a circuitous route, stopping at other sites in this culturally and anthropologically rich region. At Monasterboice, supposedly founded in the 5th century by a follower of St. Patrick, we roamed smooth paths through a cemetery and monastic ruin featuring one of Ireland's tallest round towers and a score of Celtic high stone crosses, all emblematic of Ireland's early history. Alone in the silent cemetery, amid miles of fields, I again experienced a sense of traveling back in time to when early Christians were spreading the faith or when 8th-century settlers battled Viking invaders for control of this region.

On our last evening in Dublin, we took a taxi to Chapter One, a gourmet restaurant located in the basement of the Dublin Writers Museum. Once again, an entry with stairs and no elevator foiled our plans. The apologetic proprietor offered to have his staff carry Trish and her scooter down the dozen steps, but we demurred. Instead, we accepted his suggestion to try L'Ecrivain, a comparable restaurant in a nearby neighborhood. While that establishment had an accessible entrance, a staircase led up to the dining room. But this proprietor had a workable solution. He set up a table for us in the first-floor bar area and assigned a server specially to wait on us. The staff's hospitality soon got us over any feeling of being isolated, as we feasted on prawns, Irish beef, duck breast and plum cake, accompanied by an excellent Irish pinot noir.

We wished we had allotted a couple more days to our stay in Dublin, but we had much more to see. As we drove westward from Dublin, Trish grew wistful over not being able to place her ancestry at particular locations.

"I wish I'd done more family research," she lamented while staring out the car windows at passing villages. "I'm pretty sure my ancestors came mainly from the northwestern part of the country We could be driving right near places some of them lived."

We did detour for a brief visit to Roscommon, a town Trish recalled one of her parents having mentioned. There we found a town square featuring an 18th-century stone building, once a church and now a bank; a museum incongruously bearing a Star of David on its upper front window; an Indian restaurant, several pubs; and the ruins of a castle built in the 12th century and largely destroyed by Cromwell forces 500 years later. Trish could only imagine generations of her ancestors living and working here or in nearby communities.

Over the next week, we walked the streets of Galway, drove narrow roads amid the mountains of Connemara, explored the rugged wilderness of the Burren region, viewed the soaring seaside Cliffs of Moher, and wandered the paths of Killarney National Park. As we drove along a rural road, surrounded by verdant meadows in all directions, I said to Trish, "No wonder this is called the Emerald Isle. I haven't seen so much bright green landscape anywhere else we've traveled."

On our return drive to Dublin, we stopped at the Rock of Cashel, a hilltop fortress that served as the stronghold of King Brian Boru. As I stood inside the shell of the walled enclave's domed cathedral, another visitor approached me.

"Pardon me, do you speak English?" he asked, in what sounded like an unaccented American voice.

"I do."

"Thank goodness. I was afraid you might only speak Irish. Do you know where there are restrooms up here?" Struggling to keep a straight face, I pointed him down the hill to where I had seen facilities by the parking lot.

When I later described this encounter to Trish, while driving on to Dublin, she roared with laughter. "We'll have to see about getting you honorary Irish citizenship," she said, shaking her head.

"Seriously, though, this has been great," she continued. "I'm so glad we took this trip. Even if I couldn't locate exact places connected to my family, I feel so much more in touch with my roots. I want to come back, after I've done a lot more family research."

I understood. Our trips to Eastern and Central Europe gave me the same kind of feeling of connection. Even more so, because I went with considerable information and experience relating to my family's background and places of origin.

This trip made an impact on me too, opening my eyes to a place and people I previously experienced only through their American reincarnation and allowing me to share that with Trish. Still, after all the natural, historical, and cultural wonders we experienced on this trip, the most indelible memory remains my repeatedly being mistaken for a native Irishman.

# Chapter 22
## TRAVEL IN THE TIME OF COVID

Trish on Stearns Wharf, Santa Barbara

*Santa Barbara, November 2021*
Health issues pose special concerns for disabled and elderly travelers. Those concerns take on even greater importance for people like Trish, whose MS condition compromises her immune system. Our trip to Santa Barbara during the COVID-19 pandemic brought that into sharp focus.

When the virus struck in early 2020, we had just begun planning a trip to the Florida Keys. I had wonderful memories of a previous visit and looked forward to more of the excellent scuba diving, eclectic seafood, and laid-back culture I experienced there. We also had been discussing another trip to Europe, this time perhaps driving around northern France and Germany.

Once the seriousness of the pandemic became apparent, we shelved all those plans indefinitely. Our concerns mirrored those of most potential travelers, only more so. New information and new cautions emerged constantly, often without clear direction. Even once we were fully vaccinated, what about passengers sitting close to us on airplanes, staff and guests at hotels and restaurants, and fellow divers aboard boats? Even if we wore masks in public, what about maskless people around us? When Florida emerged as a center of opposition to vaccination and mask mandates, we abandoned any immediate plans to go there. But the same concerns, if less so, applied to virtually anywhere we considered going, at least until conditions markedly improved.

While we took frequent walks around our neighborhood and along San Diego Bay, we didn't venture farther than our desert weekend home. During that time, Trish grew somewhat weaker, requiring more help from me in transferring and moving about. I wondered if, by the time the pandemic lifted enough, we still would be able to travel. Trish had the same concern.

"I'm glad we're being careful," she commented one evening as we reminisced about past travels, "but do you think we'll ever be able to take another one of our adventure trips? I feel like this has been a wake-up call. COVID makes it worse, but we're going to have to be more careful now whenever we travel."

"I know. I'd love to be in the Caribbean right now, or sitting in a sidewalk café in Paris. I'd even settle for a road trip here in California. We've just got to take all the right precautions, especially since Medicare won't cover us outside the country."

Relief came unexpectedly. We received a new wedding invitation from my long-time friend John Gilderbloom whose nuptials had been postponed twice due to COVID. He and I had worked together in California housing politics in the 1970s and 80s, and we had co-authored a couple of published articles.

The wedding originally was to take place in the San Francisco area. That would have meant flying up there, something we wouldn't have done once COVID struck. It was now set for Santa Barbara in November. We contacted the Mar Monte hotel, which would be the hub of wedding activity.

"I'm fine with this," Trish informed me afterward, even without my asking. "The hotel says they're observing COVID protocols, all the wedding events will be outdoors, and all the guests are supposed to be vaccinated."

We made hotel reservations, optimistic that the third time would be the charm. Then, as the November wedding date approached, COVID conditions in California subsided enough that we felt even more comfortable going.

We first thought to take the train from San Diego to Santa Barbara, a route we had last ridden on our way to Portland two years earlier. Then we hit our first obstacle. The wedding itself would take place in a hilltop park a considerable distance from the beachfront hotel. We could rent a car in Santa Barbara, but we wouldn't have the mechanical lift that raises Trish's scooter into the rear of my SUV or the ramp she rides into her van.

"Just as well," I told Trish. "I'd rather drive. The travel time should be shorter, and we won't have health concerns about other passengers. Plus, I'll be spared the stress on my back of lifting the scooter into a rental car."

I would drive. Trish could manage local driving in her van with its swiveling driver's seat and hand controls, but her level of comfort had declined over the years. If we traveled together, especially on longer drives, we both felt more secure with me at the wheel.

The decision to drive generated its own issues. We left home on a sunny Friday morning in the Toyota Sienna van, trying to time our departure to trail the northbound morning rush hour traffic while getting past Los Angeles before the start of weekend traffic. But we had barely made it halfway to LA on Interstate 5 when we heard a loud thumping from beneath the front of the car.

"Sounds like a tire," Trish said with a sigh.

Seeing a gas station sign ahead, I pulled off the freeway in Laguna Hills. Sure enough, tread on the right front tire had begun to peel away. The service station didn't have tires that fit our van and the tire shop to which they directed us was backed up.

During the two hours we waited for the tire to be replaced, freeway traffic thickened considerably. By the time we passed LA International Airport on Interstate 405, traffic was at a virtual standstill, forcing us to inch our way through the Cahuenga Pass over the Hollywood Hills and then up the Ventura Freeway. Traffic sped up from time to time, and we enjoyed the scenic parts of the drive, especially along the ocean north of Ventura. Still, the experience reminded us that trying to time Southern California traffic is as much a fool's errand as trying to time the stock market.

We exited US 101 at Cabrillo Boulevard in Santa Barbara around 5 p.m., three hours later than expected. I breathed a sigh of relief at pulling up to the Mar Monte minutes later and finding ample handicapped parking within steps of the main entrance. Once out of the car, we looked across the street at breakers rolling onto East Beach and the beginning of an orange-yellow sunset.

"I love the salty smell of the breeze off the ocean," Trish said. "We've got to take a walk along there tomorrow."

The hotel had been renovated recently. Their website promised "a seamless travel experience" for disabled guests. However, situated on an incline and with multiple levels, some parts of the century-old building were not accessible by elevator, only by stairs. Our accessible guest room, half a level up from the lobby and reachable by elevator, was more than adequate in size for Trish to roam about on her scooter. The bathroom too, but it suffered from the common feature in accessible rooms of having no shelving or counter around the sink.

After unpacking, we went in search of the pre-wedding party, but encountered our first on-site accessibility obstacle. Within the hotel, the poolside Café Lido could only be reached by stairs. Front desk staff apologized and explained that we would need to go out the front door, follow a sidewalk fifty yards along the busy adjacent street, and reenter through a pedestrian gate at the far end of the pool area.

As we made our way along the sidewalk, Trish commented, "I know it's an old building and they didn't make them accessible in those days. But it's still annoying that a basic amenity like the pool wasn't made accessible when they renovated this place."

That annoyance dissipated once we reached the party and reconnected with John, whom I hadn't seen in person since he left California twenty years earlier to teach at a university back east and whom Trish had only met once at a long-ago conference. I spotted him immediately, as his six-foot-four frame towered over most of the crowd. He introduced us to Carla, the lively, much-shorter, blond woman who had been his high school nemesis but now prepared to marry him decades later.

As we joined the eclectic gathering of family and friends, we saw that none were masked. This marked our first attendance at a social gathering since the advent of COVID, so we blanched initially. But, knowing all were fully vaccinated, we put aside some of the caution that had guided us for the previous twenty months and mingled, while still trying to maintain a reasonable social distance. The sense of freedom and relief that brought explained a lot about how readily so many people resisted masking, but also made clear the importance of remaining vigilant.

The following morning, after a late breakfast of bagels and coffee, we crossed the street to take a walk along the beach on this cool day amid a light fog. We followed a paved path north for a mile through a park lined with skinny, fifty-foot-tall Mexican fan palms. That led us to the foot of Stearns Wharf, Santa Barbara's 150-year-old pier, still in use by fishing boats and coastal freight carriers. Pelicans floated above the shoreline and around the pier, while squawking gulls clustered on the beach and ducks bobbed in tidal pools.

Just as during our last visit here, on the way home from Big Sur a dozen years earlier, we continued onto the pier. The heavy, uneven timbers jostled Trish's scooter, even at slow speed. She grimaced with each bounce.

We rode an elevator to the second-story deck at the Harbor Restaurant, where we lunched on crab cakes and locally brewed ale. By now, the morning fog was burning off. Across the water, we could just make out the northern Channel Islands and a few offshore oil platforms.

"Nice view," I said to Trish. "I had great diving experiences around those islands."

"Yes, but those platforms bring back memories of that terrible oil spill back in the late sixties that messed up this coastline for years."

By the time we returned to the hotel, we needed to prepare for the wedding. The invitation requested that guests dress "chromatically." That was an allusion to a book John had authored, depicting colorful old homes in various cities. In keeping with his request, I brightened my grey suit with a pink silk shirt and a tie emblazoned with Caribbean beach scenes. Trish chose a navy-blue pantsuit and white blouse accented with Navajo turquoise earrings and necklace. We made for as colorful a couple as any there.

I followed directions to Elings Park—three miles north on the freeway, then a mile down a rural two-lane road, and finally up a long hill into the park. Signs directed us up a steeper, narrower road to the high point of the park, restricted to those attending the wedding. We found handicapped parking at the top, then followed a winding pathway to the wedding venue in Godric Grove. The site offered an unobstructed view of the Santa Ynez Mountains towering over Santa Barbara like miniature Rockies. In the opposite direction, between ridge lines, we glimpsed the blue-green ocean.

We paused at the top of the amphitheater where the wedding would take place, seeing only stairs leading down one side. Trish frowned and said, "I hope we won't have to watch the ceremony from up here."

As if on cue, an usher appeared and directed us to an obscured, paved pathway leading down the other side. Following it to the bottom, we settled in at the center of the first row of stone benches, below the hundred or so other guests. Trish opted to remain seated on her scooter. Golden oldies music played in the background as children danced on the stage beneath an ancient oak.

At the appointed time, John appeared at the head of the stairs, dressed chromatically in a black, western-style jacket with multi-colored stitching over a polka-dotted white shirt, accented by a bola tie with a turquoise slide. As he danced his way down the stairs on one side, Carla, attired in a more traditional white sleeveless dress, appeared on the other side. Carla's rabbi and a minister who happened to be John's sister conducted the service, as sunset glow bathed the entire scene.

We followed the crowd back up the hill to a flat outcropping in the midst of a grove of mature oaks and liquid amber trees. Trish's scooter performed fine on the paved pathways and the firm ground at the dinner venue. When we found our assigned table, she remained on the scooter through dinner, rather than transferring to one of the low folding chairs. She knew from experience how difficult getting up again from one of those chairs would be.

We congratulated the newlyweds and chatted at length with our tablemates. Then, as the band music became more raucous and younger people danced into the night, we made our way back to the car and returned to the hotel.

The wedding had brought together a number of people with common professional and academic interests. John arranged to have a dozen of us meet for brunch on Sunday in a hotel conference room. Trish and I looked forward to meeting more of John's colleagues. But, if reaching the pre-wedding party had been inconvenient, the obstacles we encountered in getting to this conference room made it a virtual search-and-rescue mission, as multiple stairways seemed to bar any way for a scooter to get there.

We inquired at the front desk, where a young woman, perhaps new to the hotel, gave us what she apparently thought were simple directions but involved multiple elevators and corridors. That quickly broke down when the second elevator deposited us in the bowels of the hotel's maintenance facilities. By chance, a manager came along, saw our plight, and offered to lead us to our destination. That required going up the elevator a couple of levels, out of the building, back into a vacant meeting room, through the restaurant kitchen, and finally to the conference room.

"How will we ever find our way back when we're done here?" I asked our guide.

"Don't worry, we won't leave you stranded," she said with a laugh. "Ask anyone on the hotel staff to bring you back to the lobby."

The meeting went fine. John had assembled college professors, lawyers, federal officials, and consultants—all people interested in urban planning and housing—to talk about our work and share ideas. I also had an opportunity to describe my recently published memoir, *Becoming American*.

Midway through the meeting, Trish excused herself to find a restroom. The nearest one was unreachable, at the foot of a staircase, so she went in search of another. She didn't return. Perhaps she had gone off exploring or had run into someone from the wedding party whom she wanted to talk with more. Or perhaps, I realized, she may have gotten lost in the hotel labyrinth.

When the meeting ended an hour later, I took a more direct route, via hallways and stairs, back to our room. Still no Trish. That concerned me, though I doubted she would have left the premises. Moments later, as I bounded down stairs to the lobby to inquire about her, I spotted her by the front door. She had just arrived, after fruitlessly wandering the premises until she came across a hotel employee able to help her.

Back in our room, Trish vented, saying, "What a frustrating experience! I found an accessible restroom, but then I got totally lost. For thirty minutes, every way I went led to a dead end or a set of stairs. No signs, and most of the staff here haven't dealt with this problem. They can do stairs, so they apparently never thought about accessible routes."

That brought a close to what otherwise was an enjoyable weekend. We packed up and headed back toward San Diego. Along the way, we stopped for a picnic lunch with our friends John and Patty Kelly, now relocated from Visalia to nearby Santa Paula. Both had recently recovered from COVID, despite being vaccinated. In a park just off the freeway in Ventura, we talked politics and caught up on personal lives over a lunch of egg salad sandwiches and homemade chocolate chip cookies. We then resumed our drive, with hopes of not getting caught in weekend returning traffic.

We made good time at first, but that changed as we neared Los Angeles. We soon found ourselves creeping south over the Hollywood Hills, through West LA, and past the airport, backtracking on the most congested part of our northbound route two days earlier. But then conditions suddenly improved, and the rest of our drive back to San Diego was swift and uneventful.

As we passed Trish's onetime college neighborhood in Irvine, she remarked, "I'm glad we did this. I had my concerns from a health standpoint. But this experience made me feel more confident about traveling again."

After a pause, she continued, "I'm not ready to fly quite yet. Hopefully, that'll come soon. Then, St. Martin or Paris, here we come!"

# Chapter 23
# HOMECOMING

Trish and Cary on Nordkette, Innsbruck

*Austria and Germany, May 2023*
By late 2022, with the COVID pandemic receding, Trish and I felt ready to take another long-distance vacation. As we considered returning to Paris or Dublin, or maybe taking a first trip to New Zealand, an unexpected third party intervened.

For the previous year, I had been working with Andreas Maislinger, then head of the Austrian Service Abroad program (similar to the US Peace Corps, but with an emphasis on aiding Holocaust-related projects). I met Maislinger through Eduard Schmiege, a Viennese urban planner whom I got to know when he was working in San Diego. I responded with great enthusiasm when Maislinger invited me to join in his effort to convert the Adolf Hitler birthplace (commonly called the Hitlerhaus) in my hometown of Braunau am Inn into what he called a House of Responsibility — a conference and study center for international cooperation and opposition to fascism. He soon had me sending government officials email messages explaining my connection to Braunau and declaring my support for his proposal. I saw this as a great opportunity to help Braunau shed the stigma related to that building.

When I mentioned to Maislinger the possibility of coming to Europe, he laid out a plan to use my visit to promote the campaign through press interviews and meetings with public officials. With that inducement, Trish and I designed an ambitious, two-week itinerary through western Austria and southern Germany. We considered including an excursion into Switzerland, but gave up on that when we found accessible accommodations nonexistent in the smaller Alpine towns we would have liked to visit.

I remembered from our last European trip that many cities and roadside rest stops offered free accessible restrooms, but they required a special key. This Eurokey can only be obtained through the German CBF Darmstadt organization serving disabled people and requires proof of disability. I made multiple unsuccessful attempts to order the key through their website until I received a message that they could only deliver to European addresses. Our solution was to have the key delivered to our friend Karin Zinecker in Braunau, though that meant not getting the key until a few days into our trip. An alternative would have been to have the key sent to our first hotel stop, but that seemed riskier.

Lufthansa offered non-stop flights from San Diego to Munich, and our previous experience with them had been good, so we booked a round-trip for the following May. We expected nice springtime weather by then.

For years, we relied on commercial van services like SuperShuttle to transport us and Trish's scooter from home to the airport and back. Then we tried Lyft and found we could request an SUV with ample room for us, the scooter, and our luggage, at far less cost.

On checking in at San Diego International, we hit our first potential obstacle. Lufthansa had required us to submit detailed information about Trish's scooter, particularly the battery. They approved both, but no one entered that into our reservation record. The young agent at the check-in counter had no experience with this issue and seemed conflicted about what to do.

"We provided all the documentation you required, including the manufacturer's safety data for the battery," I told her. "We received this from the airline approving it all," I said, showing her an email from the airline's disability assistance staff.

She still vacillated. At that point, an older agent intervened and telephoned someone with apparent authority to confirm the approval. After a wait of several minutes, she smiled and nodded.

"It is all good," she assured us, to our great relief. With that, she tagged the scooter to be checked at the aircraft door and to be returned there at our destination.

As we headed for our gate, I said to Trish, "I'm hoping that was a good omen. I would have been so disappointed if we had run into a major accessibility issue before we even got out of San Diego."

Outbound, we reserved seats in the airplane row closest to restrooms, a useful preparation for an eleven-hour flight. While en route, I maneuvered Trish in small steps to the restroom while a flight attendant kept it open for us. Unfortunately, such convenient seats were not available on our return flight. As a result, we needed to use an aisle chair—a mini-wheelchair similar to the kind used in boarding—to transport Trish to the restroom on that flight.

On arriving at Munich's Franz Josef Strauss Airport, we encountered a more significant obstacle. We expect to wait until all other passengers deplane and for Trish's scooter to be brought up from the aircraft belly. Typically, that takes about twenty minutes. Here, it took a little longer, and there remained the need to transport Trish off the plane to her scooter. That required an aisle chair, but one with larger wheels than the one used aboard the plane, so it could handle the step from the door onto the jetway. We waited and waited for the chair to arrive. So did the flight crew, who may not leave the aircraft until all passengers are off. After an hour, with the captain becoming upset, I made a suggestion.

"Let me drive the scooter to her seat and take her off the plane on it. We just would need a little help with the step at the door."

I knew that was contrary to regulations, but desperate situations require desperate measures. The captain agreed, my plan succeeded, and we all went on our way.

After collecting our baggage and making a quick passage through passport control and customs, we picked up the rental car that would transport us nearly a thousand miles over the next two weeks, a white VW Tiguan with a rear hatch that provided easy access for loading and unloading the scooter. Because we would be on the move among several cities, we packed as lightly as possible. Trish's suitcase did, however, include the portable grab bars which we always carry to deal with hotels lacking them.

The spring weather we had hoped for eluded us. From the time of our arrival through most of our stay, it was chilly and often drizzling. Trish stayed bundled up in a black leather jacket and an Irish wool scarf, while I made do with a hooded windbreaker over sweaters. But we were not going to let a little unpleasant weather interfere with a long-anticipated trip.

Two hours after leaving the airport, we arrived in Nuremberg and checked in at the Hampton/Hilton. European "accessible" hotel rooms, even at American-affiliated establishments, vary a lot in their degree of accessibility, as we would experience passing through six hotels on this trip. This room was spacious enough for Trish to maneuver about and had the usual bathroom grab-bars and roll-in shower. As much as anything, we had picked it for its location, a few minutes' walk from the Altstadt, the historic Old Town within the original city walls from the 11th century.

As much as we enjoyed walking the Altstadt and taking in the centuries-old sites there, it took a toll on Trish and the scooter.

"Oh no, cobblestones everywhere," she moaned on our first venture up Königsstrasse through the heart of the Altstadt, once the capital of the Holy Roman Empire. Still, she gamely bounced over them for the next two days as we wandered alongside forty-foot stone walls; circled the sprawling central marketplace, the former site of a Jewish ghetto cleared out in 1349; viewed the soaring Gothic façade of the Frauenkirche cathedral; and passed over the Henkersteg covered wood bridge crossing the slow-moving Pegnitz River.

Food choices surrounded us. On our first evening, we dined on Nuremberg's famous mini-sausages and mugs of local pilsner in a beer garden amid dozens of umbrella-covered tables. As we walked around the Altstadt the next day, we experienced a barrage of aromas from produce stands, street vendors, and food trucks. One evening, we ate Wiener schnitzel and dumplings in the courtyard of a former hospital building, again accompanied by draughts of local beer. Trish found the food a bit heavy, but for me, it was a nostalgic dive straight back into my youth.

One day, we drove an hour out of Nuremberg to visit a stretch of the Romantic Road, a 260-mile route passing through forests, mountains, and vineyards, and connecting numerous historic towns. Rothenburg and Dinkelsbühl both had been constructed as fortified towns during a long-ago era of constant warfare and, while damaged during the Second World War, had been well restored. Though the cobblestone streets here challenged Trish even more than those in Nuremberg, viewing the half-timbered houses, arched gateways, clock towers, and ancient stone walls made the inconvenience worthwhile.

But we were in Nuremberg primarily to visit places of more recent historical significance. My father had worked on the prosecution staff at the war crimes military tribunals after the Second World War, just before my birth. I hadn't been in Nuremberg since my childhood and had never visited the courthouse where the trials were held or other places associated with this onetime Nazi stronghold.

Our guidebook cautioned about parking around the District Court (formerly the *Justizpalast* or Palace of Justice), so I sighed with relief at finding a dozen handicapped parking spaces close to the courthouse entrance, several of them vacant. I hung our California handicapped parking placard from the rearview mirror, assuming as always that no one would challenge it.

Today, the complex houses local and regional courts but, nearly eighty years ago, it played host to one of the most significant legal proceedings in history. An elevator took us to the top floor, where the splendid Nuremberg Trials Memorial exhibits spread through several rooms, connected where necessary by ramps for accessibility. The exhibits focused mainly on the initial trials of the major Nazi defendants, placing them in the context of development of international law and recognition of genocide as a crime against humanity.

I was happy to see the memorial also included panels about the subsequent military tribunals that tried officials involved in operating concentration and forced labor camps, as well as prominent jurists, lawyers, doctors, journalists, and others who enabled and participated in the Nazi regime. Those were the trials in which my father was involved as a translator and investigator. He seemed proud to have had a role in those proceedings, but he rarely talked about them. Nonetheless, as I surveyed the exhibits, I felt satisfaction that the trials took place at all and that my family had a close connection to them. All the more so because of our many relatives killed in the Holocaust.

"Stand over here," Trish urged me, pointing to a panel that displayed the Nuremberg Principles, the set of guidelines that emerged from the trials to define what actions constitute war crimes. I posed at the side of the panel while Trish snapped a photo to remember that day. The picture showed me looking somber and intense, with lips pursed and eyes narrowed, certainly capturing my feelings of the moment.

Nuremberg suffered heavy bomb damage during the war, but an important historical structure survived—the Kongresshalle, a nearly completed stadium alongside the site of the Nazi Party Rally Grounds. The grey stone outer structure now houses a documentation center showing the rise of Naziism and Nuremberg's role in that. We followed a long concrete ramp into the brick-faced inner arena, planned to seat 50,000 Nazi supporters.

"When I close my eyes, I can almost see and hear Hitler exhorting his followers, and tens of thousands of them roaring their support," I said to Trish.

"Yes, just like in the old newsreels."

"I'm really glad we came to Nuremberg. I feel connected on a whole new level to my parents' experiences before I was born."

•———————————•

With that on our minds, we made the three-hour drive the next day to my hometown of Braunau, just across the Inn River from Germany. A first face-to-face meeting with Andreas Maislinger awaited me there. Eduard Schmiege, the urban planner from Vienna, would be there too. But first, we stopped for a reunion and meal with my childhood friend, Karin, a lifelong resident of Braunau and now-retired principal of a local school for children with special needs. Trish's scooter managed to climb the short step at the entrance to Karin's townhouse. Amid hugs, bowls of homemade vegetable soup, and cups of cappuccino, the three of us sat around her kitchen table and caught up on events since our last visit six years earlier. We also retrieved the restroom Eurokey.

From Karin's home, we followed a familiar route into the historic town square lined with colorful medieval buildings. Along the way, we passed the Hitlerhaus, which would play an important role in our visit here. As always, driving through this old part of town resurfaced childhood memories of walking here with my parents or my nanny, like I was slipping back into comfortable, familiar terrain.

We checked in at the Mayrbräu Hotel, in a onetime inn and brewery just off the town square. Trish and I had stayed there on our previous visit and found a particular room to be the closest thing to accessible quarters available in this small, centuries-old town. We used rolled-up towels to create a makeshift ramp at a small step between the elevator and our room, and our portable grab bars made the bathroom more accessible.

Andreas had arranged for me to speak to students at two local schools—a high-tech vocational school in Braunau and a conventional high school in Simbach, Germany, just across the river. Trish accompanied me to both. The audience of a hundred or so students at each school was attentive as I described my early years in that area, my family's Holocaust experiences, and our transition to becoming Americans. They asked excellent questions: What issues did I face in moving to a new country and assimilating? As a Jewish American, how did I feel about the rise of neo-fascist groups in both Europe and the US? Did I have any regrets about having left Austria? I thought how much more focused and intellectually curious these teenagers seemed than most of my former university students back home. The most intriguing question, asked in similar form at both schools, had to do with what I learned from my immigrant experience, growing up in two widely separated cultures.

"The most significant thing," I told them, "is the importance of learning from history. The histories of Central Europe and the United States both include inspiring events, but they also include great tragedies. Remember the saying that those who forget history are condemned to repeat it."

Andreas complimented me on the school presentations. The students' positive reactions seemed to energize him as much as it did me. Meanwhile, hoping for a breakthrough on the future of the Hitlerhaus, he had set up a meeting for us with Braunau Mayor Johannes Waidbacher. Out of consideration for Trish, the Mayor arranged for us to convene at modern city offices in a former convent near my onetime home in the suburban Ranshofen neighborhood rather than in the inaccessible medieval town hall on the central square.

A jovial, fortyish fellow, the mayor seemed uneasy at first, and I expected this to be a short meet-and-greet with him and his advisors. Then, as we conversed about the town and its future, not yet addressing the main topic, he relaxed. Seated around a square conference room table, eating pastry from a local bakery and drinking strong coffee, we plunged into an animated, bilingual dialogue that lasted over two hours. Like many of the public officials with whom I had corresponded, he expressed reluctance to go against the plan of the federal government to convert the Hitlerhaus into a police station. Still, while he remained non-committal, he showed sympathy for Maislinger's House of Responsibility proposal, leaving the door open for further discussion. At the end of the meeting, I gave the mayor a signed copy of my book, *Becoming American.* And I thanked him for holding the meeting at a location where Trish could attend and take part in the discussion.

On our last day in Braunau, a reporter from the German ORF public television network interviewed me for a feature report on the Hitlerhaus controversy. Seated in a meeting room in the Gugg restaurant, across the street from our hotel, with kitchen aromas wafting in, she quizzed me about my connections to Braunau, my feelings about the Hitler birthplace, and the arguments over its future use. Trish sat to the side on her scooter, giving me a smile of amusement.

"Turning it into a police station as the government suggests would create a terrible image, in light of the history of police agencies aiding the Nazis," I told the reporter. "It would suppress the history of the place and trivialize the significance of the events that began here."

Afterward, her crew filmed me walking up to the Hitlerhaus and pausing to look at the monument in front, a granite block from the Mauthausen concentration camp quarry, inscribed with a memorial to the victims of fascism. As on previous visits to this site, I felt moved by the enormity of what that the building represented, but also by the positive significance of the town's placement of that monument. It especially troubled me, I told the reporter, that the plan for a police station there might require moving the monument to some less-meaningful location.

The show aired a few days later, viewed by nearly half a million people in Germany and Austria. Interview requests from two major newspapers soon followed.

"You're becoming better known over here than back home," Trish said with a laugh, after watching the television show.

Andreas couldn't have been more pleased. Meanwhile, he had taken the train back to his home in Innsbruck, where we would rendezvous with him again a few days later.

•———————•

Imagine Shangri-La relocated from the Himalayas to the Austrian Alps. That's Bad Gastein, a village perched on the north-facing slope of the Hohe Tauern, flanked by snowy peaks, with a multi-drop waterfall on the western side, and views as far as one can see down the sloping, emerald Gastein Valley.

We drove there from Braunau on a windy, rainy day. The drizzle turned to serious rain most of the way. But then, as we left the *autobahn* and turned west up the Salzach River valley, the rain stopped, the sun broke through the clouds, and the Alpine peaks appeared to our left.

As the road rose into the mountains, past classic chalets with geranium-decked balconies and steep roofs to shed winter snow, backed by slopes sprouting spring blooms, I smiled and turned to Trish. "This is perfect," I said. "This is exactly the point in our trip where I most wanted the weather to be with us."

We had planned for just an overnight stay at Bad Gastein on the way to Innsbruck. I had forgotten from my childhood how stunning the views were and how pristine it felt high up there on the steep mountain slopes. The Hapimag Kaiserhof, a late 19th-century, Belle Époque structure, was the only hotel there that could offer us an accessible room. I found that odd for a spa resort town that has always catered to an older clientele. For the price of a plain hotel room elsewhere, we got a multi-room, accessible suite with floor-to-ceiling windows facing what had to be among the town's best views.

"It's breathtaking," Trish said. "Looking down from here, it feels like we're defying gravity."

We made the most of our brief stay. At sunset, we strolled along a path that offered views across the mountain scenery in all directions. We then repaired to the hotel dining room for meals of venison and trout with parsley potatoes from the regional menu.

I had hoped to take a car-carrying train south from there through a tunnel beneath the mountains, and then come back by a parallel route past the Grossglockner Glacier. But the train tunnel was closed for repairs and the Grossglockner Highway was closed by snow. Instead, we struck out for Innsbruck the next morning, initially cruising along on a route that was much improved from my childhood days.

"You wouldn't believe how much harder a drive this was in the old days," I told Trish as we sped westward down the valley below a row of towering peaks. "The road through here used to wind over every ridgeline, through every little mountain town."

I had no sooner spoken than signs warned of highway construction ahead, one of many post-winter repair projects we encountered on this trip. Traffic was shunted onto the very local road I had just described, and would continue that way for many miles. I hoped we would not be delayed too much, as accessible facilities would be scarce in these remote villages.

After eventually finding the *autobahn* into Innsbruck, we arrived midafternoon and checked into the Schwarzer Adler Hotel downtown. The Altstadt here, a pedestrian-only zone close by our hotel, was older and even more colorful than the one in Nuremberg. Along central Herzog Friedrich Strasse, 14th-century stone structures stood side-by-side with mural-covered, late-medieval buildings and a scattering of post-war construction. Again, lots of cobblestones, but mostly larger, flatter ones, so not as bumpy. Standing by the river that flows past the Altstadt, I realized, maybe for the first time, that this was the same Inn River that flows past Braunau.

Andreas hung out with us on-and-off. One evening, he joined us for dinner at the Goldener Adler restaurant, which had been serving famous composers, politicians, and other celebrities since 1390. Our second day there, we accompanied him to a meeting with Anton Mattle, Governor of the Austrian State of Steiermark. We traveled the several blocks to the state offices on smooth sidewalks that provided relief for Trish from the cobblestones in the Altstadt. Mattle already supported the House of Responsibility proposal in Braunau, but Andreas wanted to cement the relationship and thought the Governor would find my perspective interesting. We had a warm, hour-long conversation at his office, in a mix of German and English, after which I gave him a signed copy of my book and posed with him for photographs.

Also at Andreas' instigation, Trish and I were invited to join in the thirty-year anniversary celebration of reopening of the sole synagogue in Innsbruck. The Jewish community there had fled or been wiped out and the previous synagogue destroyed during the war, but a few Jewish residents had returned and over time formed a sufficient nucleus to reestablish their community. On arriving, I noted several police outside the inconspicuous, single-story building, as well as private security inside.

"It's pretty shocking that a synagogue needs that kind of security, that they're so vulnerable," I said to Trish. "And we've seen that in other cities too."

"Yes," she replied, "but the situation is getting that way at home too, after the shootings and arsons at temples in different cities."

Once we made it to the meeting room where the event was to be held, an usher directed us to a convenient spot along an aisle, where Trish could remain on her scooter while I sat on a chair next to her. Two hundred other guests soon joined us, including a few in wheelchairs.

The event was deemed significant enough to draw as speakers most of the local elected and civic officials, all of whom emphasized the importance of this community's rebirth. To our pleasant surprise, the most heartfelt of the speeches was delivered by the local Catholic bishop, who emphasized the historical and cultural contributions of the Jewish community.

Security issues notwithstanding, seeing this institution thriving gave me a sense of pride and satisfaction. So many Jewish communities here and in Eastern Europe were obliterated by the Nazis and their collaborators, Most, especially in smaller towns, never saw a revival like this. I wished my father could have been there with me. Experiencing this day would have given him some comfort after his family's flight from Vienna following the antisemitic rampage of *Kristallnacht* seventy-five years earlier.

Innsbruck is surrounded by mountains that were obscured by low clouds during most of our visit. When the weather began to clear on our last morning there, we did a quintessential tourist thing, riding first a funicular and then two cable cars up the Nordkette mountains. As at airports, Trish was allowed priority boarding on each conveyance. From an observation deck surrounded by ice and snow, we took in views of the city, the surrounding countryside, and the peaks on the far side of the valley.

"This is so cool that I could get way up here on my scooter," Trish remarked. "It reminds me of going up on the cogwheel railroad in Zermatt to see the Matterhorn."

Our last stop in Austria was the resort town of Bregenz, on the easternmost shore of the Bodensee (also known as Lake Constance), a forty-mile-long body of water fed by the Rhine River. Our room at the Hotel Germania was spacious and had the usual accessible features, except that the bathroom had a small step at the doorway and was too narrow for the scooter to maneuver. I helped Trish move about in there, and we managed well enough for a short stay.

I recalled happy times walking along the lake with my family on sunny summer days decades earlier and looked forward to a similar experience with Trish. This time, however, a cold drizzle greeted us. Since we would be there just a single night, I braved the elements, walking down to the lakefront park and watching ships decorated with ornate designs motor off into the mist, carrying passengers to other lake towns. The weather cleared enough by morning that Trish joined me in a final walk on a smooth pathway by the lake. Geraniums and iris bloomed alongside us as if oblivious to the wintry weather.

The route from there to Munich was *autobahn* all the way. And the rain had moved on, giving us fair weather for the last few days of our visit. Navigating into downtown Munich was challenging, and would have been near-impossible without GPS. The Flemings Hotel, part of a German chain, sat across from the central train station, a few blocks west of Munich's Altstadt. With no more events or meetings, we had ample time to explore the many medieval churches, the Gothic town hall, public gardens, and the unusual cube-shaped synagogue. And we had more traditional meat-and-dumplings dinners, mainly at restaurants associated with local breweries.

Adjacent to the onetime Nazi Party administrative center and parade grounds now stood the Documentation Center presenting detailed exhibits on the rise of Naziism and the central part that Munich played in that. I knew a lot of the history but was still shocked at how openly public officials and civic institutions enabled or even directly supported the growth of the National Socialist movement, and how deviously the Nazis insinuated themselves into every aspect of political and civic life.

I was glad to see groups of school-age children making their way through the three floors of exhibits. As with the student groups in Braunau and Simbach, I hoped they came away with an understanding of the events illuminated by the exhibits and that they would be influenced to prevent repetition of that history.

As we exited the building, Trish commented, "Munich sure has owned up to what a huge role it played in the Nazi era. I wish more Americans could handle coming to terms with negative parts of our own history, and learning from it."

---

The museum visit made for a somber conclusion to our time in Munich, but it did not overshadow all the positive aspects of the trip. Now, we just needed to drive to the airport, return the Tiguan to Hertz, check in at the Hilton adjacent to the terminal, and fly out the next morning.

All the hotels at which we stayed offered substantial breakfast buffets with the rooms, but the one here was particularly lavish, giving us a nice send-off to home. The crew on our Lufthansa flight was especially helpful to Trish, aiding her in getting to and from the one accessible restroom and checking regularly if she needed anything else. I had given the flight attendants a box of Austrian *Mozartkugeln* — balls of dark chocolate filled with marzipan, pistachios, and hazelnuts — but I imagined they would have been just as helpful even without that.

As we crossed the coast and started over the Atlantic, I could feel myself decompressing from the intense activity of the past two weeks. The trip had exceeded all our expectations, in terms of the cities we visited, the people we met, the architecture and scenery we saw, and the food and drink we enjoyed. And I had revisited so many places of which I had wonderful, if sometimes vague, childhood memories.

"I'm so happy about how this all worked out," I said to Trish. "So many memories and so many new experiences, in places I hadn't seen in sixty years or more. This trip, more than our previous ones, gave me a sense of my personal roots. It wasn't just a vacation. It felt like a homecoming."

Most important, we had successfully navigated a maze of marginally accessible places in numerous locations, dealing with physical obstacles and refusing to let them undermine our plans. Flexibility and determination got us through yet again.

# THE CHALLENGE MET

Trish and I have been traveling together for twenty years. We're both now in our seventies. Her MS symptoms continue to progress. We have no intention of letting that condition or our age keep us from traveling, though the destinations and activities may become tamer over time.

More than fifty million Americans are aged sixty-five and over, and their numbers are growing faster than younger age groups. Over fifteen percent of them, nearly eight million, have physical conditions that limit their mobility. That increases to nearly half among people aged eighty-five and over. More than twelve million younger people have similar disabilities.

Most of this population can travel well into their later years. They simply need to believe that they can continue to enjoy traveling and its associated experiences despite their age or physical limitations.

When we travel, we notice relatively few people our age or older. We especially notice the almost complete absence of people with mobility constraints. We are more likely to see travelers utilizing scooters or wheelchairs in the United States, almost never outside the country. That frequently makes Trish's scooter an object of curiosity.

From the time Trish's condition began to restrict her mobility, we have recognized travel for us would be challenging, and increasingly so. Yet, it has not stopped us. As we age and continue to travel, we hope to remain a model for other older and disabled potential travelers. We have met the challenge. They can too. Hopefully, we will inspire them with our two legs and three wheels.

## THE END

# About the Author

Cary D. Lowe, Ph.D., is the author of the award-winning memoir *Becoming American*, the story of his growing up in post-war Europe with parents who were Holocaust survivors, immigrating to the United States, and becoming deeply engaged in law, politics, and academia. He has published eighty non-fiction pieces, appearing in the Los Angeles Times and other major newspapers, and taught at several universities.

Apart from his writing, he loves outdoor adventures — scuba diving for over forty years, climbing Mt. Whitney, running a marathon in San Diego, among other things. He can often be found in the kitchen perfecting his Eastern European cuisine, with Mexican and Cajun thrown in for spice. Interested in Native American culture, he has advocated extensively for tribes in California.

## Other Titles by Cary D. Lowe

## Note from Cary D. Lowe

Word-of-mouth is crucial for any author to succeed. If you enjoyed *On Two Legs and Three Wheels*, please leave a review online—anywhere you are able. Even if it's just a sentence or two. It would make all the difference and would be very much appreciated.

Thanks!
Cary D. Lowe

We hope you enjoyed reading this title from:

www.blackrosewriting.com

Subscribe to our mailing list – *The Rosevine* – and receive **FREE** books, daily deals, and stay current with news about upcoming releases and our hottest authors.
Scan the QR code below to sign up.

Already a subscriber? Please accept a sincere thank you for being a fan of Black Rose Writing authors.

View other Black Rose Writing titles at www.blackrosewriting.com/books and use promo code **PRINT** to receive a **20% discount** when purchasing.